Translation and Meaning. New Series, Vol. 1

ŁÓDŹ
STUDIES IN LANGUAGE

Edited by
Barbara Lewandowska-Tomaszczyk
and Łukasz Bogucki

Vol. 41

PETER LANG
EDITION

Marcel Thelen / Gys-Walt van Egdom /
Dirk Verbeeck / Łukasz Bogucki /
Barbara Lewandowska-Tomaszczyk
(eds.)

Translation and Meaning. New Series, Vol. 1

PETER LANG
EDITION

Bibliographic Information published by the Deutsche Nationalbibliothek
The Deutsche Nationalbibliothek lists this publication in the Deutsche Nationalbibliografie; detailed bibliographic data is available in the internet at http://dnb.d-nb.de.

This publication was financially supported by
Zuyd University of Applied Sciences, Maastricht.

ISSN 1437-5281
ISBN 978-3-631-66390-5 (Print)
E-ISBN 978-3-653-05899-4 (E-Book)
DOI 10.3726/978-3-653-05899-4

Peter Lang – Frankfurt am Main · Bern · Bruxelles · New York ·
Oxford · Warszawa · Wien

This publication has been peer reviewed.

www.peterlang.com

Preface

The papers in this volume by a number of authorities in the field discuss current hot topics in Translation Studies and translator/interpreter training, viz. translation/interpreting didactics, competence acquisition and assessment, curriculum design, and the so-called skills gap between training and actual professional practice. The ideas and practices presented are new and unique and are valuable contributions to Translation Studies and translator/interpreter training. The book is of interest to trainers/students/practitioners of translation/interpreting, translation companies, as well as the whole discipline of Translation Studies, but also to linguists, terminologists, terminographers, lexicographers, publishers, etc., and anyone with a general interest in translation and interpreting.

The editors
Marcel Thelen, Gys-Walt van Egdom, Dirk Verbeeck, Łukasz Bogucki and Barbara Lewandowska-Tomaszczyk

Table of Contents

Introduction

1. General

The present volume contains a collection of selected articles that are a reflection of the papers read at the Maastricht Session of the 6th International Maastricht-Łódź Duo Colloquium on "Translation and Meaning" on 21 and 22 May 2015 at the Maastricht School of Translation and Interpreting of Zuyd University of Applied Sciences. The total number of papers presented was 43 by scholars and practitioners from 17 countries. The (co)authors of these selected articles are based in 13 countries: Belgium, Denmark, France, Germany, Italy, Mozambique, Netherlands, Poland, Portugal, Republic of South Africa, Spain, United Kingdom, and United States of America.

All the articles in this volume have been peer reviewed by an international committee of reviewers. Only those were included that were found to represent one or more of the special themes of the Maastricht Session well and to be solid academic papers in a proficient language. The special themes of the Maastricht Session were:

1. The didactics of translation and interpreting
   a. Teaching methods
   b. Testing and assessment criteria and methods
   c. Learning strategies
   d. Competences and levels of competences
   e. Entrance requirements and required prior education/training
2. The translation/interpreting student
   a. The ideal translation/interpreting student
3. The translation/interpreting trainer
   a. The ideal translation/interpreting trainer
   b. Requirements/qualifications for translation/interpreting trainers
   c. Quality register for trainers
   d. Train the trainer
4. The training curriculum for translation/interpreting
   a. The ideal training curriculum
   b. Curriculum building and planning
   c. BA vs. MA
   d. Working towards graduate employability
   e. "Professionalisation" vs. "academisation" of the curriculum

f. Attuning the curriculum to needs and requirements of the professional world
g. Involving external professional experts in the curriculum

The articles in the present volume do not cover all these special themes, and some articles deal with a combination. Consequently, the following three sections were established for this volume:

1. The didactics of translation and interpreting: assessment, competences, student and trainer, training
2. Curriculum design
3. Specialised domains and specific issues of translation and interpreting.

Up to this volume of proceedings, the proceedings of previous Duo Colloquiums have been published by the Maastricht School of Translation and Interpreting, in total ten volumes containing 428 articles by both leading as well as coming scholars and practitioners in the field of translation and interpreting. An anthology of the most important articles was published by Peter Lang in 2010 under the title *Meaning in Translation* (eds. **Barbara Lewandowska-Tomaszczyk** and **Marcel Thelen**). From the present volume onwards the proceedings of the Maastricht-Łódź Duo Colloquium will be published by Peter Lang with the title *Translation and Meaning, New Series*.

The Maastricht-Łódź Duo Colloquium is a five-yearly conference with two Sessions in one and the same year, one in Maastricht and one at the Institute of English Studies of the University of Łódź in Poland. Both Sessions and all the editions of the Duo Colloquium have one and the same central theme, viz. Translation and Meaning, with a common set of sub-themes, although these may vary between the two venues depending on local interests and (inter)national topicality at the time of the Session. The working languages are always English, French and German. The first Duo Colloquium took place in 1990 after the plan for it was conceived by **Barbara Lewandowska-Tomaszczyk** and **Marcel Thelen** in 1987 in former East-Berlin. The Maastricht-Łódź Duo Colloquium has become an internationally well-known event and its proceedings have become standard works. Initially, it brought together scholars and practitioners from former East and West, followed by North and South.

2. Brief description of the articles included

SECTION I contains seven articles on five important aspects of the didactics of translation and interpreting, viz. assessment, competences, student and trainer, and training. The first article by **Henri Bloemen** and **Winibert Segers** (*Evaluating literary translation competence*) deals with the assessment of competences in literary translation and gives a few suggestions of how this might be done. They, furthermore, elaborate on whether the traditonal translation test is adequate enough for testing and assessing the quality of literary translation.

The second article is by **Elsa Huertas Barros** and **Juliet Vine** (*Translator trainers' perceptions of assessment: an empirical study*) who report on a survey among translator trainers at their university. Their objective was to find out more about the practice, perception, criteria, and instruments of translator competence assessment by means of summative assessment as applied in the academic context. One of their findings is that only half of the competences could be tested in a product-oriented assessment.

In her article (*Wissensrevolution, Generation Z und die Translationsdidaktik*), **Iwona Jacewicz** discusses the intriguing question whether the current methods of translation/interpreting didactics suit the learning needs of translator/interpreting students of the current and coming generations and (can) keep pace with the ongoing knowledge and technical evolution. It would be good, she argues, for universities to give students internet access to their programmes.

Armando Magaia (*Assessing translation competence at Eduardo Mondlane University*) reports on his research among undergraduate students of his university into their translation competence in order to identify the major obstacles for translation competence development, and concludes by suggesting that a reforming of the curriculum is necessary to cater for this development, as well as investing in modern technology and giving students access to research resources.

In the next article (*Can subjectivity be avoided in translation evaluation?*), **Winibert Segers** and **Hendrik Kockaert** outline the evaluation method PIE (Preselected Items Evaluation) that they developed in order to minimize subjectivity in translation assessment as much as possible. In PIE, a preselection of items is made and afterwards tested; results are then mathematically calculated. The preselection of items requires much time, but this, they hope, may be limited by automation.

The topic of objectivity of assessment is also taken up by **Marcel Thelen** (*Quality and objectivity of testing and assessing in translator training: dilemmas and suggestions*). He argues for not restricting assessment to training institutes, but for also including criteria and methods applied in professional translation practice in order to maximize its quality. This can best be done by introducing professionalisation in the curriculum, one possible realisation of which is the so-called skills lab, an in-house simulated translation bureau run and managed by students under the supervision of trainers and with the cooperation of external professionals.

Such a skills lab requires a combination of assessment criteria and methods applied in training and practice. The Maastricht School of Translation and Interpreting has more than 25 years of experience with this and has been able to reduce the perceived skills gap between training and professional practice considerably.

In the last article in this section (*Negotiating meaning at a distance: peer feedback in electronic learning translation environments*), **Donata Lisaité, Sonia Vandepitte, Bruce Maylath, Birthe Mousten, Susana Valdez, Maria Castel-Branco** and **Patricia Minacori** present their Transatlantic & Pacific Project (TAPP) on online peer feedback and its effect on the development of translation competence. The timing of these per feedback activities appeared to influence the quality of meaning-related items.

SECTION II on curriculum design contains four articles. The first article (*Crafting the training and testing of interpreting students towards employability*) by **Linda Dewolf** describes the consequences for the curriculum of the academisation process imposed on higher education in Flanders, in particular interpreting training, while having to keep abreast of the demands of the professional world and having to increase graduate employability. The solution has to be found in blended courses, e-learning and web-based coaching tools.

In the second article (presented as a keynote paper at the Maastricht Session) titled *Beyond the static competence impasse in translator education*, **Don Kiraly** – in line with his earlier work on translator education – argues for a dynamic translator training curriculum based on an emergentist pedagogical epistemology enabling students to develop translation competence along with workplace competence in a socio-constructive learning environment. Key instruments in this process are work placements.

The third article (*On "general" and specialised texts in the translation training programme: conjectures, assumptions, refutations and implications*), **Gys-Walt van Egdom** tackles the problem of text selection in training programmes. Instead of selecting general pragmatic texts in the first stages of training and subjecting these to discourse analysis, and specialised texts only in the later stages, he argues for selecting specialised texts right from the first stages onwards. This would provide students with a more solid basis for developing specialised translation competence. This does not mean, however, that general pragmatic texts should be discarded altogether, as these enable students to focus on the translation activity and not to be distracted by subject matter.

Hildegard Vermeiren concludes this section with her article on *L'Interprétation à l'ère des TIC* in which she argues in favour of incorporating ICT in interpreter training. By way of illustration she describes the situation at her university where a useful threefold distinction is applied between ICT for research, for education and for a professional context.

SECTION III deals with a variety of aspects relating to the training of translators and interpreters under the title *Specialised domains and issues of translation and interpreting*. It is the largest section containing 11 articles. The first one (*The influence of machine translation and CAT tools on creativity and quality*) by **Marcos Aranda** reports on a quantitative experimental study he conducted on the impact of MT and CAT tools on creativity and quality of translation. Results show that there is indeed a decrease of creativity and quality, but this decrease does not outweigh the increase in productivity which is considerably higher. This does not mean that MT and CAT tools should not be used in translator training, he argues; far from this, as these are unstoppable. What should be done instead is to give more weight in the curriculum to post-editing and proofreading.

In his article on *Rendering otherness in film – Techniques for translating multilingual audiovisual material*, **Łukasz Bogucki** addresses – with ample examples – the problem of audiovisual translation of multilingual dialogues. Multilingual material, he argues, may come in various forms: both aural-verbal and visual-verbal, making the translation of this type of communication a real challenge. He provides a useful taxonomy of techniques to tackle this problem. All this has great relevance for the training of audiovisual translation.

The third article (*Exploring and developing legal translation competence: learning from old dogs*) by **Eleanor Cormelius** explores, by means of an experiment, legal translation competence, in particular the difference between inexperienced and experienced legal translators (in way of working, consulting resources, etc.), and compares these with general translators and gives a number of useful suggestions for trainers on the basis of her findings.

A completely different issue is discussed in the next article (*Katalanische Übersetzungen der griechischen und lateinischen Klassikern unter der Franco-Diktatur*) by **Montserrat Franquesa Gòdia**. She analyses the origin and ideology of three library collections with translations of Greek and Latin classics, and goes deep into one of them, the Catalan collection that was prohibited under the Franco dictatorship. Her findings are, though not mentioned explicitly, certainly also of relevance to (research into) Translation History in translator training.

The fifth article in this Section (*Variation in the translation of terms: corpus-driven terminology research*) by **Koen Kerremans** deals with the problem in translation-oriented terminology that existing specialised terminology resources such as terminological glossaries, dictionaries, thesauri or databases do not always give a full account of the linguistic features and options of textual items a translator might benefit from, not even the European term bank IATE. The translator could benefit in such cases from a corpus-driven analysis. The research that he carried out confirms this and its methodology is now taught at his university.

In the following article (*Principle of cluster equivalence and parallel corpora*), **Barbara Lewandowska-Tomaszczyk** understands translation as cycles of re-conceptualisation in terms of cognitive linguistics and deals with parallel corpora containing source texts and their translations, together representing cluster equivalence by way of meaning clusters. Cluster equivalence opens up a number of options for the translator to use. This was analysed in a study carried out on Polish and English. Such parallel corpora, in particular cluster equivalence, she argues, may be very useful in translator training in that they contribute to semantic awareness with students.

The seventh article (*Marking plural forms in Tshivenḓa and the study of translation and mass nouns*) by **Munzhedzi James Mafela** discusses an indigenous African language Tshivenḓa that may cause translation problems arising from differences in grammar relating to mass nouns and their meaning, and leading to miscommunication, especially in translations from a non-African language such as English into Tshivenḓa. A thorough analysis of the problem is given, illustrated by ample examples. These problems may be overcome, in his opinion, if grammar courses on both source and target language are included in the translator training curriculum.

The next article (*Functionalism in literary translation. The use of a functionalist approach in translating contemporary Swiss-German poetry*) by **Lucia Salvato** gives an account of the application of Nord's functionalist approach to translation (her translation-oriented ST analysis) to the translation of a Swiss-German poem into Italian. She describes various translation problems and finally addresses the question whether a scientific theory as Nord's developed for non-literary translation can be applied integrally to non-literary translation; literary translation is, after all, more than non-literary translation an art where creativity and instinct are essential.

The one but last article in this Section is *Researching and teaching the translatability of neologisms* by **Rita Temmerman**. By means of a thorough analysis of two cases she discusses translation problems that may arise in the translation of English neologisms into French and Dutch in the domain of molecular biology, and raises the question whether term creation is language and culture-bound, making it difficult to translate. In an elaborate conclusion she gives a number of detailed and valuable suggestions for translator training.

The last article in this Section and the very last one of this whole volume is by **Sergiy Tyupa**. In *Cognitive debriefing of patient questionnaires: how to capture meaning as understood by respondents?*, he addresses medical questionnaires used to measure the reactions and evaluations of testees on a particular treatment. Mostly, these clinical trials are carried out in more countries, which makes the translation of these questionnaires and data provided by the testees important since their comprehension of the questions asked in these questionnaires, as well as efficiency and safety of new medicines are at stake. In a linguistic experiment he tested existing methods and an alternative method for cognitive debriefing or linguistic validation. Cognitive debriefing may be important for translator training, especially for translation quality assessment.

The editors
Marcel Thelen, Gys-Walt van Egdom, Dirk Verbeeck, Łukasz Bogucki and Barbara Lewandowska-Tomaszczyk

Section I: The Didactics of Translation and Interpreting: Assessment, Competences, Student and Trainer, Training

Winibert Segers and Henri Bloemen

Evaluating Literary Translation Competence

Abstract: In 2014, the *Leerlijn Literair Vertalen* (*Learning Line Literary Translation*) was published (Antwerp / Utrecht: Expertise Centre for Literary Translation (ELV)). This 'learning line' was further developed on a European scale into a 'Framework for the Education and Training of Literary Translators' (the PETRA-E-project). The Framework consists of eight competencies (translation competence, linguistic competence, textual competence, heuristic competence, literary-cultural competence, professional competence, evaluative competence and research competence) and five levels (preparatory, beginner, advanced, professional and expert).

A learning line is an important first step, but should not be the last one. The learning line describes the various competences, but those competences must be tested at some point. The evaluation is important because its outcome can have a major impact on the career of a literary translator (granting of scholarships, translation prizes, literary translation jobs).

The learning line is competence-based. The evaluation must also be competence-based. We will have to try to develop instruments that measure the eight competences in a reliable and valid way.

A competence is a combination of knowledge, skills and attitude. A competence test must contain those three elements. Testing only knowledge is too narrow and goes against the competence approach.

Is the traditional translation test (Translate this text in the target language x from source language y) a good competence test? Does this evaluation, which is synthetic, not clash with the fundamental analytical competence approach? Is there a relationship between the competences of a literary translator and the quality of his translation products? Does a competent literary translator make good translations? We will try to answer these questions and we will give examples of a competence test.

Keywords: literary translation competence, PETRA project, linguistic competence, textual competence, heuristic competence, literary-cultural competence, professional competence, evaluative competence, research competence, competence evaluation.

1. Introduction

It is a well-known fact that in the field of translation, evaluation and assessment often give rise to questions of validity and reliability. A lot of effort has been made to cope with these problems, especially in those fields of translation in which, at first sight, problems of validity and reliability can be overcome quite easily. For example in so called 'specialised translation' several aspects of translational competence (terminology, syntax, cohesion and coherence, style) can be evaluated in a more a less valid and reliable way.

When it comes to evaluation and assessment of literary translations however, the discussion becomes more complicated (and often rather harsh), because attitudes of what, for the sake of simplicity, we could call 'aesthetic ideology' enter into it. The ideological position assumes that literary translation is a kind of art and that the evaluation of artistic texts is mainly a matter of individual taste and preference. The quality of a literary translation then often depends on its accordance to the aesthetic standards and convictions of the evaluator or to the accepted norms a literary translation has to meet in a certain context. The factor of subjectivity – central in the discussion on reliability and validity – is dominant in the evaluation of literary translation. This might turn out to be problematic, because evaluation and assessment have become important issues in literary translation ever since the emergence of master's degrees in literary translation and other developments in the training and education of literary translators. Admittance to master's programs or other training trajectories is often made dependent on preliminary tests. Subsidizing institutes often give grants on the basis of the quality of the translation. Also translation prizes are often awarded on the basis of translation quality. Valid and reliable evaluation then becomes a question of justice, which is hardly served when grants are given or candidates are admitted on the basis of personal taste and preference or of idiosyncratic norms and convictions.

2. Competences of a Literary Translator

In order to focus not so much on the quality of the translation product but rather on the skills, knowledge and attitude of the translator, initiatives have been taken to line out the competences of a literary translator. Recently the Dutch/Flemish 'Centre of Expertise in Literary Translation' (ELV, Expertisecentrum Literair Vertalen), a joint institute of the University of Utrecht and Leuven University, has developed a 'learning line' or 'framework' for literary translators. This learning trajectory is competence-based and therefore subject-related, which means something else than 'subjective': it concentrates on the 'properties' of a translator rather than on those of a translation. The learning line lists the competences a literary translator should have in order to be called a competent translator. It is about the competences a translator should have acquired in the course of a training trajectory or an education program. Taking the learning line as a starting point for evaluation constitutes the first, and major, difference to the more classical forms of evaluation that care about the properties of the translation product: Does it meet certain quality standards? Whereas the more interesting question should be: has a translator acquired such and such competences?

The learning line in question distinguishes eight competences or sub-competences that together make up the overall competence 'literary translation competence'. The eight (sub-)competences as defined in the learning line are:

1. *Translation competence:* the knowledge and skills needed to translate literary texts into the mother tongue at a required level. It comprises the ability to recognize translation problems and the ability to solve these problems in an appropriate way, and to account for the result.
2. *Linguistic competence:* this competence refers to the grammatical, stylistic and pragmatic mastering of the source and target language especially on the domains of reading and writing.
3. *Textual competence:* the knowledge of literary genre and styles and the ability to apply this knowledge in the analysis of source texts and the production of target texts.
4. *Heuristic competence:* is the ability to gather linguistic and thematic knowledge needed to understand a source text and to produce a target text. It is also about the application of textual criticism and the differentiation between text editions and their consequence for the production of a target text.
5. *Literary-cultural competence:* is the ability to apply knowledge about the source and target culture and their literary systems (synchronic and diachronic). It also includes the ability to handle cultural differences.
6. *Professional competence:* is the ability to gather knowledge about the working field (institutes, subsidies, prizes, professional organizations etc.) and to show the appropriate attitudes expected by the working field.
7. *Evaluative competence:* is the ability to evaluate and assess translations, the translation process and the competences of a literary translator.
8. *Research competence:* is the ability to submit literary translations to methodical research.

There is some discussion among theorists and practitioners whether competence 7 and 8 are essential for a literary translator. For some they only constitute 'flanking' competences. For the sake of completeness we don't distinguish here between flanking and essential competences.

The vertical line of the framework lists the competences of a literary translator, the horizontal line distinguishes five levels of a learning path from 'breakthrough' to 'beginner', 'advanced', 'professional' and 'expert'. If we consider the framework as a whole, the question of evaluation is decisive (a) between every level shift and (b) for the final competence of a literary translator.

3. Descriptors

Just as the overall competence 'literary translation competence' is analytically subdivided in eight partial competences, each of these are in turn defined in detail by so-called descriptors. A descriptor mentions a certain aspect of a competence. For example, one of the descriptors of the translation competence reads like 'can identify translation problems'; one of the descriptors of the textual competence is 'can recognize stylistic features of the source text', and one of the descriptors for literary-cultural competence reads like: 'knows a number of literary traditions in the source and target language'. It is important to cover all aspects of a competence by as much descriptors as necessary, but no more. As every descriptor should ideally be the object of a valid and reliable evaluation, the number of descriptors should be limited to those who in essence define the competence in question. We cannot discuss the 'right' number of descriptors for the moment, but it should be emphasized that the analytic nature of the model is extremely important when it comes to evaluation. Evaluation based on this analytic model puts it in opposition to all kinds of holistic evaluation. On the other hand, the number of descriptors should be limited to those essential to a certain competence in order to keep evaluation feasible.

In competence evaluation it is necessary to keep in mind that competences are a combination of knowledge, skills, and attitudes. Competence-based evaluation has to evaluate all three aspects: what does a translator know? Does he/she have the skills to translate a literary text? Does he/she show the appropriate attitudes of a literary translator?

4. Reliability and Validity

Competence evaluation should meet the requirements central to every serious – and just – testing: reliability and validity. An evaluation is reliable when the evaluation tool produces stable and constant results. The circumstances of the testing may not have any influence on the result of the test. The same holds for the person of the corrector: when two or more people correct the test independently from each other, the result must be the same. If this is not the case, the test is not reliable. The requirement of reliability is a central argument against any form of evaluation based on artistic ideology where differences resulting from subjective predilections and convictions are accepted as normal.

A competence-based evaluation is valid when the evaluation tool evaluates what it is purported to evaluate. When evaluating translation competence only translation competence should be tested and not, for example, literary-cultural competence or heuristic competence. A translator who makes a grammar error may well be competent in the domain of translation competence, for example because he/she is able to choose the right translation strategy. As a consequence, when evaluating, the several (sub-)competences should not be mixed up. It is clear that on this point, again, the analytical scope of competence-based evaluation puts it in opposition to any kind of synthetic or holistic evaluation that takes the translation itself (and not the translator) as a starting point and that judges the translator by the qualities of the product he/she has delivered.

In our view, an analytical model is more suitable for a reliable and valid evaluation than synthetic forms of evaluation. The generally known tools of competence evaluation, especially in bachelor and master programs are:

- a case study
- internship report
- interviews
- portfolio
- project work

Regarding all these widely used forms of evaluation, the overriding question is: are they reliable and valid? There may be some justified doubts about that.

5. Dichotomy

Another important property of competence-based evaluation is the fact that competences are dichotomic by nature: either you have a competence or you don't have it. Someone is either is competent or not competent at all. It is difficult to say that someone is 'a little bit competent'; it does not make very much sense to say, as is often heard, that someone is 'very competent' either . The dichotomic nature of competences makes it difficult to distinguish 'levels of competence'. If these are part of a framework, as is the case in the ELV-learning line, these levels should be very strictly distinguished from one another.

6. Examples

What could competence-oriented tests look like? The main difference would be the fact that the competence of a translator is not only measured by the qualities of the translation product he/she has produced. Every single competence, every single descriptor should ideally be object of a valid test, i.e. the test should only test what it purports to test: the competence in question. Once again this shows the radical analytical nature of these kinds of tests.

Admittedly, also a translation could prove that a translator is competent in a certain field of his profession. For example, if the source text contains some specific cultural elements, a translator can show how to handle them by translating them correctly. Nevertheless, in the correction of such ways of testing several extra steps will have to be made.

We give some – simple – examples of what (possibly) valid and reliable test questions could look like.

Evaluation of literary-cultural knowledge
Example 1
Who is the author of *Pride and Prejudice*?

- o Jane Austen
- o Emily Brontë
- o George Eliot
- o Henry Fielding

Evaluation of literary-cultural knowledge
Example 2
'It was a bright cold day in April, and the clocks were striking thirteen' is the opening sentence of

- o *A Clockwork Orange*, by Anthony Burgess
- o *Great Expectations*, by Charles Dickens
- o *Nineteen Eighty-Four*, by George Orwell
- o *The Sea, The Sea*, by Iris Murdoch

Evaluation of literary-cultural knowledge
Example 3
Who was the Nobel Prize winner for literature in 1983?

- o William Golding
- o Graham Greene
- o Aldous Huxley
- o Virginia Woolf

7. Doubtful Questions

The question remains whether a reliable and valid competence-based evaluation is feasible: if all the aspects, expressed in descriptors, are to be evaluated, the evaluation may take quite some time. Can one decide whether a translator is competent or not, when a test has to take into account all 152 descriptors that are now part of the framework? And what if the framework were to be introduced on a European scale: can we imagine a test that is reliable for the whole of Europe? Is it possible to exclude all 'national' circumstances in a reliable European test regarding the multiple European traditions in the education and training of literary translators?

Elsa Huertas Barros and Juliet Vine

Translator Trainers' Perceptions of Assessment: An Empirical Study

Abstract: Since translation established itself as a profession and an academic discipline, assessment in translator training has developed and become more complex due to the fast and significant changes affecting the industry and the emergence of new approaches to quality in translator training (Drugan, 2013: 185; Saldana and O'Brian, 2014: 95). As pointed out by Williams (2009: 5), while translations are constantly assessed in a variety of contexts, ensuring the validity and reliability of assessment criteria remains problematic. Indeed, translation evaluation within university training courses is problematic, with a recognition that individual impressionistic assessments need to be made more valid through the introduction of more objective assessment criteria, but as yet with no rigorous research into assessment practices having been carried out (Melis and Hurtado Albir, 2001: 272–273).

This paper will explore some complex aspects linked to assessment criteria and instruments in translator training in order to gain a clearer understanding of the current practice and situation of assessment within the academic context. For the scope of this paper, we will present the first preliminary results obtained from a survey carried out among translator trainers at the University of Westminster (UoW). We will analyse translator trainers' perceptions of assessment, and particularly summative assessment, by focusing on how trainers approach assessing translator competence.

Keywords: assessment criteria, assessment instruments, summative assessment, survey, trainee translators, translation assessment, Translation Studies, translator competence, translator trainers, translator training.

1. Assessing Translator Competence

Competence-based training has been the cornerstone of the EHEA harmonisation process. Although there is undeniably a wide range of conceptual approaches to translation competence (TC), there is also agreement as to what the main skills or areas of competence are. In this paper we will take as reference point Kelly's (2002, 2005, 2007), PACTE's (2003, 2005) and EMT's (2009) TC models, since they set themselves as some of the most recent integrated competence-based approaches for teaching, learning and assessment in translator training.

Despite the trend towards competence-based training, there are few research studies on the evaluation of the acquisition of TC and how to assess students' performance in translator training. As pointed out by Galán-Mañas and Hurtado

Albir (2015: 6), most of the TC models do not describe exhaustively the operationalisation (i.e. components and indicators, performance levels) of each competence.

Some of the existing research in this area includes the volume edited by Schäffner and Adab (2000), which devotes an entire section to TC assessment and the evaluation of the product as concerns expected levels of TC. Beeby (2000: 185–198) presents an empirical study that compares the results of summative and diagnostic evaluation into non-mother tongue. The author concludes that a typical examination environment is limited, and a variety of innovative methods such as introducing take away exams or requesting translation diaries in which students explain how they deal with translation problems may be used in order to make evaluation more complete, effective and balanced (*ibid.*: 196). Adab (*ibid.*: 215–228) proposes a clearly defined framework (based on specific categories and weighting criteria) for summative assessment through the evaluation of the product, which allows for measurement of students' ability to transfer a message from the source text to the target text. McAlester (*ibid.*: 229–243) focuses on assessing translation into a foreign language and highlights the need for a standard criterion referenced evaluation framework for translation adequacy. More recently, other proposals advocate for ways to assess translation processes formatively. For instance, Way (2008), presents a systematic assessment of students competence that encourages self-assessment and self-criticism in students in the course of their training in translation but also throughout their professional careers. Garant (2009), presents a case study for holistic translation assessment, particularly focusing on the assessment of students' TC in translation practice courses. Massey (2012, 2013), proposes assessment methods that explore translation processes in laboratory-based and workplace research projects to complement traditional product assessments.

2. A Practical Case Study: Assessment on MA Translation Courses at the UoW

The following section presents a practical case on assessment on MA Translation courses at the UoW. We will first provide an outline of the MA Translation courses offered at our university and the assessment practices used in translation modules. Next, we will present the preliminary results obtained in a survey that analyses translator trainers' perceptions of assessment, particularly the summative assessment used in the translation modules they teach.

2.1 Overview of MA Translation Courses at the UoW

The UoW has been training translators in its various previous guises since 1967. It is claimed to be the first specialised training course for translation in the UK (Pedrola, 1999:19). The original course, a diploma in Translation, was designed by both Peter Newmark, and Anthony Crane, the chair of a professional body of technical and specialist translators. The translation programme was solely vocational and remained so until the introduction of a Masters in Translation in 1992, when elements of translation theory were incorporated in to the programme.

The emphasis on vocational training has permeated the ethos of the courses offered and it is reflected in the emphasis on professional experience in those teaching on the courses. As mentioned in section 3, at present, of the 16 trainers surveyed, over 90% define themselves as freelance translators and state they combine their teaching with work as commercial translating. In a course taught predominately by staff whose translation experience was prioritised over consideration of pedagogical training, the assessment of translations was a matter of professional judgement and supported by a rigorous system of second marking. There was an assumption that all translation trainers knew what was required and these requirements did not need to be made explicit. Indeed, Peter Newmark (1982: x) in the introduction said of 'detailed schemes of assessment' that they were 'dead ducks, either too theoretical or too arbitrary.' However in the last ten years assessment has become more explicitly formalised with assessment criteria being matched to learning outcomes.

The UoW offers two MAs courses: Specialised Translation MA and Translation and Interpreting MA. Both MAs have core translation modules, which involve 40 hours of language specific taught seminars which encompass an introduction to specialist topics and text types, group discussions of prepared work, and individual or group translation assignments, with emphasis on subject and terminology research. Detailed formative feedback is provided on the work undertaken and, on completion of the translation modules, students should be able to work in professional settings as junior translators.

2.2 Overview of Summative Assessment in MA Translation Courses at the UoW

The translation modules are summatively assessed through two pieces of coursework, weighted at 15% each, and a final exam, weighted at 70%. The assessment practices were designed originally to reflect the ways in which translation performance was assessed in professional settings i.e. through assessment of translation products. There is an implicit assumption that a competent translator (i.e. one who has developed all the required translation competence) will be able to demonstrate this through the product of their translation practice.

The assessment weightings put considerable emphasis on the final examination and this again reflects the desire to train translators who can work competently in the professional market. It has been considered that one of the ways of determining this is through a test of the translator's ability to translate at speed and yet maintain accuracy and presentation standards, thus ensuring that the translators can translate at economically viable speeds.

In 2009, the UoW was one of the first universities to join the European Masters in Translation Network (EMT Network). Part of the process of becoming a member of the network was to match learning outcomes with the EMT competences. This process ensured that the idea of teaching competences was firmly embedded in teaching practice and this is borne out in the survey results presented in section 3, which shows that 95% of respondents consider translator competences when choosing texts for summative assessment (i.e. coursework or exam).

Pieces of summative assessment are marked using a rubric of criteria that judge the translation by appropriate professional criteria for a junior translator. To be of an acceptable standard, it must be accurate; stylistically appropriate and in an appropriate register, bearing in mind the function of the text and the target readership; follow and interpret the translation brief, being mindful of the target text audience and the client requirements; phrased in appropriate institutional or technical terminology; grammatically accurate and accurately spelled and punctuated; presented in an appropriate format and to professionally acceptable standards. These criteria are matched to the learning outcomes.

Each of these criteria is assessed individually and given a grade from Distinction (fully meet professional criteria), Merit (substantially meets professional criteria) to Pass (acceptable translation, which will require revision) and Fail (unacceptable translation, which will require considerable revision). These grades are awarded by not only deducting marks based on the number and severity of the errors, but also acknowledging good translation solutions. The grade boundaries are not explicitly defined in terms of number of errors and rely on the judgement of the marker. The module handbook states that 'These marking criteria are inevitably open to some subjectivity, as the translation may not satisfy all criteria equally.'

3. Survey Results on Trainers' Perception of Assessment

The following section presents the preliminary results obtained from a survey carried out among translator trainers at the MA translation courses offered at the UoW. While the survey broadly looks at translator trainers' perceptions of assessment, particular emphasis is paid to how trainers approach assessing TC in the pieces of summative assessment in the translation modules they teach. The survey was created using Google Forms and was submitted to 29 members of staff (including full-time, fractional members and Visiting Lecturers) teaching on MA Translation courses. A total of 16 trainers completed the survey. Given the large proportion of Visiting Lecturers and staff on fractions below 0.5 (i.e. over 75% of the whole staff group), a response rate of 55% is not surprising. However, from the responses, it is clear that most of the full time and higher fraction staff did indeed complete the survey. While we can only draw tentative conclusions from this size sample, we feel this is a representative sample for a case study at university level that can serve as a useful starting point for identifying aspects of improvement in terms of assessment practices at our institution. The main results obtained refer to the following categories: 1) Assessing TC in pieces of summative assessment; 2) Assessing translation product vs. assessing translation process; 3) Academic assessment criteria vs. industry assessment criteria; 4) Proportion of subjectivity to objectivity in assessment practice; 5) Acceptability of the assessment methods used and the weighting allocated to the pieces of summative assessment.

When asked to rank different areas of TC[1] in terms of how important it is to assess them in pieces of summative assessment, the respondents' rankings can be grouped as follows: 1st) language competence and strategic competence; 2nd) professional competence, information mining and thematic competence; 3rd) intercultural competence; 4th) interpersonal competence and technological competence. The ranking given to the translation competences reflects those competences which are explicitly addressed in the learning outcomes of the modules. In addition, these answers were broadly in agreement with what trainers thought was measured most accurately by an exam, which shows that trainers felt that those competences which are most important to assess are in fact the ones which are assessed. On the other hand, some trainers highlighted the need of complementary assessment methods that take into account other important aspects of TC, particularly interpersonal competence. One respondent stated that they had rated this competence low in the ranking of importance in the university context, but felt that it would be rated much higher in a professional context.

Strategic competence, from the spread of rankings allocated to it, is the competence which the respondents disagreed most about. Although the survey provided a definition of this competence, perhaps the respondents were still not clear about

---

1 As we have mentioned in section 1, the TC model used is an adaptation of Kelly's (2002, 2005, 2007), PACTE's (2003, 2005) and EMT's (2009) models.

what exactly it encompasses or this could reveal that models of competences are not fully understood, since the strategic competence and its equivalents in other models are the overarching competence (PACTE, 2005; Kelly, 2007; EMT, 2009). Alternatively, like processes in general, perhaps the trainers felt that this competence is not directly assessed, but rather is reflected in the products.

Over 93% of respondents agreed that assessing translation product accurately reflects the TC of the learner. This result chimes with the original ethos of the course as professional training taught by professionals who apply the assessment instruments of their professional experience to the training courses, as one respondent says 'they will be judged professionally on the basis of the product alone'. Many of the responses state that the translator competences are in fact assessed indirectly through this assessment method, but there were also concerns that by looking exclusively at the product some competences (i.e. interpersonal competence) are not addressed and the process 'which reflects a deeper understanding of the competence' is overlooked. Consequently, some trainers feel that 'alternative assessment methods are needed to evaluate all competences.'

In contrast to the positive view of assessing products as a way to reflect TC, when asked if exam performance was an accurate representation of TC only 44% agreed. This ambivalence about exams is also reflected in the response to questions about the assessment weightings. One respondent stated 'exam conditions are generally not representative of the translation work done by a professional, whereas coursework is: like the student, the practitioner will want to take time to go through the different stages, including laying it aside and revisiting it for the final polish.'

When asked about the modules that the trainers themselves taught on, they were more positive about the correlation between the assessment methods they used and the level of translation competence attained by students, with over 62% agreeing that the assessment accurately reflects the students' translation competence. However, this leaves 38% who felt ambivalent or disagreed.

When asked if they thought assessing the translation product was the most practicable method of assessing TC within an academic institution, there was slightly less strong agreement (i.e. 75% compared to the 93% of trainers who believe assessing translation product accurately reflects TC). This answer may reflect lack of clarity over the term 'practicable' or may indicate trainers belief that other assessment tools could be used as practicably as assessing product alone.

When asked if assessing the translation process was an important aspect of assessing translation competence within an academic institution almost 70% agreed that it was important, but over 30% neither agreed nor disagreed. Some of the comments show that trainers were thinking about processes as a vehicle to 'un-teach any unproductive thinking' and that considering processes offers 'explicit learning opportunities' and 'reflects a deeper understanding of TC and of how students approach a translation'. Other responses showed that trainers felt it was not possible to directly assess what are essentially mental states and therefore inaccessible, although the process 'should be evident in the success of the product'. Other respondents felt that focus on the process was a reflection of the academic environment and was not 'necessary on a programme that aims to produce professional translators.'

When asked if the academic assessment criteria should match professional ones, only 56% agreed with this statement and almost 44% were either ambivalent or disagreed. Those that agreed did so as they felt that the aim of MA Translation courses is to equip students with the skills required in the professional environment and, consequently, academic training courses need to adopt industry assessment criteria, particularly 'for a Masters to have credibility in the industry'. This also provides students with an understanding of the standards required professionally. Those that did not agree felt that, in academic environments, the students as learners 'need to be assessed on their learning' and it would not be fair to assess them using professional criteria at the beginning of the course. However, these respondents also felt that towards the end of the course, the academic assessment criteria applied should match professional ones, 'as students should be ready to work as junior translators in the translation industry.' Another respondent said that academic courses are teaching 'a wide range of competences which may or may not be explicitly reflected in a piece of translation.'

Although 44% of participants were either ambivalent or disagreed about whether the academic assessment criteria should match professional ones, almost 69% agreed that the criteria used on the modules they teach on were representative of industry standards of quality. Those who felt that both criteria were not representative stated that 'the industry standards of quality are higher and stricter', since some errors would not be tolerated in the industry. In connection with this, another respondent raised the interesting point that 'the industry provides clearer guidelines on levels of tolerance.'

The questionnaire also included two questions on the balance of subjective vs. objective nature of assessing. One was asking what the ideal balance would be and the second question asked the trainers to evaluate their own assessment practice in this respect. There were interesting differences between the two sets of answers: whereas almost 44% of respondents thought that ideally marking should be completely objective or at least 90% so, in fact, none of the respondents evaluated their own performance in this way, and three quarters said their marking was 70 to 80% objective. While in an ideal situation, a third of respondents felt marking would have a lower than 80% objectivity, in reality half of the respondents felt their marking had lower than 80% objectivity. Interestingly, a 20% of respondents stated that the ideal balance of subjectivity to objectivity would be 50/50, compared to 12.5% of trainers who consider this was in fact the balance in their assessment practice.

In terms of the clarity of the assessment criteria used to assess pieces of summative assessment, although over 81% of trainers felt they were clear about the criteria, many still thought that some aspects of performance should be more clearly defined, particularly the 'accuracy', 'comprehension' and 'readability (style/register)' criteria.

When asked about the acceptability of the assessment methods used, over 62% felt that these instruments (i.e. an exam and two pieces of coursework) can accurately measure the level of TC attained by students, compared to over 31% who neither agreed nor disagreed. Those who did not strongly agree felt there should be more pieces of coursework. In fact, some trainers suggested the inclusion of alternative assessment methods 'that reflect the learning process' since the current pieces of summative assessment 'do not allow for the assessment of all translator competences', particularly interpersonal competences. In particular, some respondents felt that coursework could include annotations in which students justify their decision-making, or incorporate a group task to measure parameters such as 'cooperation and social skills.'

Asked if they agreed with the present weightings allocated to the pieces of summative assessment (i.e. 15% for each of the two courseworks and 70% for the exam), the percentage that agreed (44%) was identical to the percentage of those that disagreed. Interestingly, of those who disagreed, the vast majority (90%) felt the current weighting allocated to the exam is 'excessive' and, consequently, 'more weighting should be attached to coursework.' Most suggestions agreed on decreasing the percentage assigned to the exam to 50% and increasing the proportion of both pieces of coursework accordingly (i.e. to 25%). One respondent mentioned the possibility of leaving the current weighting of the exam, but reflecting the expected progression of the learner by assigning a higher percentage to the second piece of coursework (i.e. CW1 – 10%; CW2 – 20%; Exam – 70%). The rest of the proposals (40% of those who disagreed) suggested decreasing the weighting of the exam to between 30% to 60% and increasing the weighting of the coursework proportionally. According to the respondents, the main reasons of this change are that while coursework reflects real-life situations in which students have access to all resources, exams are 'artificial' or 'unrealistic' and 'the time limitations do not allow students to produce quality products.'

Finally, despite over 81% of trainers affirming that the assessment criteria used in translation modules were clear to them, almost 44% would add or remove certain parameters from the current feedback sheet used for pieces of summative assessment. Some trainers suggested including parameters that reflect 'professionalism' or 'professional usability'. Other proposals included adding 'intercultural awareness' and 'coherence and grammatical cohesion' criteria. The only criteria trainers said they would remove from the feedback sheet was 'presentation', as they do not normally find this an issue in translations and, if necessary, these could be flagged up in the comments section. One trainer suggested an interesting way to incorporate an element of formative assessment to the feedback sheet by adding an extra column next to each criteria in which trainers or students themselves would specify 'what to do next' to resolve specific problems. Over 56% of respondents were happy with the current feedback sheet and would not include any modification at all.

4. Conclusions

Over the last decade, there has been a gradual shift in translator trainers' focus from a previous preoccupation with products of translation to the processes involved in translating. These processes have been formalised into a set of competences which should be explicitly addressed in training courses. This has had an impact on how trainers perceive the value and effectiveness of summative assessment which consists of evaluating the product of assessment. Both the shift in focus towards a competence-based understanding of the translator training and the shift in the value placed on exams as an assessment instrument can be seen in the responses to the survey of translator trainers at UoW. The use of coursework (i.e. translations completed by students in their own time) has not lost as much favour, but again the shift to process-centred teaching has also led trainers to consider whether and how coursework could integrate more of the processes.

Summative assessment demonstrates competences through ability to produce an acceptable product. Matching aspects of translation competence demonstrated both directly and indirectly in the summative assessment tools used at UoW to the list of 47 EMT sub-competences (2009) showed that only half of the competences were capable of being assessed in a product- orientated assessment. Exams as the main element of summative assessment have long been considered the most effective way of measuring the student translator's ability at the UoW, evidencing students' ability to translate under pressure and at economically viable speeds.

However, these two parameters are not reflected in the TC models under study neither are they taken into consideration by professional organizations such as the Institute of Translators and Interpreters (ITI) in the UK. The result of the survey showed some trainers call for a widening of the focus of the assessment, and suggest the inclusion of alternative assessment methods that reflect the learning process and evaluate the competences that are presently overlooked.

References

Adab, B. J. (2000) "Evaluating Translation Competence". In: Schäffner, C. and Adab, B. J. (eds.). *Developing Translation Competence.* Amsterdam: John Benjamins.

Beeby. A. (2000) "Evaluating the Development of Translation Competence". In: Schäffner, C. and Adab, B. J. (eds.). *Developing Translation Competence.* Amsterdam: John Benjamins.

Drugan, J. (2013). *Quality in Professional Translation Assessment and Improvement.* London: Bloomsbury.

EMT Expert Group (2009). "Competences for Professional Translators, Experts in Multilingual and Multimedia Communication." Available at: http://ec.europa.eu/dgs/translation/programmes/emt/key_documents/emt_com peten ces_translators_en.pdf [Last access: 01/04/2015]

Galán-Mañas, A. and Hurtado Albir, A. (2015). "Competence assessment procedures in translator training." *The Interpreter and Translator Trainer.* DOI: 10.1080/1750399X.2015.1010358.

Garant, M. (2009). *A Case for Holistic Translation Assessment.* AFinLA-e Soveltavan kielitieteen tutkimuksia 2009. 1. 5–17.

Kelly, D. (2002). "Un modelo de competencia traductora: bases para el diseño curricular." *Puentes*, 1. 9–20.

Kelly, D. (2005). *A Handbook for Translator Trainers: Translation Practices Explained.* Manchester: St. Jerome.

Kelly, D. (2007). "Translator Competence Contextualized. Translator Training in the Framework of Higher Education Reform: in Search of Alignment in Curricular Design". In: Kenny, D. and Ryou, K. (eds.). *Across Boundaries: International Perspectives on Translation Studies.* Cambridge: Cambridge Scholars Publishing. 128–142.

Massey, G. and Ehrensberger-Dow, M. (2012). "Evaluating the Process: Implications for Curriculum Development." In: Zybatow, L., Petrova, A. and Ustaszewski, M. (eds.). *Translationswissenschaft interdisziplinär. Fragen der Theorie und der Didaktik*, Frankfurt am Main u.a.: Peter Lang. 95–100.

Massey, G. and Ehrensberger-Dow, M. (2013). "Evaluating translation processes: opportunities and challenges." In: Kiraly, D, Hansen-Schirra, S. and Maksymski, k. (eds.). *New Prospects and Perspectives for Educating Language Mediators.* Tübingen: Gunther Narr. 157–180.

Martínez Melis, N. and Hurtado Albir, A. (2001), "Assessment in Translation Studies: Research Needs", *Meta* 46 (2). 272–287.

McAlester, G. (2000). "The Evaluation of Translation into a Foreign Language." In: Schäffner, C. and Adab, B. J. (eds.). *Developing Translation Competence.* Amsterdam/ Philadelphia: John Benjamins. 229–242.

Newmark, P. (1982). *Approaches to Translation.* Toronto: Permagon Press.

PACTE (2003). "Building a Translation Competence Model". In: Alves, F. (ed.). *Triangulating Translation: Perspectives in Process-oriented Research.* Amsterdam/ Philadelphia: John Benjamins. 43–66. Available at: http://www.fti.uab.es/pacte/publicacions/. [Last access: 18/04/2015].

PACTE (2005). "Primeros resultados de un experimento sobre la Competencia Traductora". In: Romana, Mª. L. (Coord.). *AIETI Formación, Investigación y Profesión: II Congreso Internacional AIETI, Información y documentación.* Madrid, 9–11 de febrero de 2005. Madrid: AETI. 573–587.

Pedrola, M. (1999) "Interview with Peter Newmark" in Anderman, G. and Rogers, M. (eds.) *Word, Text, Translation: Liber Amicorum for Peter Newmark.* Bristol: Multilingual Matters.

Saldanha, G. and O'Brien, S. (2013). *Research Methodologies in Translation Studies.* London and New York: Routledge.

Schäffner, C. and Adab, B. J. (eds.). (2000). *Developing Translation Competence.* Amsterdam/ Philadelphia: John Benjamins.

Way, C. (2008). "Systematic Assessment of Translator Competence: in Search of Achilles' Heel". In: Kearns, J. (ed.). *Translator and Interpreter Training. Issues, Methods and Debates.* London: Continuum International. 88–103.

Williams, M. (2009). "Translation Quality Assurance." *Mutatis Mutandis.* 2 (1). 3–23.

Iwona Jacewicz

Wissensrevolution, Generation Z und die Translationsdidaktik

Abstract: This paper serves as a starting point for the debate on the future of translation didactics in the digital age in view of the knowledge revolution effected by rapid technological, economic and social developments and the new mindset and attitude of the next generation to studying translation and to their future professional life. To further illuminate the problem, the three Generations X, Y, and Z, their worldviews, lifestyles, learning methods, perceptions of the future and their professional situation will initially be compared. An attempt will then be made to illustrate the extent to which the views of translation teachers (post-war generation and Generation X) on the current study programmes meet the expectations of Generation Z (and Y).

This is followed by an examination into the new challenges translation didactics should face as soon as possible as it confronts the current knowledge revolution if Translation Studies are to meet the expectations of the job market and of future translators and interpreters. A number of specific suggestions on how to solve this problem will then be presented.

Keywords: translation didactics, knowledge revolution, Generation Y, Generation Z, Translation Studies, study programme, digital age, internet society, data mountains, information flood.

1. Einleitung

Der vorliegende Beitrag versteht sich als Auslöser der Diskussion über die Zukunft der Translationsdidaktik angesichts der durch die rasche technologische, wirtschaftliche und gesellschaftliche Entwicklung hervorgerufenen digitalen Wissensrevolution. Der Wissensrevolution, die nur für die Generationen der Hochschullehrer ein Novum darstellt, für die Generationen der Studierenden jedoch zum Alltag gehört. In Hinsicht auf den Lebenseinstellungs- und Denkunterschied der Generation der digitalen Eingeborenen und der digitalen Immigranten (Prensky 2001) sind folgende Fragen von Interesse:

- Ist die digitale Wissensrevolution als eine positive oder negative Erscheinung zu betrachten?
- Ist es durch das Treffen der digitalen Immigranten und der digitalen Eingeborenen an den Universitäten zum Zusammenstoß der Generationen gekommen, der nur Probleme mit sich bringt?

- Welche Vorstellungen vom künftigen Berufsleben eines Translators haben die heutigen Studierenden dieses Studienfaches und welche Lehre sollten daraus die Hochschullehrer ziehen?
- Mit welchen neuen Herausforderungen soll sich möglichst schnell die Translationsdidaktik in Konfrontation mit der Wissensrevolution messen?

Um die Antworten auf die oben formulierten Fragen zu erarbeiten, wird zunächst auf die digitale Wissensrevolution und ihre Konsequenzen für die Translationsdidaktik eingegangen. Nachfolgend wird der Vergleich der drei Generationen X, Y, und Z im Hinblick auf ihre Weltanschauungen, Lebensarten, Lernmethoden, Zukunftsvorstellungen und Berufssituation dargestellt. Da im Fokus des Interesses die Translationsdidaktik steht, wird als Grundlage für die Überlegungen neben der Literatur zu dem Thema auch die von der Autorin in den letzten Jahren im Institut für Fach- und Interkulturkommunikation an der Universität Warschau unter den StudentInnen der letzten Semester des Masterstudiums, d.h. kurz vor ihrem Studienabschluss, durchgeführte Umfrage über ihre Bewertung des Studienprogramms, ihre Berufspläne und die damit verbundenen Ängste und Hoffnungen dienen.

Danach wird der Versuch unternommen, zu veranschaulichen, inwieweit die Vorstellungen der Translationsdidaktiker (Nachkriegsgeneration und Generation X) über die gegenwärtigen Studienprogramme den Erwartungen der Generation Z (und Y) entsprechen.

Zum Abschluss soll beleuchtet werden, mit welchen neuen Herausforderungen sich die Translationsdidaktik in Konfrontation mit der gegenwärtigen Wissensrevolution möglichst schnell messen soll, wenn das Translationsstudium den Erwartungen des Arbeitsmarktes und der angehenden ÜbersetzerInnen und DolmetscherInnen entsprechen sollte. Es werden also ein paar konkrete Vorschläge der Lösung dieses Problems dargestellt.

2. Digitale Wissensrevolution – eine Bedrohung oder ein Segen?

Digitale Wissensrevolution, mit der wir seit Anfang der 90er Jahre, d.h., seitdem das Internet für viele zugänglich wurde, zu tun haben, wird als die größte seit der Erfindung der Schrift bezeichnet. Wie jede Revolution hat auch sie ihre positiven und negativen Seiten. Ihre Gegner sehen den Umbruch als Krise, da Wissenschaftler, Forscher und Lehrer keine Türsteher des Wissens sind, sie nehmen heutzutage wie all die anderen Internetnutzer an der Diskussion teil. Die Wissensrevolution wird auch mit der Informationsanarchie verglichen, da die Querulanten den gleichen Zugang zum Netz wie wir alle haben. Dies verursacht, dass das Wissen wilder wurde und schwerer zu kontrollieren ist. Vertrauenswürdiges Wissen ist also schwerer herauszufinden und verlangt von jedem Internetnutzer eine sehr kritische Einstellung. Gerade diese Eigenschaft – die kritische Einstellung – ist für die jungen Generationen keine Offensichtlichkeit und bringt viele Probleme mit sich, die ihrerseits eine Herausforderung für die Didaktik, also auch für die Translationsdidaktik, mit sich bringt (vgl. Reuter 2013, Weinberger 2013, Gleick 2012).

Aber der Wissensrevolution verdanken wir auch sehr viele positive Erscheinungen: neues Wissen kann sofort diskutiert und kommentiert werden, Wissenschaftler und Forscher haben also heutzutage sofort die Chance, gehört (gelesen) zu werden, Dank der Wissensrevolution wird sofort alles verlinkt, was verursacht, dass neue Ideen viel schneller viel größeres Publikum als je zuvor erreichen können und mit den Ideen der anderen konfrontiert werden. Die Digitalisierung des Wissens machte uns alle zum Medium und führte dazu, dass die Welt des Wissens keine Veranstaltung nur für Eliten ist, sondern ein Labor für neue Ideen, in dem das Wissen demokratisiert wurde. (vgl. Reuter 2013, Weinberger 2013).

3. Dozenten und Studenten – Zusammenstoß der Generationen?

Zum ersten Mal haben wir an den Universitäten mit einer neuen Situation zu tun, es trafen sich nämlich die sogenannten digitalen Immigranten (Nachkriegsgeneration) in der Rolle der Hochschullehrer mit den digitalen Eingeborenen, d.h. der Generation X (auch als Hochschullehrer), der Generation Y und der Generation Z. Um die Herausforderung besser verstehen zu können, werden nachfolgend all die oben angeführten Generationen kurz charakterisiert.

a) Nachkriegsgeneration, die sog. Babyboomer

Vertreter dieser Generation wurden in den Jahren 1945–1964 geboren, sie sind also immer noch an den Universitäten als Lehrende aktiv. Die Soziologen bezeichnen sie als die Generation, für die neue Technologien ein Tabuthema sind. (Small/Vorgan 2011: 264) Trotzdem wird von ihr verlangt, im Berufsleben von den Neuen Medien Gebrauch zu machen (z. B. E-Mail-Adresse). Da, wo es aber kein absoluter Bedarf besteht, will diese Generation mit den technischen Neuigkeiten nichts zu tun haben. Es ist ein Grund, warum sie sich in der Hinsicht mit den Generationen der digitalen Eingeborenen nicht verständigen kann und ihre Vorstellungen von einer modernen Universität nicht teilt.

b) Generation X

Angehörige der Generation X wurden in den Jahren 1965–1979 geboren. Das Internet und neue Medien waren in ihrem Leben zwar nicht immer da, aber es ist diejenige Generation, die zu der Entstehung und Entwicklung der Neuen Medien aktiv beigetragen hat. An den Universitäten unterrichten heutzutage die Vertreter gerade dieser Generation neben den Vertretern der Nachkriegsgeneration. Die Unterschiede zwischen ihnen sind groß, was für die Studierenden sichtbar ist. Angehörige der Generation X werden von den Soziologen als skeptisch, materialistisch und eigenbrötlerisch charakterisiert (vgl. Scholz 2014).

Ihre Einstellung sowohl zum Leben als auch zu der digitalen Welt und zu der Wissensrevolution ist kritisch. Diese Eigenschaft ist besonders wichtig in der Didaktik, da sie der Generation X ermöglicht, die nächsten Generationen auf die Nutzung der neuen Medien verantwortungsbewusst vorzubereiten.

c) Generation Y

Vertreter der nächsten Generation werden auch als Millennials oder Ypsiloner bezeichnet. Sie wurden in den Jahren 1980–1994 geboren. Die letzten Jahrgänge werden die Universitäten in den Jahren 2018 und 2019 verlassen. Generation Y ist die Generation der positiv eingestellten Idealisten, die gut im Team arbeiten können. All ihre Vertreter sind mit dem Internet aufgewachsen. Sich selber betrachten die Millennials als sehr anspruchsvoll, selbstbewusst und gut qualifiziert. Es ist die Generation des schnellen Aufstiegs und ihre internationale Ausbildung hat dazu geführt, dass sie auch globalorientiert, offener und toleranter als die älteren Generationen ist. Facebook, Twitter und iPhone garantieren ihr die beste Vernetzung, weswegen sie dem langen Sitzen am Schreibtisch ein lautes „Nein, danke!" sagt. Wozu auch? Mit dem Smartphone ist man ohnehin immer online! Der unbegrenzte Zugang zu Informationen, zum Wissen im Internet und die Überzeugung, dass sie sich in der digitalen Welt viel besser orientieren als die älteren Generationen, hat dazu geführt, dass die Generation X von klein auf gewohnt war, sich mit Autoritäten auf Augenhöhe auseinanderzusetzen und kein Blatt vor den Mund zu nehmen, wenn ihr etwas unsinnig erscheint. (vgl. Scholz 2014, Buchhorn/Werle 2011).

Da die Vertreter der Generation Y immer noch an unseren Universitäten präsent sind, wäre es interessant, zu fragen, welche Vorstellungen die Generation Y von dem Beruf des Translators hat. Als Grundlage für die Antwort auf die Frage wird die von der Autorin unter den Studierenden der letzten Semester (drittes und viertes) des zweijährigen Masterstudiums im Institut für Fach- und Interkulturkommunikation an der Universität Warschau in den Jahren 2013–2015 durchgeführte Umfrage[1] dienen. An der Umfrage haben 53 ProbandInnen teilgenommen. Unten, auf dem Diagramm, wird prozentuell der Anteil der einzelnen Jahrgänge dargestellt.

Abb. 1: Geburtsjahr der ProbandInnen.

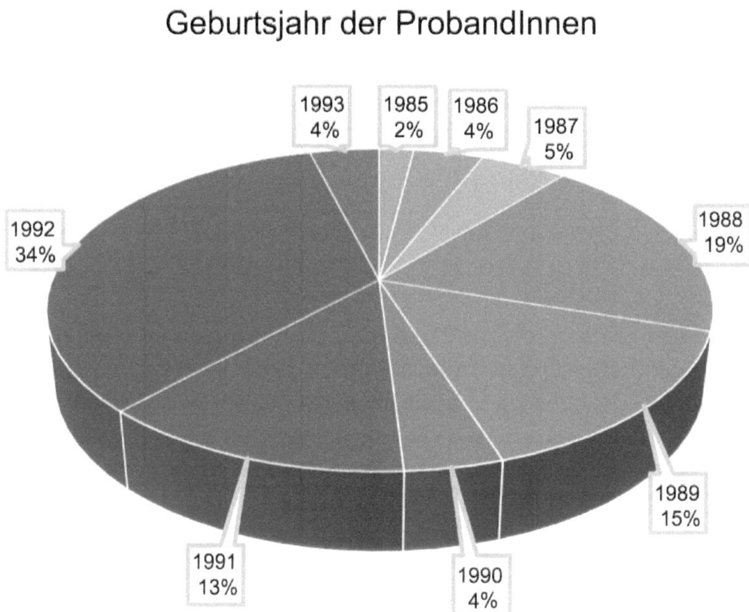

Im Rahmen der durchgeführten Umfrage wurden den Studierenden von der Autorin 23 Fragen gestellt. In dem Beitrag wird jedoch nur, im Zusammenhang mit dem Thema, auf einige von ihnen hingewiesen.

So betraf eine der Fragen das Prestige des Translatorsberufs in der Öffentlichkeit.

1 Quelle einiger der in der durchgeführten Umfrage gestellten Fragen: Göpferich 2008.

Abb. 2: Welches Prestige genießen Übersetzer/Dolmetscher in der Öffentlichkeit?

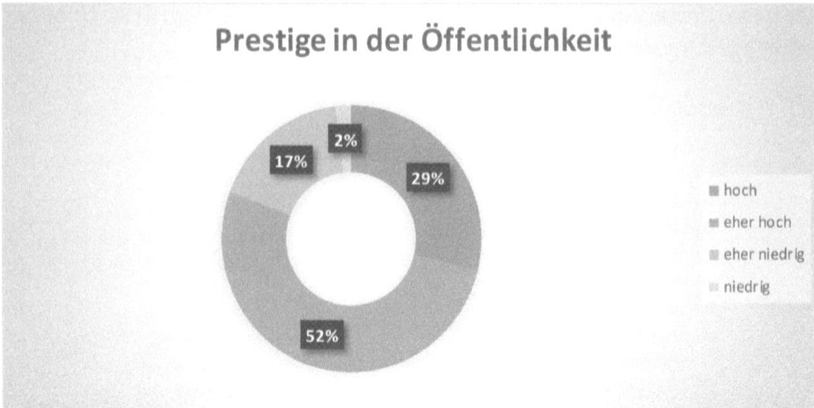

Wie es dem oben dargestellten Diagramm zu entnehmen ist, wird es von der Mehrheit der ProbandInnen (81%) als hoch und eher hoch eingeschätzt.

Die nächste Frage bezog sich auf die Eigenschaften der Übersetzer. An der Stelle muss ergänzt werden, dass die Eigenschaften für die ProbandInnen fertig formuliert wurden, sie hatten also nur zu entscheiden, welche sie für sehr wichtig, wichtig, eher nicht wichtig oder unwichtig halten.

Abb. 3: Wie wichtig sind Ihrer Meinung nach folgende Eigenschaften für Übersetzer?

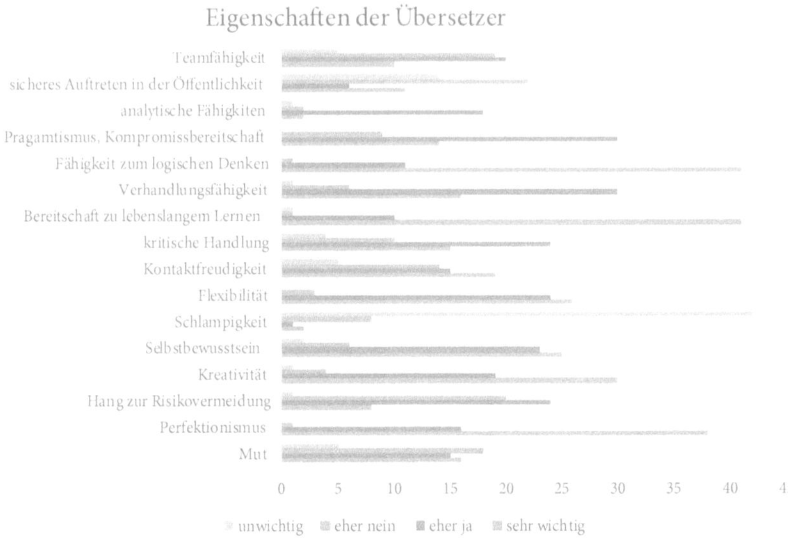

Es lässt sich feststellen, dass – nach der Meinung der VerterInnen der Generation Y – die Übersetzer sich vor allem durch folgende Eigenschaften auszeichnen wie: logisches Denken (41%), Bereitschaft zu lebenslangem Lernen (41%) und Perfektionismus (38%). An der zweiten Stelle platzieren sich Kreativität (30%), Verhandlungsfähigkeit (30%), Pragmatismus und Kompromissbereitschaft (30%). Ziemlich hoch werden auch Flexibilität (26%), Selbstbewusstsein (25%), kritische Handlung (24%) und Hang zur Risikovermeidung (24%) geschätzt. Wodurch sich die Übersetzer definitiv nicht auszeichnen sollen ist die Schlampigkeit. Sehr interessant, in Bezug auf die früher angeführten Eigenschaften der Generation Y, scheint insbesondere eine Antwort zu sein, und zwar diejenige, die die Teamfähigkeit betrifft. Nach der Meinung der Soziologen (s. Kap. 3c) ist es für die Generation Y charakteristisch, dass sie gut im Team arbeiten kann und offen ist. Die Meinungen der Studierenden waren aber bei der Beantwortung dieser Frage beinahe zu 50% geteilt: 20% haben diese Eigenschaft als eher wichtig und 10% als sehr wichtig eingeschätzt, was insgesamt 30% der positiven Antworten ergibt. Für 5% der ProbandInnen war diese Eigenschaft unwichtig und für 18% eher unwichtig, was insgesamt 23% ausmacht. Das Ergebnis bedarf einer Bemerkung: da an der Umfrage Vertreter der Generation Y nur aus einem Land (Polen)

teilgenommen haben, kann davon ausgegangen werden, dass es vielleicht eine nationale Eigenschaft ist.

Die nächste Frage betraf die Eigenschaften der Dolmetscher.

Abb. 4: Wie wichtig sind Ihrer Meinung nach folgende Eigenschaften für Dolmetscher?

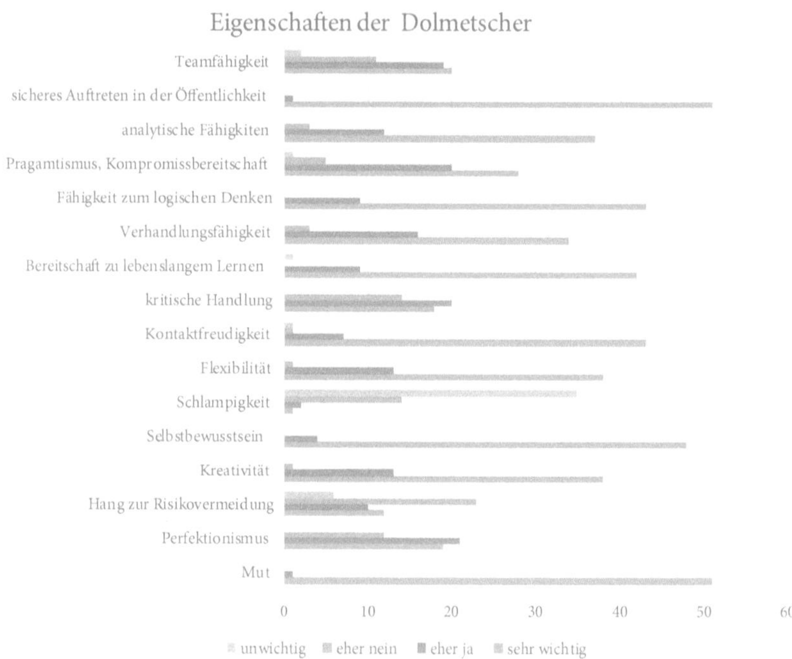

Hier lässt sich auf den ersten Blick bemerken, dass fast alle Eigenschaften von den ProbandInnen als genauso wichtig im Beruf des Dolmetschers eingeschätzt wurden. Eine von denen gehört jedoch definitiv nicht dazu, und zwar die Schlampigkeit. Wenn es um Hang zur Risikovermeidung geht, waren die Meinung geteilt, es überwogen jedoch die negativen Antworten.

Im nächsten Schritt wurden die Probandinnen gefragt, wie sie sich selber als Kandidaten für künftige Übersetzer bzw. Dolmetscher einschätzen.

Abb. 5: In welchem Maße treffen folgende Eigenschaften auf Sie zu?

Nur bei einer Eigenschaft hat die Mehrheit der ProbandInnen sehr deutlich mit „sehr wichtig" geantwortet, und zwar bei der Bereitschaft zu lebenslangem Lernen. Was andere Eigenschaften anbetrifft, waren die Studierenden mit ihren Antworten eher bescheiden, da sie mit „eher ja" geantwortet haben. Nur eine Eigenschaft haben sie als unakzeptabel eingeschätzt, und zwar die Schlampigkeit, obwohl auch diese Frage mehr als 20% der Befragten wieder mit „eher nein" zu 26%, die diese Frage mit „absolut nicht" beantwortet haben.

Zusammenfassend lässt sich also sagen, dass die Vertreter der Generation Y den Beruf des Translators für eine schwierige Aufgabe halten, bei der praktisch alle der aufgelisteten Eigenschaften von Bedeutung sind. Weiter, nach der Vorstellung der Generation Z, wird der Versuch unternommen, zu zeigen, was für eine Einstellung die Generation Y zu den Universitäten hat. Die Antwort auf eine so gestellte Frage wird auch die Ergebnisse der durchgeführten Umfrage besser erklären.

d) Generation Z

Vertreter der jüngsten Generation, der Generation Z, die ab dem Jahre 1995 geboren wurden, treffen wir schon an unseren Universitäten im erstem bzw. im zweiten Studienjahr. Für diese Generation, anders auch „Net Generation" genannt, ist die virtuelle Welt eine Selbstverständlichkeit, weil sie ihr die uneingeschränkte Mobilität und Kommunikation garantiert. Gerade diese Generation wird sehr oft dafür kritisiert, dass sie nicht mehr im Stande ist, traditionell, d.h. face to face zu kommunizieren. Sie tun es, nur sie tun es anders. Die Vertreter der Generation Z sind hochgradig auf eigene Zeile konzentriert und es ist an der Stelle zu bemerken, dass sie sich in dem Sinne von der Generation Y unterscheiden. Für die Generation Y war an der ersten Stelle die Karriere, der möglichst schnelle Aufstieg am wichtigsten. Die Generation Z sieht es anders, das eigene Ziel muss nicht unbedingt mit dem Berufsleben verbunden sein. Was für diese Generation ansonsten charakteristisch ist, ist Bindung nur zu interessanten Projekten, sie weiß also ihre Zeit zu schätzen und wird dem, was ihr nicht interessant scheint, nicht loyal sein. Darin liegt eine große Gefahr für die Universitäten und für uns Didaktiker (vgl. Scholz 2014).

Generation Z wird als Hoffnungsträger und Problemfall zugleich gesehen, da auf der einen Seite ihre Lebensweise, vor allem in der zweiten Welt, für die früheren Generationen (vor allem die Nachkriegsgeneration) schwer zu akzeptieren ist, auf der anderen Seite jedoch sehr ansteckend ist. Im Grunde genommen sind sich heutzutage Vertreter aller Generationen dessen bewusst, dass sie ohne entsprechende Fähigkeiten im Bereich der Neuen Medien in der Berufswelt keine Chancen auf Erfolg haben. Und wir alle wissen auch ganz genau, dass die Generation Z diejenige ist, die sich in diesem Bereich am besten auskennt und nicht unbedingt will, uns mit dem ganzen ihr zur Verfügung stehenden Wissen vertraut machen.

Zum ersten Mal ist es also in der Geschichte dazu gekommen, dass die Lebensweise der jüngsten Generation von den älteren, ob sie es wollen oder nicht, zu akzeptieren ist. Das ist der Bedarf der neuen, der digitalen Welt, in der wir alle heutzutage leben.

Was die Generation Z ansonsten noch auszeichnet ist eine räumliche Unabhängigkeit und eine fließende Verbindung von Berufs- und Privatleben. Diese Generation weiß ganz genau, was auf sie im Berufsleben zukommt, da sie eine sehr realistische Einstellung zu der Zukunft hat. (Scholz 2014: 33)

Im Vergleich zu den anderen Generationen wird die Generation Z als cleverer als die Generation Y, jedoch als leichter zu beeinflussen als Generation X bezeichnet.

Den Vergleich aller vier oben charakterisierten Generationen veranschaulicht am besten die folgende Tabelle.

Tab. 1: Diskontinuierliche Merkmale der vier Generationen (Scholz 2014: 33)

	Babyboomer 1945–1964	**Generation X 1965–1979**	**Generation Y 1980–1994**	**Generation Z 1995–…**
Grundhaltung	Idealismus	Skeptizismus	Optimismus	Realismus
Hauptmerkmal	Selbsterfüllung	Perspektivenlosig-keit	Leistungsbere-itschaft	Flatterhaftigkeit

Die angeführten Grundhandlungen weisen ein paar wichtige Parallelen auf. Die Generation der Babyboomer, die Idealisten, waren auf die Karriere orientiert, wie die Generation Y, die Optimisten. Im Unterschied dazu, die von der Perspektivlosigkeit überzeugten Skeptiker (Generation X) scheinen besser die Realisten aus der Generation Z, die die sog. Flatterhaftigkeit, die im nächsten Kapitel erklärt wird, auszeichnet, zu verstehen. Die von Scholz gegenübergestellten Eigenschaften der einzelnen Generationen veranschaulichen uns, Didaktikern, mit welchen Erwartungen die nächsten Generationen der Studenten zu uns kommen werden und vor welche Herausforderungen es uns alle stellt. Im Zusammenhang damit wird im nächsten Kapitel eben die Einstellung der Generationen Y und Z zu der Universität besprochen.

4. Generationen Y und Z an der Universität

Generation Y, was oben schon angedeutet wurde, ist bedingungslos karriereorientiert. Was sie also von der Universität erwartet hat, war ein kurzes praxisorientiertes und selbst-gestaltbares Studium, unbedingt mit Praktika und Auslandsaufenthalten. Die im Rahmen vom Bologna Prozess entwickelten Studienprogramme wurden von ihr als Erfolgsformel ohne kritische Distanz akzeptiert. (Scholz 2014: 47) Sehr oft war es der Fall, dass sie sich ihre Studienprogramme selbst zusammenstellen konnten, frei entscheiden konnten, wann sie welche Module/Kurse absolvieren werden, ohne dass die Lehrenden Rücksicht darauf genommen haben, dass auf diese Art und Weise die logische Kontinuität und die allmähliche Einführung in ein Thema verletzt wurde.

Anders sieht die Situation mit der Generation Z aus. Sie spürt keine emotionale Bindung und Loyalität zu irgendwelchen Gruppierungen, inbegriffen die Universitäten, sie sucht nach Kurzzeitbeziehungen, da das Leben für sie eine Ansammlung aus Lebensabschnitts-partnerschaften aus unterschiedlichen Bereichen ist. Für sie ist es nicht mehr interessant, an ein paar Fakultäten parallel zu studieren wie die Generation Y, da sie sich durch Flatterhaftigkeit auszeichnet. Die Generation Z wird nämlich mit den Insekten verglichen, die Suche nach Nahrung von Blume zu Blume zieht. (Scholz 2014: 33) In Hinsicht darauf, dass sie nicht loyal ist und Bindung nur zu interessanten Projekten empfindet, verlangt sie von uns, Didaktikern, dass wir ihr den richtigen Weg in der digitalen Welt zeigen, dass wir ihre Lebensweise nicht kritisieren, sondern versuchen, sie zu akzeptieren und uns ihr anpassen. Wenn wir auf diesen Schritt nicht vorbereitet sind, werden wir Studierende aus der Generation Z verlieren, da sie sich zu einer anderen Blume gezogen fühlen wird und sich von uns ohne Bedauern verabschieden wird.

Gibt es einen guten Ausweg aus dieser neuen Situation? Wie soll die Translationsdidaktik auf die Herausforderungen reagieren, um sich mit ihnen möglichst erfolgreich messen zu können? Im nächsten Kapitel wird der Versuch unternommen, Antworten auf diese Fragen zu finden und zur Diskussion zu stellen.

5. Neue Herausforderungen für die Translationsdidaktik – was tun?

Im letzten Kapitel setzt sich die Autorin zum Ziel, von den Herausforderungen für die Translationsdidaktik bezogen auf die Generation Z und ihre Erwartungen an die Universitäten zu sprechen. Diese Entscheidung ist dadurch begründet, dass die letzten Vertreter der Generation Y ihr Studium bald absolvieren werden und die Änderungen in den Studienprogrammen immer viel Zeit bedürfen, bevor sie ihre praktische Anwendung finden können.

Die Vertreter der Generation Z wurden als Realisten bezeichnet, die ganz genau wissen, was auf sie zukommt. So sollten wir die Studienprogramme in unseren Instituten weiterhin individualisieren, aber mit Sinn und Verstand. Sie sollten also an die einzelnen Studierenden, ihre persönlichen Eigenschaften und Interessen angepasst werden. Die Lösung lautet also: Individualisierung mit der bewussten „an-der-Hand-Führung". Die jungen Leute fühlen sich in der digitalen Welt sehr verloren, deswegen suchen sie nach Autoritäten, klaren Regeln, interessanten Möglichkeiten, sich das Wissen anzueignen. Geben wir ihnen diese Chance.

Alle Institute und Universitäten, nicht nur in einem konkreten Land, gerade, was das Übersetzen und Dolmetschen angeht, sollten sich den Studierenden und den Lehrenden gegenüber öffnen. Die Generation Z fühlt sich räumlich unabhängig, sie möchte einen unbegrenzten Zugang zu interessanten Veranstaltungen in anderen Instituten und an anderen Universitäten im Internet haben. Für angehende Übersetzer und Dolmetscher ist es ansonsten sehr wichtig, die Chance während des Studiums zu bekommen, sich das entsprechende Fachwissen aus anderen Wissensgebieten anzueignen. Dies setzt voraus, es den Studenten zu ermöglichen, ihr

Translationsstudium mit dem Studium an der Fakultät der Rechtswissenschaften, der Technik, der Medizin u. dgl. zu ermöglichen. Dazu ist es zu bemerken, dass ein idealer Fachübersetzer/Fachdolmetscher das Fachwissen in zwei/drei Sprachen besitzen muss. Es ist jedoch nicht möglich, im Rahmen des fünfjährigen Studiums zugleich, z. B. in Polen, Deutschland und England zu studieren. Das Internet macht es jedoch möglich.

Solche Ideen werden schon entwickelt und erfolgreich in der Praxis eingesetzt. An der Stelle wird solch ein gutes Beispiel angeführt. An der Jagiellonen Universität zu Krakau im Institut für Philosophie schuf Prof. Michał Ostrowicki die sog. Academia Electronica (www.academia-electronica.net). In der digitalen Welt kann absolut jeder Internetnutzer sich einen Avatar basteln und an den dort organisierten Veranstaltungen aktiv (!) teilnehmen. Auf der Plattform werden Vorlesungen gehalten und Seminare geführt. Den Teilnehmern wird außerdem ein Forum zur Verfügung gestellt, wo sie, auch während der Vorlesungen, ihre Kommentare abgeben können und dem Lehrenden die Chance geben, seine Gedanken mit den Zuhörenden austauschen zu können.

Das Leben in den zwei Welten ist heutzutage eine Tatsache. Die Zukunft der Translationsdidaktik liegt darin, die Möglichkeiten, die uns die digitale Welt und die Wissensrevolution gibt, richtig und erfolgreich zu nutzen.

Literatur

Buchhorn, Eva/Werle, Klaus, "Generation Y. Die Gewinner des Arbeitsmarkts", in: http://www.spiegel.de/karriere/berufsstart/generation-y-die-gewinner-des-arbeitsmarkts-a-766883.html, eingestellt am: 7.06.2011, abgerufen am: 15.06.2015.

Gleick, James, 2011, *The Information. A History, A Theory, A Flood,* Pantheon Books.

Göpferich, Susanne, 2008, *Translationsprozessforschung. Stand – Methoden – Perspektiven,* Tübingen: Gunter Narr Verlag.

Prensky, Marc, 2001, "Digital Natives, Digital Immigrants", in: *On the Horizon* (MCB University Press, Vol. 9, No 5, October 2001), in: http://www.marcprensky.com/writing/Prensky%20-%20Digital%20Natives,%20Digital%20Immigrants%20-%20Part1.pdf, eingestellt 2001, abgerufen am: 25.04.2015.

Reuter, Benjamin, 2013, "Interview mit David Weinberger, Lernen, wie Wissen entsteht", *WirtschaftsWoche,* Nr. 15, 8.04.2013, S. 96–97.

Scholz, Christian, 2014, *Generation Z. Wie sie tickt, was sie verändert und warum sie uns alle ansteckt,* Weinheim: Viley-VCH Verlag.

Small, Gary/Vorgan, Gigi, 2011, *iMózg. Jak przetrwać technologiczną przemianę współczesnej umysłowości,* Poznań; Vesper. (Originalausgabe: Small, Gary/Vorgan, Gigi, 2008, iBrain. Surviving the Technological Alternation of the Modern Mind).

Weinberger, David, 2011, *Too big to know: das Wissen neu denken, denn Fakten sind keine Fakten mehr, die Experten sitzen überall, und die schlaueste Person im Raum ist der Raum,* Bern: Huber.

Armando A. Magaia

Assessing Translation Competence at Eduardo Mondlane University[1]

Abstract: This paper assesses the translation competence of Eduardo Mondlane University (UEM) students in order to establish the major barriers to translation competence development in undergraduates and to provide suggestions for improving the didactics of translation. The research was designed as a multiple case study and was conducted at UEM from 2013 to 2014, involving 50 students and 11 lecturers. A questionnaire and a corpus of texts translated by the students were used for data collection. According to the questionnaire data, lecturers and students disagree about the UEM students' level of translation competence, but both groups identify curricular, attitudinal/motivational, pedagogical and infrastructural/instrumental factors, coupled with substandard bilingual skills, as the main barriers to translation competence development. Moreover, the macro- and micro-textual analysis corroborates concerns regarding the poor quality of students' translations and suggests that two types of translation errors negatively impact translation competence development: (i) Source-language-originated errors and (ii) Target-language-originated errors. These findings have two major implications for UEM: (1) reviewing the current curriculum to make it more conducive to translation competence development; and (2) investing in modern infrastructure, translation technology and research resources. Furthermore, in respect of UEM translation instructors, translation competence development in students necessitates the use of teaching strategies specifically designed to help students to: (1) get a grasp of the source-language text message, (2) maximize message accuracy during the transfer process and (3) hone their target-language text production skills.

Keywords: didactics of translation; translation competence; translation competence development; translator training; translation quality assessment; translation errors; macro-level errors; micro-level errors; source-language-originated errors; target-language-originated errors.

---

1 This paper is based on an MA dissertation titled *Investigating Translation Competence: A Case Study of Undergraduates at Eduardo Mondlane University*, submitted to the University of South Africa (Unisa) in November 2014. The author would like to thank Prof Claribel Koliswa Moropa, from Unisa, for her guidance and encouragement during and after the MA research, Dr Cynthia Donovan, from Michigan State University, and Donal Anthony Conlon, a former co-lecturer at UEM, for reading and critiquing this paper.

1. Introduction

Despite enough evidence suggesting that translations produced by undergraduates at Eduardo Mondlane University (UEM) are poor, comprehensive research aimed at identifying the major barriers to translation competence development in Mozambican students has been scanty. For example, previous research available has tended to focus on Portuguese language error analysis with a view to developing the didactics of Portuguese as though the students' translation competence could be measured – and developed – merely by improving their Portuguese language competence. As a result, the role of English as the source language has been omitted, not to mention that such an approach has done little or nothing to develop the didactics of translation as a whole.

Considering that "Ever since Translation Studies has been recognized as a separate academic discipline, translation quality has been a significant focus for research" (Drugan 2013, 54), this paper assesses the translation competence of UEM students, particularly by measuring their translation quality. To this end, the following key questions have been proposed:

(1) How do UEM lecturers and students perceive the current level of students' development of translation competence? and
(2) What are the main barriers to translation competence development in UEM students, as evidenced by macro- and micro-textual analysis?

To provide the background to this research, however, a summary of relevant studies available at UEM prior to this research is given below.

1.1 Summary of Previous UEM Research Findings

Since the introduction of the current translator-training programme at UEM in 2001, only two studies have been conducted with relevant contributions to the didactics of translation. The first study found that the students' translated texts, up to a point, reflected some knowledge of Portuguese grammar rules and of translation procedures and strategies, although lacking in target language quality (Felimone 2007, 39). Furthermore, according to Felimone (2007, 42–61), lexical level errors are the most important translation problems at UEM (with 35.2%), followed by text production errors (32%) and syntax errors (30%), while errors of form are quite irrelevant (at 3.8%). The second study was conducted by Companhia (2009, 4) with the goal of undertaking a descriptive analysis of some idiosyncrasies resulting from linguistic interference, arising from the translation process. He concluded from his language error analysis that the students' written production is characterized by "deviations" from the European Portuguese norm (ibid, 45). Such deviations are related to problems in the lexical, lexical-syntactic, syntactic and morphosyntactic domains. Companhia (ibid) suggests that such errors are due to source-language (English) interference during the translation process.

Although such studies are praiseworthy for shedding light on the quality of UEM students' translations (showing that, overall, it is poor), they only give a partial view of the reasons behind poor quality. More importantly, they do not assess translation competence as such, but rather Portuguese language competence in the translation context. Thus, such studies leave some critical questions unanswered. For example: Why do students underperform when it comes to lexical selection in translation? Why are students' translations marred by source-language (English) interference?

1.2 Defining and Measuring Translation Competence

Needless to say, the assessment of translation competence is compounded by the lack of a uniform definition or model of translation competence in the first place (Orozco and Albir 2002, 375). However, the ultimate goal of any translator-training programme should be to help students acquire or develop translation competence because, as Ardi (2012, 320) argues, by having it, "a translator could choose the best way to solve the problem in translation".

Several authors have proposed models of translation competence consisting of multiple sub-competences or components. For example, for Nord (2001, 28), translation competence entails a nine-component profile encompassing skills and knowledge such as professional knowledge, meta-communicative competence, intercultural competence, distribution skills, writing abilities, media competence, research competence, and the like. Despite using different terminology, the PACTE group (PACTE 2005, 610), Göpferich (2009, 21–23) and the EMT group (EMT 2009, 3) present comparable sets of skills and knowledge they believe a translator should have. By contrast, Pym (2003, 487) disagrees with multi-componential models of translation competence arguing that they "are heavy with assumptions not just about what translation is and how it should be taught, but more especially about the level at which specific teaching is needed, and for how many years". Accordingly, Pym (2003, 489) argues for a minimalist approach under which the training of translators involves the creation of a two-fold functional competence, namely:

- The ability to generate a series of more than one viable target text (TT_1, TT_2 … TT_n) for a pertinent source text (ST); and
- The ability to select only one viable TT from this series, quickly and with justified confidence.

It goes without saying that measuring translation competence is just as difficult a task as that of defining it. Significantly, Drugan (2013, 45) refers to a paradox in translation quality assessment when she states that "theorists and professionals overwhelmingly agree there is no single objective way to measure quality", although different actors do just this on a daily basis. Nevertheless, it could be argued that translation quality can be assessed according to the degree to which it is acceptable or relevant. In this regard, Derrida (2004, 426) suggests that a relevant, or "good", translation is the one that "performs its mission, honors its debt and does its job … while inscribing in the receiving language the most *relevant* equivalent for an original, the language that is *the most* right, appropriate, pertinent, adequate, opportune, pointed, univocal, idiomatic". Thus, it follows that assessing students' translations – to see the extent to which they are good, acceptable, relevant, functionally and stylistically adequate, etc. – is usually the most convenient way for instructors to measure their students' translation competence. Concurring with this view, Khodabakhshi (2009, 11) states that "although evaluation is made on students' performance, it is meant to assess their translation competence." She justifies that argument with "the fact that translation competence is not directly measurable" (ibid).

When assessing the quality of students' translations, it is important for instructors to use clear criteria which the students themselves are able to understand. Thus, while acknowledging the lack of broad-based empirical studies that can validate a typology of errors, Melis and Albir (2001, 281) suggest that the main questions that need to be considered in translation error classification are the following:

(i) The difference between errors relating to the source text and errors relating to the target text;
(ii) The difference between functional errors and absolute errors;
(iii) The difference in individual translators between systematic errors (recurrent) and random errors (isolated); and
(iv) The difference between errors in the product and errors in the process.

Against this background, the next section is on the methodology used in this study.

2. Methodology

This research was designed as a multiple case study and was conducted at UEM in 2013/2014, covering 50 students and 11 lecturers. The data collection tools consisted of a questionnaire and a corpus of texts translated by students for macro- and micro-textual analysis. The questionnaire had three sections containing

11 questions. The first section captured the respondents' profiles. The second section asked the respondents to rate the students' bilingual, extra-linguistic, knowledge about translation, instrumental and strategic sub-competences as well as their psycho-physiological components according to the PACTE model (PACTE 2005, 610). This section also probed the lecturers' and students' perceptions about the quality of UEM students' translations. The last section asked about the customisation of the classes by lecturers to students' specific needs and ended with two open-ended questions enquiring about the factors perceived to hinder or enable the development of translation competence. Macro- and micro-textual analysis was conducted based on 65 Portuguese texts translated from 13 English texts.

In this paper, no hard-line distinction is made between the concepts of "mistake" and "error". Thus, a translation error is defined as an instance of underperformance during a translation act, observed through the lack of translation message accuracy and target text effectiveness. All mistakes or errors are identified and analysed under two broad categories of errors, or macro-level errors: Source-Language-Originated Errors (SLOEs) and/or Target-Language-Originated Errors (TLOEs). The first category affects translation message accuracy and the second affects target text effectiveness.

A SLOE is any error being caused by flawed interpretation of the source-language text, in part or in whole. SLOEs are usually seen when the translated text is compared to the source-language text and distortions of meaning are found. Since the translator's message is not primarily of his/her authorship, its production is contingent upon full comprehension of the source-language text. Thus, any propositional mismatch between the intended meaning of the source-language text and that of the target-language text is construed as due to poor linguistic competence in the source-text language. Thus, all manifestations of poor source-text comprehension or inadequate problem-solving at every imaginable level (morphosyntactic, semantic, extra-linguistic, pragmatic, cultural, etc.) are classified as SLOEs. Likewise, a TLOE is any mistake or error exposing a translator's poor mastery of the target language/culture norms and conventions, but which is not necessarily identifiable through source-text vs. target-text comparison. An effective (translated) text does not usually contain (or contains very few cases of) syntactic or morphosyntactic errors, or even errors of form (spelling and punctuation, for example). Since these errors are usually observable from the target-language point of view, they are considered to be TLOEs.

Accordingly, the major micro-level errors making up SLOEs are: wrong meaning, wrong lexical choice, nonsense and omission. Wrong meaning and nonsense errors usually occur at structural level, while wrong lexical choice errors always occur at word/terminological level and omission occurs both at structural and word level. On the other hand, the main micro-level errors composing TLOEs are: norm-deviation, misspelling, unclearness, unnaturalness, ambiguity and punctuation errors.

It should, however, be pointed out that the above categories and subcategories of errors do not exclude each other as they can sometimes co-occur and therefore explain the same phenomenon in translation error analysis. Hence, in a situation where a SLOE and a TLOE occur simultaneously to explain one same phenomenon, the two-angle analysis may prove beyond doubt that the translation quality is low. Moreover, it should be noted that this taxonomy mainly serves the purpose of assuring that the translation quality assessment criteria used by translation instructors are fair, transparent and practical. In line with Waddington's (2001, 313–314) translation error analysis methods, it is hereby suggested that the weight of a TLOE penalty should be half that of a SLOE.

3. Findings and Analysis

3.1 Findings from Questionnaire Analysis

Respondents' Profiles

Regarding the students' linguistic background, while 58% had an African language as their mother tongue, almost all (98%) reported Portuguese as their first language of formal education. Moreover, each UEM student, on average, had been learning English for 11 years. Nearly all participants claim to be fluent in reading and writing both English (96%) and Portuguese (98%). As for the lecturers, they have taught different levels of English, Portuguese, Terminology, Lexicology, Translation Theory/Methodology and Translation Practice.

Perceptions Regarding Translation Competence

A remarkable finding regarding the students' perception of their own translation competence was the fact that most of them rated themselves in all five sub-competences and psycho-physiological components of the PACTE model as either "good" or "very good". This is in stark contrast to lecturers' perceptions, whose majority rated the students' sub-competences from "poor" to "average".

Confidence in Students' Translation Competence

Most students (68%) feel "confident" about translating any type of text into Portuguese or English. However, only 28% feel "very confident" about translating into Portuguese, a figure that drastically shrinks to as low as 4% when it comes to translating into English. Equally remarkable is the fact that when it comes to translating into English, the number of those rating themselves as "a little confident" significantly rises to 26% compared to the percentage of those claiming to be "a little confident" to translate into Portuguese (4%). By contrast, UEM lecturers in general do not trust the quality of their students' translations. For example, while 2 out of 11 lecturers would refer a client to "most" of their students for Portuguese translation services, 4 would only opt for "some" and 5 would only recommend "very few". For English translation services, 7 out 11 lecturers would recommend "very few" students.

Customization of Subject Contents to Students' Needs

The students' opinion regarding the customisation of subject contents to their needs is positive, which is consistent with most lecturers' own claim that they "sometimes" customise the contents of their subjects to suit their students' needs.

Factors Hindering Translation Competence Development

By and large, both lecturers and students identified curricular, attitudinal/motivational, pedagogical and infrastructural/instrumental factors as well as the students' lack of a balanced bilingual background as the most relevant barriers to the development of students' translation competence at UEM. For instance, the respondents converged in remarking that the UEM curriculum is very heavy in linguistics or that it is too theoretical. On the other hand, lecturers are perceived to be too busy to assist students, and the latter are seen as only aiming at a university degree at any cost – or even at the cost of translation competence. Likewise, lecturers are perceived to be lacking in teaching skills or methods that genuinely cater to translation students' needs. Moreover, respondents recurrently mentioned that the university lacks technological equipment or materials for translator training, including dictionaries, translation manuals, computers and the internet, which could be used for practical classes. Finally, substandard bilingual skills were seen by most lecturers – and acknowledged by *some* students – as gravely limiting UEM students' development of translation competence as they have no mastery of either English or Portuguese.

3.2 Macro- and Micro-Textual Analysis

To give readers a glimpse of the macro- and micro-textual analysis conducted during the study, two examples illustrating SLOEs and TLOEs are provided below:

Source Text 1:

"Many conflicts erupt due to clashes over access to resources, for instance as a result of the encroachment of one party on lands traditionally considered by another to be on its own terrain" (NIC 2020 Project 2010).

Student Translation:

"Muitos conflitos ~~entram em erupção~~ devido a conflitos por acesso a recursos, ~~por exemplo~~ como resultado da ~~usurpação de um partido em terras tradicionalmente consideradas por outro estar em seu táctico militar~~".

Translation Error Type		
Macro-level:	*SLOE*	*TLOE*
Micro-level:	**Wrong Lexical Choice, Nonsense**	**Norm Deviation, Ambiguity, Unnaturalness, Unclearness, Punctuation**
Detailed accuracy analysis		***Detailed text effectiveness analysis***
The student fails to determine the correct meaning of some lexical items. As a result, he uses the expression "***entram em erupção***" for "erupt", which is not natural in this context as it usually applies to volcanic eruptions (WLC). Likewise, he translates "party" as "***partido***", which would be more appropriate for a political party (WLC). Finally, the expression ***usurpação de um partido em terras tradicionalmente consideradas por outro estar em seu táctico militar***" makes no sense at all (NS).		In the expression that was viewed as a SLOE (NS), the student also displays poor mastery of Portuguese grammar. For example, in his text, "***usurpação***" selects the preposition "***em***" instead of "***de***" (ND). Another problem is that "***usurpação de um partido em terras***" is both ambiguous (A) and unnatural (UN), not to say unclear (UC). Finally, the absence of a comma after "***por exemplo***" reveals poor punctuation skills (P).

Source Text 2:

"Given that these very same issues still dominate the news agenda in modern-day Britain, it's only too tempting to speculate what Dickens would have made of London today" (Hewitt 2012).

Student Translation:

"Tendo em conta que esses mesmos problemas continuam a dominar a agenda de notícias na Grã-Bretanha moderna, é apenas demasiado tentador deduzir o que Dickens ~~teria feito de~~ Londres hoje".

Translation Error Type	
Macro-level:	*SLOE*
Micro-level:	Wrong Meaning/Wrong Lexical Choice
Detailed accuracy analysis	
The translated text is effective in Portuguese. However, the meaning of the idiom "make of" is misunderstood. As a result, the literal translation, "teria ***feito de*** Londres", does not correspond to the intended meaning in English and thus distorts the message (WM/WLC).	

3.3 The UEM Students' Typology of Translation Errors

The macro-level textual analysis leaves no doubt about the UEM students' tendency to, concomitantly, make two types of translation errors: SLOEs and TLOEs. However, as depicted in Graph 1, UEM students tend to make more SLOEs than TLOEs. This suggests that the students' ability to correctly analyse and interpret the source-language text in English is far from sufficient, resulting in their conveying incorrect messages into Portuguese.

Graph 1: Macro-level translation error occurrence at UEM.

Key: *SLOEs=Source-language-originated errors; TLOEs=Target-language-originated errors*

On the other hand, micro-level textual analysis suggests that SLOEs (Graph 2) are mainly characterized by message distortions or **wrong meaning** (48%), which often stem from poor understanding of the source-language text. The second main characteristic of SLOEs at UEM is the **wrong lexical selection** of equivalents in the target-language text (34%). This also contributes to message distortion. Finally, **nonsense** errors (13%) are less frequent at UEM and **omission** errors (5%) are quite negligible.

Graph 2: Micro-level SLOE occurrence at UEM.

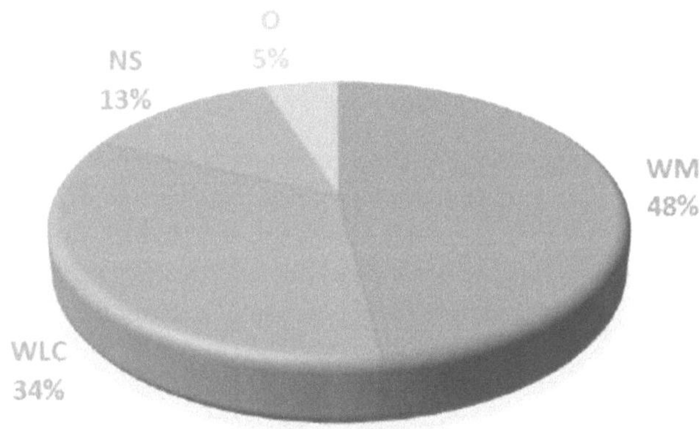

Key: *WM=wrong meaning; WLC=wrong lexical choice; NS=nonsense; O=omission*

Finally, Graph 3 shows that the main characteristic of TLOEs among UEM students is the presence of **unclearness**, **unnaturalness** or **ambiguity** in the translated texts, which cumulatively account for 45% of the cases. However, a closer look at the graph reveals that, in terms of relevance, target-language/culture **norm deviation** errors are the most notable, accounting for 32% of TLOE occurrences alone. In addition, it appears that **misspelling** (17%) also hampers the UEM students' development of translation competence during their training. Lastly, **punctuation** problems (6%) do not seem prominent among factors hindering UEM students' development of translation competence.

Graph 3: Micro-level TLOE occurrence at UEM.

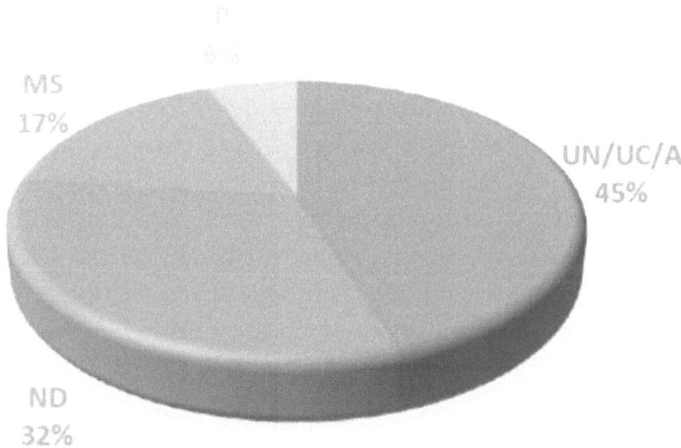

Key: *UN/UC/A=unnaturalness/unclearness/ambiguity; ND=norm deviation; MS=misspelling; P=punctuation*

4. Final Considerations

The study has demonstrated that UEM lecturers perceive their students' translation competence to be poor. Moreover, although the students somehow feel confident to translate any type of text, they share the same opinion as their lecturers regarding factors hindering their development of translation competence. These are: curricular, attitudinal/motivational, pedagogical and infrastructural/ instrumental factors, compounded by the students' poor mastery of their language pair. This finding is corroborated by the macro- and micro-textual analysis of students' translations, which reveals that they lack sufficient English text analytical skills and Portuguese text production skills, resulting in their failure to convey accurate, clear and natural messages. The finding on insufficient English mastery on the part of UEM students is particularly relevant because it also unveils the reason why their lexical selection is often incorrect, as well as the reason behind English interference in their translations, as observed in previous research at UEM. One could also speculate that the fact that UEM students are being trained to translate from L3 (English) into L2 (Portuguese) is a major bottleneck, considering that most Mozambican students have an African language as their mother tongue.

Significantly, the repeated occurrence of SLOEs, where the target-language text was grammatically correct, provides sufficient proof that a student's translation competence cannot be achieved merely by improving his/her target-text linguistic competence. Moreover, under a typical Portuguese error analysis, content or message errors, due to poor source-language text comprehension, would certainly have gone unnoticed, with the resulting biased assessment of the students' translation competence.

The study findings have two major implications for UEM. First, to ensure translation competence development in undergraduate students, UEM should create an enabling environment by providing adequate infrastructure such as a translation lab equipped with computers and modern translation technology. Such a lab should also be fitted with research and learning materials such as dictionaries, thesauri, grammars and basic literature on translation theory and practice. Second, UEM should review its curriculum, which may entail the deletion of certain subjects and the introduction of new ones to allow students more time to focus on Translation Studies.

Finally, the study findings suggest that improving students' source-language-text comprehension skills could go a long way toward improving their translation competence. Nevertheless, it is evident that UEM students still need a significant amount of assistance with their command of Portuguese as the target language, particularly in relation to text production skills. Thus, it is incumbent upon translator trainers to develop and apply teaching methods that are specifically aimed at helping students to achieve three goals in tandem: (1) getting a good grasp of the source-language text message, (2) maximizing message accuracy during the transfer process and (3) sharpening one's target-language text production skills. A translation practice lesson plan, therefore, should clearly reflect these goals through all its stages.

References

Ardi, H. 2012. "Is Theory of Translation Needed to Build Students' Translation Competence?" Proceedings of the International Seminar on Languages and Arts (ISLA), conducted by FBS Universitas Negeri Pa: 320–28, accessed 31 March 2013, http://english.unp.ac.id/wp-content/uploads/2012/02/A-Proceeding-havidse.pdf.

Companhia, C. 2009. *Transferência interlingue no âmbito da prática da tradução: análise de "erros" de selecção categorial em estudantes do ensino superior em Moçambique.* MA Dissertation, Universidade Eduardo Mondlane.

Derrida, J. 2004. What is a "relevant" translation? In *The Translation Studies Reader, Second Edition*, ed. L. Venuti, 180–192. New York: Routledge.

Drugan, J. (2013). *Quality in Professional Translation. Assessment and Improvement.* London: Bloomsbury.

EMT. 2009. "Competences for professional translators, experts in multilingual and multimedia communication", accessed 31 March 2013, http://ec.europa.eu/dgs/translation/programmes/emt/key_documents/emt_competences_translators_en.pdf.

Felimone, L. M. C. C. 2007. *Desenvolvimento da competência comunicativa para tradução.* MA Dissertation, Universidade Eduardo Mondlane.

Göpferich, S. 2009. "Towards a model of translation competence and its acquisition: the longitudinal study TransComp." In *Behind the Mind: Methods, Models and Results in Translation Process Research, ed. S.* Göpferich, A. L. Jakobsen and I. M. Mees, 11–37. Copenhagen: Samfundslitteratur, accessed 4 May 2013, http://gams.uni-graz.at/fedora/get/o:tc-095-187/bdef:PDF/get.

Hewitt, D. 2012. "Rich London, poor London – a tale of two cities." New Internationalist magazine, accessed 20 August 2013, http://newint.org/features/web-exclusive/2012/02/07/london-inequality-what-would-charles-dickens-think/

Khodabakhshi, M. "Translation Evaluation in Educational Settings for Training Purposes: Theories & Applications." TranslationDirectory.Com, accessed 4 August 2013, http://www.translationdirectory.com/article32.htm.

Melis, N. M. and Albir, A. H. 2001. "Assessment In Translation Studies: Research Needs." *Meta*: Translators' Journal 46(2): 272–287, accessed 31 March 2013, http://id.erudit.org/iderudit/003624ar.

NIC 2020 Project. "Conflict Resolution in Africa. Discussion Paper", accessed 15 June 2012, http://www.docstoc.com/docs/3558509/CONFLICT-RESOLUTION-IN-AFRICA

Nord, C. 2001. "Training Functional Translators." In *Training Translators for the New Millenium,* ed. M. Tennent, 27–46. Amsterdam: John Benjamins, accessed 10 September 2013, http://www.wds-portal.de/mfmedia_downloads/3/10/5707_Nord,%20Training%20translator.pdf.

Orozco, M. and Albir, A. H. 2002. "Measuring Translation Competence Acquisition." *Meta:* Translators' Journal 47(3): 375–402, accessed 31 March 2013, http://id.erudit.org/iderudit/008022ar.

PACTE. 2005. "Investigating Translation Competence: Conceptual and Methodological Issues." *Meta:* Translators' Journal 50(2): 609–619, accessed 5 April 2013, http://id.erudit.org/iderudit/011004ar.

Pym. A. 2003. "Redefining Translation Competence in an Electronic Age. In Defence of a Minimalist Approach." *Meta*: Translators' Journal 48(4): 481–497, accessed 31 March 2013, http://id.erudit.org/iderudit/008533ar.

Waddington, C. 2001. "Different Methods of Evaluating Student Translations: The Question of Validity." *Meta:* Translators' Journal 46(2): 311–325, accessed 31 March 2013, http://id.erudit.org/iderudit/004583ar.

Winibert Segers and Hendrik J. Kockaert

Can Subjectivity be Avoided in Translation Evaluation?

Abstract: Is translation evaluation a subjective, personal matter? Is evaluating translations the same as beer tasting or listening to a piece of music? Is the judgment determined by personal taste? We will try to answer those questions and show how the subjectivity of the evaluation can be curtailed.[1]

The evaluation method that we use is the PIE method (Preselected Items Evaluation). (Kockaert & Segers 2012, 2014; Anckaert *et al.* 2006, 2008; Eyckmans *et al.* 2009, 2012; Van de Poel & Segers 2007; Segers 2012). PIE has five stages:

- Preselection of items in the source text (before the test taking)
- Determination of correct and incorrect solutions of the preselected items
- Calculation of the scores of the candidates
- Calculation of the difficulty degree (p-value) and the discriminatory power (d-index) of the preselected items
- Calculation of the final scores of the candidates (This calculation is based on the preselected items with a good p-value and a good d-index.)

Keywords: translation evaluation, subjectivity, PIE method, p-value, d-index, dichotomous method, criterion-referenced method, norm-referenced method, transparent method, automation.

1. Evaluation Method

The PIE Method is a

- Dichotomous method. The translation solutions are correct or incorrect. There is no grey zone. No weight (e.g. minor, serious, critical) is accorded to the incorrect solutions. Evaluation methods with a weighting component have a risk to be subjective. Evaluators often disagree about the weight of an incorrect solution. What one evaluator considers as a minor error, can be a serious error for another evaluator.

---

1 The subjectivity degree of the evaluation can be statistically measured by calculating the intra-rater reliability and the inter-rater reliability.

- Criterion-referenced and norm-referenced method. Stage 1 and 2 are criterion-referenced (These stages are based on predetermined criteria). Stage 4 and 5 are norm-referenced (The norm is determined by the performance of the tested group of candidates).
- Transparent method. Candidates can exactly see how their final scores are calculated.

You can use the PIE method

- In different domains. Administrative, cultural, economic, legal, medical … translations can be evaluated with PIE.
- In educational and professional contexts. Translation teachers can select items based on the material treated in class. In professional contexts the selection of the items will be related to the required competencies of the translator.

2. Example

In order not to overload this contribution with quantitative data, we will give an example with a limited number of candidates. Twelve students (Master in Translation, KU Leuven, academic year 2014–2015), translated the following English source text into French. They could make use of all resources: dictionaries, websites etc. The chosen text is a urological text from Princess Alexandra Hospital (Essex) and gives information to patients about uroflowmetry.

Original English text
What is a Uroflow?
The uroflow study is a simple test to measure how much urine you pass, the strength of the flow and how efficiently your bladder empties.

What does having the procedure involve?
You will be asked to urinate into a special uroflow study container which measures the speed of your urination. After the uroflow study, an ultrasound probe <u>will be passed</u> [PI 1] over your lower abdomen. This will measure how much urine you have left in your bladder after you urinate.

What will this show?
This study provides some information on how your bladder functions and if something is obstructing the flow of urine. This study is being performed on you to help determine if you have a different <u>pattern</u> [PI 2] of urination compared to people who do not have an issue with how their bladder functions.

How do I prepare for <u>this procedure</u> [PI 3]?
Prior to beginning the study, you will be asked to <u>drink enough water</u> [PI 4] or fluids to fill your bladder. You may start filling your bladder from home providing your travelling

distance is within one hour [PI 5]. It is important that the bladder should feel full (to a point that you would normally pass urine) but not be uncomfortably full. Do not overfill the bladder [PI 6].

When the bladder feels full, you will be asked to urinate [PI 7] into the special uroflow study container. It is important that you pass urine in as normal a pattern (for you) as possible. If you think that this urination was not normal (for you) tell the nurse [PI 8] and you may be asked to repeat the study.

If you have any mobility problems, or any other special needs, please let us know in advance so that we can make any necessary arrangements to accommodate you.

What happens after the procedure?
Immediately after the uroflow, an ultrasound probe will be passed over your abdomen. The nurse performing the procedure [PI 9] will lightly press the probe into the lower part of your abdomen and measure the amount of urine left in your bladder.

The results of these studies [PI 10] will be discussed with you on your next visit.

3. Ten Preselected Items

In the English source text we preselected ten items. We have underlined and numbered the ten items. The candidates have translated the English text without knowing which items we had selected. They worked on a version of the text without the underlined and numbered items.

4. Correct and Incorrect Solutions of the Ten Preselected Items

The twelve candidates gave the following translation solutions for the ten preselected items.

PI 1 will be passed
= on passe, on passera, on fera, on effectuera, sera passée, sera prise, l'infirmière glissera, Ø (candidate 3, 4, 5, 6, 7, 9, 10, 11, 12)
≠ passe, sera posé, on insérera (candidate 1, 2, 8)
p-value: 9/12 = 0.75

PI 2 pattern
= façon, manière, mode, miction, excrétion (candidate 2, 4, 5, 6, 10)
≠ habitude, patron, modèle, procès, comportement, patron d'excrétion (candidate 1, 3, 7, 8, 9, 11, 12)
p-value : 5/12 = 0.41

PI 3 this procedure
= l'examen, le test, cet examen (candidate 1, 2, 4, 6, 9, 10, 11)
≠ ce procédé, cette procédure, la procédure (candidate 3, 5, 7, 8, 12)
p-value: 7/12 = 0.58

PI 4 drink enough water
= boire suffisamment d'eau, boire assez d'eau, vous buvez assez d'eau (candidate 3, 4, 5, 6, 7, 9, 11, 12)
≠ boire assez de l'eau, boire suffisamment de l'eau (candidate 1, 2, 8, 10)
p-value: 8/12 = 0.66

PI 5 within one hour
= moins d'une heure, maximum une heure, ne dépasse pas une heure, inférieure à une heure, moins qu'une heure (candidate 3, 5, 6, 8, 9, 10, 11)
≠ n'est plus qu'une heure, à moins qu'une heure, se passe dans une heure, une heure (candidate 1, 2, 4, 7, 12)
p-value: 7/12 = 0.58

PI 6 Do not overfill the bladder.
= Ne remplissez pas trop la vessie., la vessie ne doit pas être trop remplie, Ne surchargez pas la vessie., Evitez donc d'avoir la vessie trop pleine., mais pas bondée (candidate 1, 2, 5, 9, 10, 12)
≠ Ne déborde pas la vessie., Ne remplissez votre vessie pas trop., Ne fait pas déborder la vessie., Ø, Ne buvez pas trop. (candidate 3, 4, 6, 7, 8, 11)
p-value: 6/12 = 0.50

PI 7 you will be asked to urinate
= on vous demandera d'uriner, on vous demande d'uriner, vous urinerez, il vous sera demandé d'uriner, vous devez uriner, vous allez commencer à uriner (candidate 1, 4, 5, 6, 8, 9, 10, 11, 12)
≠ vous allez être demandé d'uriner, Ø, vous serez demandé d'uriner (candidate 2, 3, 7)
p-value: 9/12 = 0.75

PI 8 tell the nurse
= informez l'infirmière, dites-le à l'infirmière, informez l'infirmier (candidate 1, 5, 6, 7, 8, 11)
≠ vous l'annonceriez à l'infirmière, Ø, dites l'infirmière, Ø, dit l'infirmière, vous le diriez à l'infirmière (candidate 2, 3, 4, 9, 10, 12)
p-value: 6/12 = 0.50

PI 9 performing the procedure
= Ø, exécute ce procédé, qui effectue la technique (candidate 2, 4, 7, 8, 11, 12)
≠ performant l'examen, Ø, qui fait la procédure, (candidate 1, 3, 5, 6, 9, 10)
p-value: 6/12 = 0.50

PI 10 these studies
= ces examens (candidate 1, 4, 10, 11)
≠ l'étude, Ø, ces études, cette étude (candidate 2, 3, 5, 6, 7, 8, 9, 12)
p-value: 4/12 = 0.33

5. Scores of the Twelve Candidates

The scores are calculated on the basis of the number of correct and incorrect solutions.

Candidate 1	5/10	(5 correct, 5 incorrect)
Candidate 2	4/10	(4 correct, 6 incorrect)
Candidate 3	3/10	(3 correct, 7 incorrect)
Candidate 4	7/10	(7 correct, 3 incorrect)
Candidate 5	7/10	(7 correct, 3 incorrect)
Candidate 6	7/10	(7 correct, 3 incorrect)
Candidate 7	4/10	(4 correct, 6 incorrect)
Candidate 8	4/10	(4 correct, 6 incorrect)
Candidate 9	6/10	(6 correct, 4 incorrect)
Candidate 10	7/10	(7 correct, 3 incorrect)
Candidate 11	8/10	(8 correct, 2 incorrect)
Candidate 12	5/10	(5 correct, 5 incorrect)

Lowest score	3/10	(candidate 3)
Highest score	8/10	(candidate 11)
Mean	5.58/10	
Median	5.50/10	
Mode	7/10	
Standard Deviation	1.55	

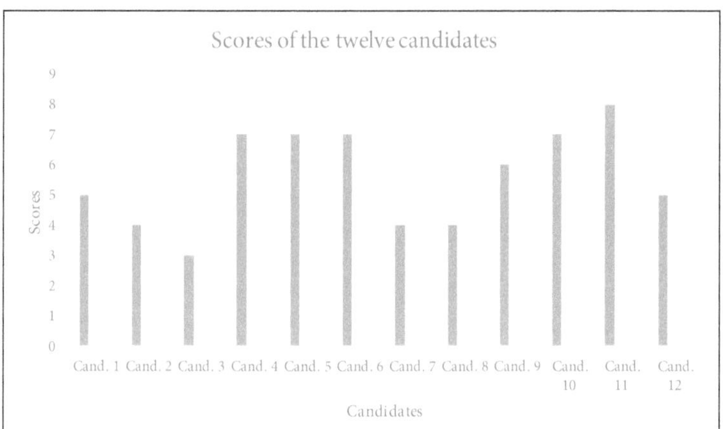

6. P-values of the Ten Preselected Items (Item Difficulty)

The p-value of an item can be calculated easily: the number of correct solutions divided by the total number of candidates.

Preselected Item 1	0.75	(9/12)
Preselected Item 2	0.41	(5/12)
Preselected Item 3	0.58	(7/12)
Preselected Item 4	0.66	(8/12)
Preselected Item 5	0.58	(7/12)
Preselected Item 6	0.50	(6/12)
Preselected Item 7	0.75	(9/12)
Preselected Item 8	0.50	(6/12)
Preselected Item 9	0.50	(6/12)
Preselected Item 10	0.33	(4/12)

Preselected Item 1 ('will be passed') and 7 ('you will be asked to urinate') are the easiest items. Preselected Item 10 ('these studies') is the most difficult. Good items have p-values between 0.27 and 0.79 (not too difficult and not too easy). The ten preselected items have p-values between 0.33 and 0.75. From a difficulty level point of view, the ten items are good items.

The average p-value of the ten preselected items is 0.55. The difficulty of a translation test is very often subjectively determined by the evaluator on the basis of his impression of the difficulty of the source text and his estimation of the translation capacities of the candidates. Calculation of the average p-value can help to avoid the subjectivity of the evaluator. The average p-value gives an objective image of the difficulty of a translation test.

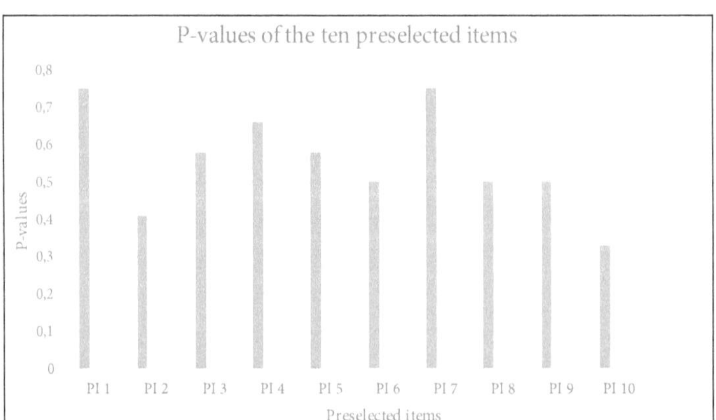

7. D-indices of the Ten Preselected Items (Discriminatory Power)

To calculate the discriminatory power of the ten preselected items, we use the top-group-bottom-group method (extreme group method). For each item, the p-value in the bottom-group is subtracted from the p-value in the top-group.

Top-group (tg) = Candidate 4, 5, 6, 10 and 11.
Bottom-group (bg) = Candidate 2, 3, 7 and 8.

Preselected Item 1	0.50	(5/5 (p-value tg) – 2/4 (p-value bg))
Preselected Item 2	0.55	(4/5 (p-value tg) – 1/4 (p-value bg))
Preselected Item 3	0.55	(4/5 (p-value tg) – 1/4 (p-value bg))
Preselected Item 4	0.30	(4/5 (p-value tg) – 2/4 (p-value bg))
Preselected Item 5	0.30	(4/5 (p-value tg) – 2/4 (p-value bg))
Preselected Item 6	0.15	(2/5 (p-value tg) – 1/4 (p-value bg))
Preselected Item 7	0.75	(5/5 (p-value tg) – 1/4 (p-value bg))
Preselected Item 8	0.10	(3/5 (p-value tg) – 2/4 (p-value bg))
Preselected Item 9	-0.35	(2/5 (p-value tg) – 3/4 (p-value bg))
Preselected Item 10	0.60	(3/5 (p-value tg) – 0/4 (p-value bg))

d-index = 0.40 or higher	very good items
d-index = 0.30 to 0.39	good items
d-index = 0.20 to 0.29	fairly good items
d-index = 0.19 or less	poor items

An item is a good discriminating item (d = 0.30 or higher) when candidates who responded to the item correctly also did well on the overall test (in this case, the ten preselected items), while candidates who responded to the item incorrectly also did poorly on the overall test.

Item 9 (*performing the procedure*) has a negative discrimination index (d = -0.35), this indicates that candidates who performed poorly on the translation test performed better on item 9 than the candidates who performed well on the translation test. Items 6 and 8 have weak discriminating power.

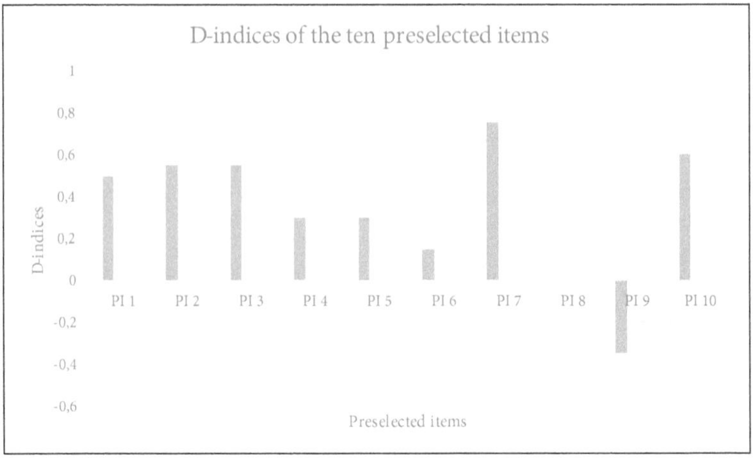

8. Final Scores of the Twelve candidates

On the basis of the seven good items (item 1, 2, 3, 4, 5, 7, 10), the items with a good p-value and a good d-index, we can calculate the final scores of the twelve candidates.

Candidate 1	5/10	→	3/7	(4.28/10)
Candidate 2	4/10	→	2/7	(2.85/10)
Candidate 3	3/10	→	3/7	(4.28/10)
Candidate 4	7/10	→	6/7	(8.57/10)
Candidate 5	7/10	→	5/7	(7.14/10)
Candidate 6	7/10	→	6/7	(8.57/10)
Candidate 7	4/10	→	2/7	(2.85/10)
Candidate 8	4/10	→	2/7	(2.85/10)
Candidate 9	6/10	→	5/7	(7.14/10)
Candidate 10	7/10	→	6/7	(8.57/10)
Candidate 11	8/10	→	6/7	(8.57/10)
Candidate 12	5/10	→	3/7	(4.28/10)

Lowest score	2/7	= 2.85/10
Highest score	6/7	= 8.57/10
Mean	4.08/7	= 5.82/10
Median	4/7	= 5.71/10
Mode	6/7	= 8.57/10
Standard Deviation	1.65	

The recalculation can have an effect on the scores. Candidates 1 and 3, for example, have the same final score (3/7), but their previous scores were 5/10 and 3/10.

The final scores of candidates 3, 4, 5, 6, 9, 10 and 11 are higher than their previous scores. The final scores of candidates 1, 2, 7, 8 and 12 are lower than their previous scores.

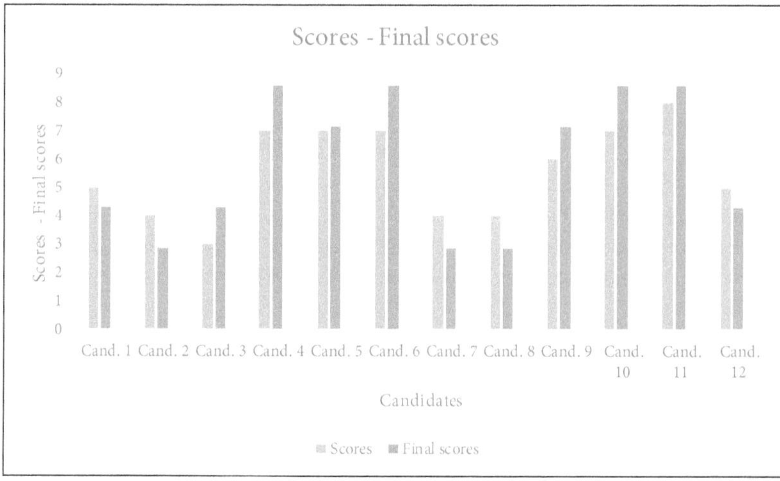

9. Non-Preselected Items

A question may arise about non-preselected items: What does the evaluator do with a candidate who proposes a wrong solution for an item that was not preselected? To answer this question we have to look at the performance of all the candidates who participated in the translation test. If the candidate is the only of the twelve candidates who proposes a wrong solution for the non-preselected item, this item should not be included in the translation test. But if the item has a good p-value (between 0.27 and 0.79) and a good discrimination index (d = 0.30 or higher), this item should be included in the translation test.

10. A Time-Consuming Method?

We have to admit that the PIE method requires a large time investment, but that is the price you have to pay to get an accurate picture of the docimological quality of the translation test.

We hope that automation can resolve the time investment problem. If we are able to automate the PIE method, a large part of the time invested can be recovered. The automation of the method is a realistic wish. For each item we have determined which solutions are correct and which are incorrect. A computer could check those solutions in the translations. Only in the case of a solution that is not in the list 'correct-incorrect solutions', 'human' intervention will be required.

References

Anckaert, Philippe, Eyckmans, June, and Winibert Segers, 'Vertaalvaardigheid evalueren: een normgerelateerde benadering', *n/f* 6 (2006), 9–27.

Anckaert, Philippe, Eyckmans, June, and Winibert Segers, 'Pour une évaluation normative de la compétence de traduction', *ITL – International Journal of Applied Linguistics* 155 (2008), 53–76.

Eyckmans, June, Anckaert, Philippe, and Winibert Segers, 'The perks of norm-referenced translation evaluation', in Angelelli, Claudia V., and Holly E. Jacobson, eds, *Testing and assessment in translation and interpreting studies* (Amsterdam: John Benjamins, 2009), 73–93.

Eyckmans, June, Segers, Winibert, and Philippe Anckaert, 'Translation Assessment Methodology and the Prospects of European Collaboration', in Tsagari, Dina, and Ildiko Csépes, eds, *Collaboration in Language Testing and Assessment* (Frankfurt am Main: Peter Lang, 2012), 171–184.

Kockaert, Hendrik J., and Winibert Segers, 'L'assurance qualité des traductions: items sélectionnés et évaluation assistée par ordinateur', *Meta : journal des traducteurs / Meta: Translators' Journal* 57/1 (2012), 159–176.

Kockaert, Hendrik J., and Winibert Segers, 'Evaluation de la traduction : la méthode PIE (Preselected Items Evaluation)', Turjuman. *Revue de Traduction et d'Interprétation / Journal of Translation Studies* 23/2 (2014), 232–250.

Poel, Chris van de, and Winibert Segers, eds., *Vertalingen objectief evalueren. Matrices en ijkpunten* (Leuven: Acco, 2007).

Segers, Winibert, 'Vertaalevaluatie. Waarover hebben we het eigenlijk?', *Ad Rem. Tijdschrift voor zakelijke communicatie* 26/6 (2012), 17–18.

Marcel Thelen

Quality and Objectivity of Testing and Assessing in Translator Training: Dilemmas and Suggestions

Abstract: Like in other sectors, in the translation sector quality assurance is important. It is required not only for the actual professional practice itself, but also for the study of translation as well as the training of students to become professional translators. Although these areas all relate to translation, they deal with it from different perspectives and focal points and with different objectives, requirements and practices. Therefore, if quality is to be required, implemented and assured, these differences should be taken into account without losing sight of the evident similarities, which undoubtedly will have a direct bearing on the quality assurance systems, quality criteria and assessment criteria in the three areas.

One of the key factors in quality assurance is objectivity of testing and assessing. The questions to be addressed are is (1) how objectivity can be implemented in the practice, study and training of translation, (2) if it is/can be identical in all three areas, and (3) – if not – how the three areas can be attuned to one another on the point of objectivity so as to guarantee the highest possible quality. As far as practice and training are concerned, there is an additional requirement, viz. to reduce the so-called skills gap as much as possible, and to make the transition from training to practice as smooth as possible.

It is these points that will be discussed in this article, as well as the various factors that translator training is facing and that have an impact on quality in general, and on the quality and objectivity of testing and assessing in particular.

Keywords: Quality, objectivity of testing and assessing, professionalisation, focal point of testing and assessing, skills lab, skills gap, standards, national accreditation standards, "educational" standards, professional standards, EN 15038/ISO 17100.

1. Introduction

The call for quality is ubiquitous in today's society. Translation is not an exception, i.e. the study of translation, as well as practice (the profession) and training. In this article, I will restrict myself to the training and practice of translation. In the area of translator training it not only relates to the actual delivery of the training, including the trainers themselves, but certainly and increasingly also to the testing and assessing of the translation (-related) products produced by students. This trend is currently reinforced by detailed requirements for testing and assessing issued by national accreditation bodies. Training institutes are required to have a documented quality assurance system in place to ensure and guarantee the quality of testing and assessing, as well as the quality of the results obtained. They have to be able to guarantee that the credits and final degrees awarded have been awarded on the basis of transparent, reliable and objective criteria, and that the level of quality is up to nationally and internationally recognised academic and professional standards, in other words, that these are "well-deserved" and have been earned and awarded without any preferential treatment, unfair practices or sloppy criteria. Compliance with professional standards is required, at least in the Netherlands, with a view to the employability of graduates, which in itself calls for professionalisation of the curriculum. As a result, translator training institutes have to pay special attention to:

1. ways to introduce and implement professionalisation in the training so as to enhance post-graduate employability and to avoid and/or reduce as much as possible the alleged so-called "skills gap" between training and actual professional practice;
2. ways to ensure the transparency, reliability and objectivity of assessment criteria and procedures; and
3. implementing a system of quality assurance to ensure the quality of testing and assessing.

Objectivity of assessing may be a requirement, the question is whether translation can be measured as objectively as this requirement stipulates, but also how objectivity and professionalisation should/can be introduced in the curriculum and what is needed for this. Two obvious factors that immediately present themselves are time and space in the curriculum. There are, however, also other factors that are equally important.

In this article, I will discuss these and other aspects and give – by way of illustration of how these requirements can be met and what is necessary for this – an outline of what the Maastricht School of Translation and Interpreting of Zuyd University of Applied Sciences has been doing since its foundation in 1981, and has done and is still doing since its previous accreditation in 2014. Let me first deal with differences in testing and assessing between training and profession.

2. Testing and Assessing: Differences between Training and Profession

There are clear differences in testing and assessing between training and profession. Represented schematically, some of the most prominent differences are:

Table 1: Differences between training and profession as regards testing and assessing

	Translator training	The translation profession
Objectives	1. to train students to become starting professionals in translation/translation-related jobs, and 2. by doing so to secure a financially sound and for students attractive training institute	1. to deliver quality translation(-related) products, and 2. by doing so to become commercially successful
People to work with	students	1. professional translators/ translation-related professionals 2. commissioners, clients
Instruments for quality management	national accreditation standards	standards of the profession
Legal stipulations	always minimally a second chance	------
Focus of quality management	functioning as a training institute	functioning as a professional (agency/bureau)
Consequences	delay in study → career ruined (+ right of appeal)	dissatisfied clients → dismissal (+ right or appeal) / business closedown

This survey is by no means exhaustive and more details may be added, but these seem to be the most prominent. As can be seen, training and profession differ considerably. Yet they deal with one and the same activity, viz. translation. They are not equal to one another, and this is not surprising because training prepares for practice and profession practices – to some extent – what has been trained. In this way, they rather complement one another. Yet there should be at least some point where the two "meet", and this will probably be quality. The question then is what is quality, is there some point of convergence in interpretation of this concept between training and profession, and how can it be accomplished so that both are "satisfied".

3. Quality and Types of Standard

Quality is a concept that is difficult to grasp. It varies between economic sectors, professions, and industries, certainly between training and practice. It also includes a certain degree of individual interpretation. It is a gradable concept.

Therefore, it is not easy to define a set of core characteristics, which would seem necessary because of the requirement of objectivity of measuring quality.

A useful definition of quality may be found in manufacturing:

Figure 1: Definitions of quality in manufacturing.

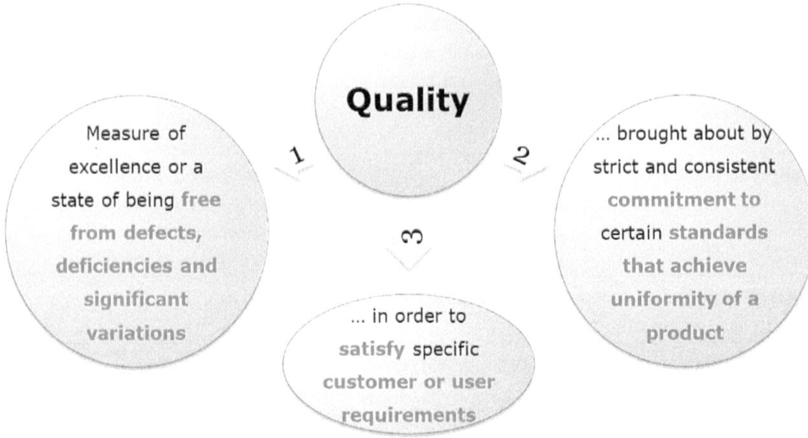

(cf. http://www.businessdictionary.com/definition/quality.html – last visited: 26 April 2015)

The bold elements form a common ground between training and profession. Element (3), viz. "[…] satisfy […] customer or user requirements" holds in both areas, albeit with a difference. Generally, in training it is in the first place the trainer and the course/task requirements that are to be satisfied for a positive assessment to result, in the profession it is the customer/client/ commissioner or the end user who has to be satisfied so that payment follows. The end user will be satisfied if the product delivered meets his expectations (e.g. it serves the purpose that he had in mind, it does what he expected it to do). In other words, client/requirement satisfaction is a point of resemblance between training and profession. Element (1) applies to training only partially, since in training defects and deficiencies are always allowed to a certain extent and their number and severity has an effect on the final score (to be) given. Element (2) applies also partially to training. The fact is that standards certainly pertain to testing and assessing by trainers so as to "achieve uniformity" of testing methods and assessment. In a way, standards also influence the way students produce their translations, and the quality of their translations. This may be the case with accreditation standards (e.g. no fraud, plagiarism) and professional standards (e.g. translations should be revised by another translator before delivering to the commissioner), but generally the objective of translation by students is not to achieve uniformity of translation. In terms of quality, elements (1) and (3) form the best common ground between training and profession as to quality. Element (2) seems to be reserved more for the work done by trainers.

Training (i.e. trainers and curriculum) has to take heed of quite a number of standards, which may make things sometimes quite difficult, and is not always possible. They can be presented as in fig. (2):

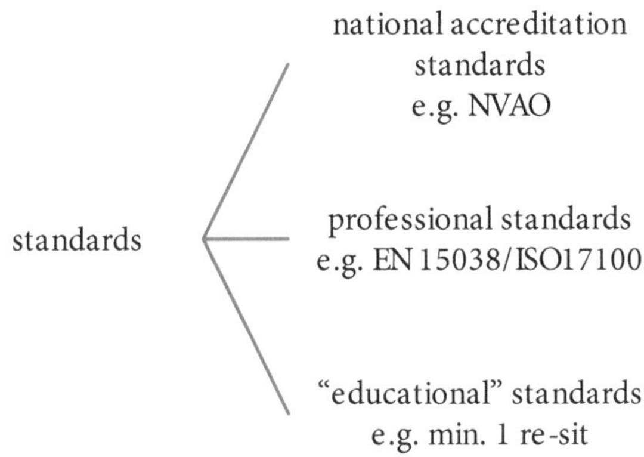

The profession is in a less complicated situation, because there at least accreditation standards do not play a separate and independent role. In addition, I doubt very much whether "educational" standards play any role at all-in the profession, on the contrary, the profession is much "harsher" than training as for testing and assessing, mainly because it does not have such an educational commitment as training.

The requirements of ***"educational" standards*** are well known among trainers and students in a training setting. Because the main objective of training is to help students prepare themselves for life after graduation, pedagogy (next to didactics) is important and implies that every student is allowed to make mistakes and should be given a "second chance" to improve his mistake so as to learn not to make the same mistake again in the future, and to learn from this mistake. On top of this, testing and assessing should be objective, excluding personal preferences on the part of the tester/assessor, and be repeatable leading to similar results. But it should also be reliable or valid, i.e. test and assess what it intended to be tested and assessed, and every result should be accountable. Finally, testing and assessing should be transparent, which means that students should know beforehand what to expect from a test and its assessment so that they may prepare themselves well, and instructions for the test should be clear.

The requirements of the ***professional standards*** EN 15038 and ISO 17100 relate to:

1. Human resources, management, competences of staff and continuing professional development of staff
2. Technical resources
3. Quality management system
4. Project management
5. Client-TSP relationship (including enquiry and feasibility, quotation, client-TSP agreement, handling project-related client information
6. Project conclusion
7. Procedures in translation services, including managing translation projects, preparation (administrative aspects, technical aspects, linguistic aspects), as well as translation process (including translation, checking, revision, review, proofreading and final verification).

The ***accreditation standards*** may be lesser known. The national accreditation standard for educational institutes in The Netherlands comprise a number of sub-standards, the most important ones being:

1. Envisaged competences/qualifications
   - ➢ Are the envisaged final competences relevant for the sector for which the programme trains students?
   - ➢ Are the envisaged final competences in line with the level and type education (in terms of Dublin descriptors?
   - ➢ Are the envisaged final competences in line with the requirements of the profession?
   - ➢ Have the envisaged final competences been endorsed by representatives of the profession?
2. Programme
   a. Orientation of curriculum = in line with developments in the relevant profession
   b. Contents of curriculum
   c. Design of curriculum
3. Testing and realisation of intended learning outcomes
   - ➢ Has the training institute an adequate system for testing and assessing?
   - ➢ Can the training institute prove that the envisaged final competences for students have been mastered on graduation? Are the final competences mastered in line with the envisaged final competences?

   These sub-standards are of direct relevance for testing and assessing.

4. Factors Influencing Quality and Testing & Assessing

4.1 Quality

Quality is a complex and not at all unequivocal term in translation (and interpreting). At the same time, objectivity that is required for quality testing and assessing is not precisely delineated either, but a gradable concept.

Quality in training and profession is influenced by associations such as branch organisations (such as FIT, national organisations such as e.g. NGTV[1] in the Netherlands and BDÜ[2] in Germany, etc.) and academic organisations (such as CIUTI[3] and EMT[4]), as well as all sorts of standards such as EN 15038/ISO 17100 and national accreditation standards. In addition, it can be addressed, on the other hand, from the perspective of training and from that of the profession.

4.2 Focal Points for Testing and Assessing

Moreover, in both training and profession, a number of focal points play a role such as product, process, service, translator, trainer, and training. This is not to say, however, that all of them are present in both training and profession. I will come back on this in section (8.3). In all these focal points, the crucial question is what is or is to be understood by **quality** (see fig. 3):

1 The Dutch Organisation of Translators and Interpreters, one of the national branch organisations in The Netherlands (https://ngtv.nl).

2 Bundesverband der Dolmetscher und Übersetzer e.V. (www.bdue.de).

3 Conférence Internationale Permanente d'Instituts Universitaires de Traducteurs et Interprètes (www.ciuti.org).

4 European Master's in Translation (http://ec.europa.eu/dgs/translation/programmes/emt/index_en.htm).

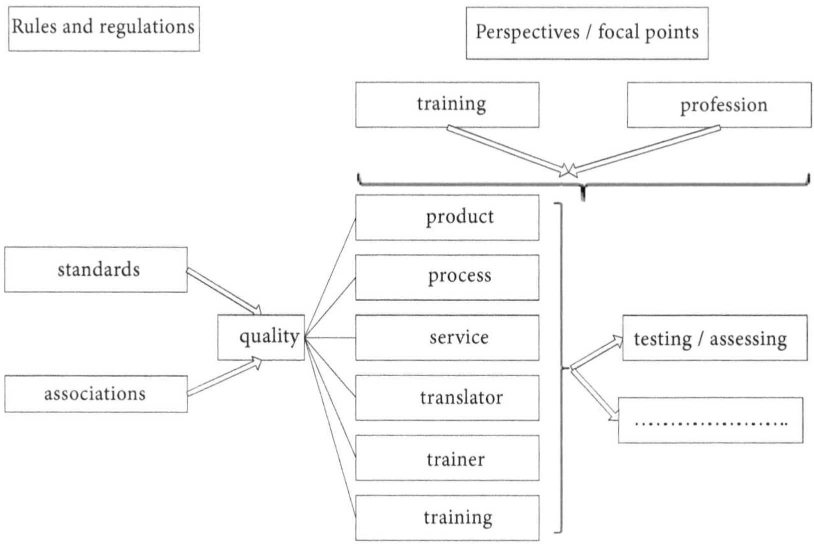

In what follows, my focus will be on the bold-italic items in the shaded boxes, viz. testing and assessing of product in training as influenced by standards, and in all this what is/may be understood by quality and how this can be tested and assessed in an objective manner. By way of illustration I will discuss these elements as they figure at the Maastricht School of Translation and Interpreting. Other perspectives, i.e. process, service and translator are also tested and assessed, but I will not go into these, since this is beyond the scope of this article.

Testing and assessing in training are in an extremely difficult position. Training prepares students for the profession, and, therefore, has to pay special attention to employability of graduates in order to avoid the perceived skills gap between training and profession. Translator training has its own dynamics, requirements and rules and regulations, on the one hand, but tries to (and is required to) tune up with the profession as much as possible, on the other. Training is in the difficult position that it has to take heed of all the other factors represented in the diagram, and at the same time face the implications of the distinction between training/education and professional world/industry. Testing and assessing in the profession, for example, differs from that in training in that in the profession the testing and assessment criteria are much more general than those in training. Another difference is the focal points employed for testing and assessing; in the profession, for example, one of the focal points is service (provision), but this is as yet present in only very few training programmes (if at all), and even if it is present, its implementation will probably be different from that in the profession. Consequently, in the light of the foregoing the questions raised at the onset of this paper may be reformulated as follows:

⇨ How can Translator Training implement objectivity of testing and assessing that is in line with
   1. requirements, rules and regulations imposed by
      i. standards (accreditations, professional standards, and educational standards),
      ii. associations (e.g. code of conduct, quality handbook),
   2. the requirement of employability, while at the same time keeping an eye to quality?

4.3 Degrees of Objectivity

The degree of objectivity of testing and assessing will undoubtedly vary depending on the focal point applied. Product requires other testing and assessment criteria than process or translator, for example, and the degree of objectivity of testing and assessing is lower than in the case of process of translator, certainly when one takes into account the definition of translation given by Newmark (1988:6): translation is "[...] a science, a skill, an art and a matter of taste". Whereas science and skill may be assessed objectively, this becomes more difficult with art and taste. The more objective the testing and assessing is, the better precise criteria may be formulated that may be checked in a rather straightforward manner. Moreover, some focal points can be implemented and provided with criteria much easier in the profession than in training. The ideal situation would, of course, be that all focal points were present both in training and the profession, but at this moment this is still very far away.

Whatever the situation, a number of minimal requirements for objectivity of testing and assessing may be formulated:

1. the aims, type, mode, and focus of criteria for testing and assessing should be determined, agreed and recorded beforehand by minimally 2 competent parties;
2. where and how aims, type, mode, focus and criteria for testing and assessing are to be recorded should be determined beforehand, as well as who does the recording, by whom these recorded data are accessible;
3. the actual testing and assessing should be done by minimally 2 competent parties;

4. the execution of testing and assessing should be monitored by a competent body;
5. the results of testing and assessing should be recorded afterwards and checked by monitoring body.

4.4 Professionalisation

Another factor of influence on testing and assessing in training is the introduction of professionalisation in the curriculum, as propagated by the EMT. Professionalisation is deemed necessary and inevitable in order to reduce the perceived skills gap to a minimum, and ideally to annihilate it completely. Professionalisation entails the introduction of different ways of working (more in line with what is done in the profession, e.g. variation in types of jobs, working with clients and with realistic and authentic materials, more practical translation exercise, etc.

5. Difficult Position of Training

Because of all the requirements imposed on training, and all the factors to be taken into account, translator training is in a very difficult position, as may become clear from fig. (4):

Figure 4: Difficult position of translator training.

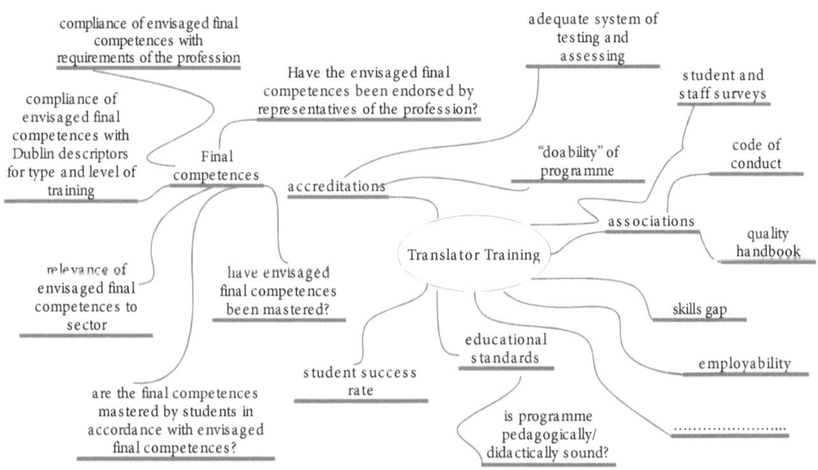

And this is not all.... Apart from the above aspects, there are issues such as conditions on government funding (e.g. requirements on student success rate *vs.* quality of training), but these are beyond the scope of this article.

6. Dilemmas for Translator Training

This situation leads to a number of dilemmas that need resolving:

1. Can translation quality (i.e. the quality of translation products) be measured at all? (cf. Newmark, 1988:6)
2. What assessment criteria are there, should there be? (profession *vs.* training)
3. Can the various perspectives of translation be measured by these criteria? (→ product, process, service, translator)
4. Are these criteria " productive"?
5. How can/should all this be done?
6. Is there enough time and space in the curriculum to accommodate professionalisation?
7. How can professionalisation be reconciled with testing and assessing of the training institute?
8. Does this affect objectivity and quality of testing and assessing?
9. Can the testing and assessing of translation (in all its perspectives and aspects) be 100%?

In the next sections, I will discuss what the Maastricht School of Translation and Interpreting does/has done to resolve these dilemmas.

7. Resolving Dilemmas: Testing and Assessing at the Maastricht School of Translation and Interpreting

Let me first outline the main characteristics of the Maastricht School of Translation and Interpreting:

1. Is was founded in 1981 by HM Queen Beatrix and the Minister of Education.
2. Its foundation was the result of elaborate study and surveys among (inter) national training institutes in the country and abroad, translation companies, clients, etc.
3. The training programme is practice-oriented → it embraces professionalisation.
4. Its mission is to train students to become starting professional translators.
5. The programme is a BA training programme of 4 years.
6. The specialist subject domains are economics, law, science/technology/IT.

7. The languages offered are Dutch (mother tongue), English, French, German and Spanish.
8. The programme has the following specialisations: translation, localisation, subtitling and interpreting.
9. There are a number of mandatory placements and in-house simulated translation bureau.
10. The School is unique in the country: it is the oldest training programme, it is the only full-time BA programme, and the only government financed BA programme.

8. Steps Taken to Guarantee Objectivity in Testing and Assessing

8.1 Organisation and Overall Testing and Assessment system

The following organisational measures have been taken and overall procedures installed:

1. Three important committees have been installed:
   a. ***curriculum board*** (responsibilities: all matters concerning form, content and execution of curriculum),
   b. ***exam board*** (responsibilities include ensuring the quality of tests and exams, annually appointing examiners, all practical aspects of examination and exams, realisation of intended learning outcomes (competences), correct implementation of Teaching and Examination Regulation), and
   c. ***assessment board*** (responsibilities include analysing tests and exams, organising annual session of realised learning outcomes).
2. The final ccompetences are based on and explicitly related to existing standard documents containing competences (e.g. EN 15038/ISO 17100), and EMT competences.
3. On the basis of these final competences, a common national set of competences has been formulated and endorsed by other translator training institutes in the country and declared a national set of competences. This set has, moreover, been endorsed by all the stakeholders in the country and has been adopted as minimal requirements for registration in the government registry for sworn translators and interpreters.
4. There is a quality register for examiners, and a quality register for lecturers.
5. A number of quality forms have been installed for testing and assessing: analysis forms, testing and assessing policy document

6. The so-called four-eyes principles has been implemented as follows: there is meeting to establish testing and assessing criteria, there is a case meeting to discuss doubtful cases as well as a validation meeting, and there is involvement of profession in testing and assessing (by means of advisory assessments). More precisely, the assessment board:

1. publishes documents on assessment policy and assessment plan
2. standardises and unifies terminology of testing and assessing, but also of working methods, etc.
3. designates 10 core exams and analyses all accompanying quality forms meticulously
4. checks and analyses at random forms of a number of non-core exams.

There are three types of test analysis forms: (1) a pre-test analysis form, (2) an exam matrix, and (3) a post-test analysis form (see fig. (5)–(7)):

Figure 5: Example of pre-test analysis form.

Exam:

- Subject:
- Academic year:
- Curriculum year/block:
- Objectives:
- Subject matter to be tested:
- Format of exam:
- Internal examiner(s):
- External expert(s):

Objectivity and standard for calculating scores

1. Did you fill in an exam matrix for his exam?	YES / NO, TO BE ADJUSTED
2. Did you indicate what components/questions the exam consists of?	YES / NO, TO BE ADJUSTED
3. Did you indicate the relative weighting of every component and every question vis-à-vis the total assessment?	YES / NO, TO BE ADJUSTED
4. Did you indicate whether the weighting of components and questions is in line with their importance?	YES / NO, TO BE ADJUSTED
5. Did you indicate per component whether it tests knowledge, skills/application of knowledge or both?	YES / NO, TO BE ADJUSTED
6. Did you indicate per component what the assessment criteria are?	YES / NO, TO BE ADJUSTED
7. Did you indicate how the final scores are calculated?	YES / NO, TO BE ADJUSTED
8. Did you indicate where the boundary between fail and pass lies and on what grounds this is so?	YES / NO, TO BE ADJUSTED
9. Did you indicate the relation between the components/questions of the exam and the final or end competences to be mastered?	YES / NO, TO BE ADJUSTED

Figure 5: Example of a pre-test analysis form (continued).

Transparancy	
1. Did you publish the study guide fort his exam on BlackBoard?	YES / NO, TO BE ADJUSTED
2. Did you include a detailed course description in the study guide?	YES / NO, TO BE ADJUSTED
3. Did you formulate all the learning objectives of the course in a clear and unequivocal way in the course outline?	YES / NO, TO BE ADJUSTED
4. Is the subject matter for this exam known to the students?	YES / NO, TO BE ADJUSTED
5. Is the whole procedure of assessment and score calculation known to the student, including consequences of fail and details of resits?	YES / NO, TO BE ADJUSTED
6. Did you submit the complete exam?	YES / NO, because ....
7. Is there a mock exam?	YES / NO, because................
Reliability	
8. Does the exam test and assess the same every year?	YES / NO, because................
9. Did you describe the assessment criteria in the exam matrix and the course outline?	YES / NO, TO BE ADJUSTED
10. Have the assessment criteria been derived from/based on the learning objectives/final competences and did you formulate them unequivocally and unambiguously?	YES / NO, TO BE ADJUSTED
11. How many questions on average relate to the same topic? (the more questions, the more reliable the exam).	

Figure 6: Example of an exam matrix.

– **Subject:** – **Academic year:** – **Curriculum year/block:** – **Objectives:** – **Subject matter to be tested:** – **Format of exam:**	
Exam components	
Assessment in terms of	
FAIL / PASS	Components ....
marks	Components ....
Relative weighting of components /questions vis-à-vis total assessment	
Is the weighting of the components / questions in line with their importance?	
Indicate per component whether it tests knowledge, skills / application of knowledge or both	
Assessment criteria per component / question	
Calculation of final scores on the basis of:	
Boundary between 5 (out of 10) / fail and 6 (out of 10) / pass defined on the basis of:	
Relation between exam components / questions and final competences:	

Figure 7: Example of a post-test analysis form.

- Subject: - Academic year: - Curriculum year/block: - Objectives: - Subject matter to be tested: - Format of exam: - Internal examiner(s): - External expert(s):	
Objectivity	
1. Have more people been involved in the assessment (both internal and external)?	YES / NO, because .... If YES: number and functions ....
2. Did you (the other examiner(s)) also teach the students on their way to this exam?	YES / NO
3. Was the assessment anonymous and indiscriminate?	YES / NO, because ....
Reliability	
4. Did the students that normally score well pass?	YES / NO
5. Did good students give correct answers to difficult questions?	YES / NO
6. Are the results of the exam comparable to those of an earlier version of the exam?	YES / NO, because ....
Follow-up	
7. Did the students get access to and/or feedback on their results?	YES (collective / individual feedback / discussion of exam in next block) NO, because ....

8.2 Implementation of Four-Eyes Principle and Overall Testing and Assessment System

For efficiency and practical reasons, not every exam is assessed by two or more internal examiners plus an external expert, instead:

1. the assessment criteria for all exams are established officially in an annual meeting of all lecturers involved (criteria meeting);
2. assessment criteria are included in course outlines and the so-called assessment policy/assessment plan;
3. all documents are published on Blackboard, in study guides, and communicated to students by mail and other means
4. deviations from established criteria are not allowed and are monitored by the Assessment Board

5. all lecturers submit pre-test analysis forms and exam matrices to the Assessment Board before the beginning of a new block (of 10 weeks), and submit post-test analysis forms after the exams;
6. the Assessment Board checks all documents submitted and analysed;
7. the Assessment Board analyses all core exams and samples of other exams;
8. there are annual meetings on all "doubtful cases" (around the boundary between fail and pass) with all the lecturers involved (case meetings);
9. the Assessment Board organises an annual session on assessment of all exams, i.e. papers, projects etc. that together make up the final examination (validation meeting). The participants are internal examiners other than those of original assessment, as well as external experts from the profession and other training institutes. All participants assess the products blindly. Moreover, all assessments are compared, and deviations are spotted and discussed, and lead to improvement measures wherever necessary.

8.3 Focal Points of Testing and Assessing

For testing and assessing students, the Maastricht School of Translation and Interpreting applies all the focal points for testing and assessing mentioned before that relate to what students do, i.e. product, process, service, translator[5]. The analysis forms and the overall testing and assessment system are identical for all focal points, the training methods and assignments to go with these focal points are, obviously, not, nor are the accompanying specific testing and assessment types (see Thelen, 2008). For product and process, for example, simple and complex translation assignments are appropriate but the focal points service and translator require different methods and assignments. These focal points are typically implemented in the form of the so-called in-house simulated translation bureau (or skills lab)[6], where students run and manage – under the supervision of a lecturer-director – a translation bureau along the lines of a real bureau. This is the ideal training form to test and assess the translator and the service provided. This is done on the basis of EN 15038/ISO 17100. Such a skills lab[7] requires the introduction of professionalisation in the curriculum. Otherwise testing the translator and service is hardly possible.

5 The focal points of trainer and training are typically applied in other settings: HR and accreditations.

6 For a more detailed description of this in-house simulated translation bureau see Thelen (2006).

7 The skills lab is comparable to Kiraly's "translation praxis class" (Kiraly, 2004:114–115).

Objectivity in testing and assessing students in the skills lab is guaranteed not only by the overall testing and assessment system mentioned before, but also because students are continuously tested and assessed during the 9-week period (40 hours per week) of the skills lab by a variety of agents: peers (co-translators, revisers, management), clients, external experts, external coach, and lecturer-director. They all follow the minimal general requirements for objectivity of testing and assessing mentioned in section (4.3) above. For a detailed survey of specific assessment procedures applied at the Maastricht School see Thelen (2013).

9. Epilogue

Quality and objectivity of testing and assessing in translator training still have a long way to go. Not only will they inevitably involve professionalisation in the curriculum, they will undoubtedly also have an effect on form and content of the curriculum. For this to be successful, more time and space should be allocated to them, and new training methods should be introduced, of which such a method as the skills lab is a promising example.

The Maastricht School of Translation and Interpreting believes that it is has come a long way since its foundation and is on the right track with its programme, particularly its skills lab, but that there is still much to do to perfect things. In all this, it is encouraged by the fact that it gets more and more recognition for what it does and how it does this from other translator training institutes, but certainly also, and not in the least, by the employment rate among graduates which is 86% within 3 months after graduation. Extra encouragement has come from the previous accreditation in 2014 which resulted in the one but highest overall score, viz. "good".

References

Kiraly, D. (2004), "Preparing Students Today to Meet Market Demands Tomorrow." In: Forstner, M. and H. Lee-Jahnke (eds.), *Internationales CIUTI-Forum. Marktorientierte Translationsausbildung.* Bern: Peter Lang, pp. 101–118.

Newmark,. P. (1988), *A Textbook of Translation.* Hemel Hempstead: Prentice Hall International.

Thelen, Marcel (2006): "Going European: A Plea for Building a Network of Simulated Translation Bureaus". *CIUTI-Forum Paris 2005. Regards sur les aspects culturels de la communication.* Bern/Berlin, etc.: Peter Lang, pp. 219–236.

Thelen, M. (2008), "Translation Quality Assessment or Quality Management & Quality Control of Translation?" In: Lewandowska-Tomaszczyk, B. and

M. Thelen (eds.), *Translation and Meaning, Part 8.* Maastricht: Zuyd University of Applied Sciences, Maastricht School of Translation and Interpreting, pp. 411–423.

Thelen, Marcel (2009): "Quality Management for Translation". *CIUTI-Forum 2008. Enhancing Translation Quality: Ways, Means, Methods*, p. 195–212. Bern/ Berlin, etc.: Peter Lang.

Thelen, M. (2013), "Translation Quality Assessment in translator training". In: Ende, A-K., S. Herold and A. Weilands (eds.), *Alles hängt mit allem zusammen. Translatologische Interdependenzen. Festschrift für Peter A. Schmitt.* Berlin: Frank & Timme, pp. 191–201.

Donata Lisaitė, Sonia Vandepitte, Bruce Maylath, Birthe Mousten, Susana Valdez, Maria Castel-Branco and Patricia Minacori

Negotiating Meaning at a Distance: Peer Feedback in Electronic Learning Translation Environments

Abstract: Recent research has contributed to an understanding of the positive impact that peer feedback has on student learning, but there is a lack of experimental studies that focus on how peer feedback affects student translation competence. Our study investigates whether the latter are enhanced in the Trans-Atlantic & Pacific Project (TAPP) with an experiment that included the explicit practice of student peer feedback competence and the negotiation of meaning among peers. Students – whether writing, translating or usability testing – collaborated online both within their own university peer group and with a partner university. The results of this intervention, however, suggest no clear tendencies or relation between peer feedback and meaning-related translation competence.

Keywords: peer feedback, negotiation of meaning, online collaborative learning, translation training, translation competence, formal linguistic evaluation items, meaning-related evaluation items, score development, translation problem, experimental design.

1. Peer Feedback: Theoretical Rationale

In modern education, peer feedback has been increasingly employed as a learning, instructional and assessment strategy. The notion of peers evaluating each other's work actually goes back to several theoretical schools of thought, in particular, Vygotsky's Zone of Proximal Development theory (1978) and his sociocultural theory (1986), which claim that individuals usually learn in the company of other people and that learning, therefore, 'presupposes a specific social nature' (1978, 34).

There are several reasons for the recent increase in interest in peer feedback. First, it has been claimed that peer-to-peer interaction facilitates the construction of knowledge, enhances learner autonomy and acquisition of various skills (Tudge 1990; Wells 1999; Swain *et al.* 2002). According to Swain *et al.* (2002, 172), for instance, learners often collaborate to 'solve linguistic problems and/or co-construct language or knowledge about language' and as such they enter a so-called 'collaborative dialogue'. In addition, research has shown that peer feedback not only encourages learners to act autonomously by thinking critically: it also enables them to acquire both domain-specific skills (e.g. writing) and transferable skills (e.g. the ability to work in a team, acknowledge and discuss different points of view, or consider the details of feedback provided by a fellow student) (Berg 1999; Paulus 1999; Tang & Tithecott 1999). This can also be linked to changing working conditions in society: for example, in order to be successful in their careers, employees need to demonstrate twenty-first century skills such as flexibility and higher order skills (e.g. problem solving, critical thinking, lifelong learning, intercultural communication) (Scardamalia 2001; Starke-Meyerring 2008; van Zundert *et al.* 2010).

Considering the fact that all the above-listed aspects underscore the co-constructional and interpersonal nature of peer feedback activities, it follows that engaging in peer feedback activities may significantly affect patterns in the generation of meaning by individuals. While research into peer feedback has been conducted in a great number of fields, the question can be asked whether peer feedback activities are a useful tool for negotiating meaning in cross-cultural and interdisciplinary writing and, in particular, in a translation setting.

2. Peer Feedback in a Translation Setting

Collaborative learning for translation has recently been pointed out as useful for translation training (Babych *et al.* 2012; Gambier 2012; Desjardins 2011; Huertas Barros 2011; O'Brien 2011; Risku & Dickinson 2009; Zili 2009; Kenny 2008; Muñoz Martín 2007; Pavlović 2007; González Davies 2004; Kiraly 2000). In addition, Babych *et al.* emphasised that both commercial and non-commercial translation are becoming increasingly reliant on collaborative activities (2012). Therefore, translation trainees will benefit from practising this learning model as early as possible.

In particular, Kiraly stressed the need for a constructivist approach towards translator education by emphasizing the impact of collaborative activities on the generation of meaning: 'individuals (…) create or construct meanings through participation in the interpersonal, inter-subjective interaction' (2000, 50–51). In addition, Kiraly states that translators enhance their competence by joining and working together. Relying on these underlying assumptions, Kiraly implemented a two-year qualitative action study in which students collaborated on a translation project and three types of data were collected: questionnaires filled out by the students, verbal data collected using tape recorders and direct observation (for example of non-verbal behaviour). The results revealed that the students were highly motivated, worked very efficiently and reported having gained a substantial insight into both translation and collaborative work.

While considerable research has been conducted to highlight the importance of and the need for collaborative translation, there is a lack of empirical studies that show the impact of peer feedback on translation competence.

3. Terminology

The terms that are used to refer to assessing and commenting on a colleague's work are numerous. For purposes of clarity, here are explanations of how we will understand some of the recurring terms:

- *Peer collaboration:* students working with each other towards a common goal (activities involve, but are not limited to, exchanging documents, assisting each other, etc.).
- *Peer interaction*: students interacting with each other, i.e. part of peer collaboration where they are actually communicating with each other (at a distance or in person).
- *Peer feedback*: students expressing their own observations about other students' work. In the context of our study, this involved students reading each other's translations and giving comments for improvement.
- *Peer revision*: students examining the translation for suitability in terms of its adequacy in representing the source text message in the target language.
- *Peer review*: students proofreading the translation for acceptability in terms of its target language.
- *Peer assessment:* students reading other students' work and giving it a mark.

4. Peer Feedback: Gaps in Research and Training

The existing body of research into peer-to-peer activities is substantial; however, some researchers warn that it should not be blindly trusted. For example, van Zundert *et al.* (2010, 270) point out that it is 'impossible to make claims about what constitutes effective PA [peer assessment]'. Furthermore, Strijbos and Sluijsmans (2010) state that the ambiguity and diversity of peer assessment practices make it difficult to see how peer assessment actually facilitates learning. One way to disambiguate the situation could be by explicitly training students to peer assess each other's work. Importantly, peer feedback training is also reported to contribute to the success of peer feedback activities (Finn and Garner 2011, 445). Such training serves a two-fold purpose: first, students learn to give constructive feedback and, secondly, research into L2 feedback has revealed that without prior training L2 revisers tend not to address higher-order – or meaning-related – problems such as content and structure (Leki 1990; Mangelsdorf and Schlumberger 1992; Flynn 1982). Further positive effects of peer feedback training on the quality of students' writing tasks are discussed in Min (2005, 2006) and Van Steendam *et al.* (2010).

5. Pilot Study

Our own experiment involved three translation tests – a Pre-test (1T), a Mid-test (2T) and a Post-test (TT) – spread out over a period of seven weeks (Appendix A) by 29 students of the Master course 'English: General Translation Practice' (Autumn 2013) at Ghent University. In between the tests, students were familiarized with and did peer feedback activities within the Trans-Atlantic and Pacific Project (TAPP), a translation training setting which is described in more detail elsewhere (Humbley *et al.* 2005; Vandepitte *et al.* 2015) and which aims to prepare translation students to work in a context that adheres to industry norms EN 15038 (2006) and ISO 17100 (2015). This involves the provision of quality assurance, including revision and review, in other words, assessment of (each other's) translations. The students carried out the usual project activities except for the fact that half of the class performed them in the former half of that period, while the other half of the class performed them in the latter half of the period. Throughout these activities, students formed triplets of students to translate a popular science article that was drafted by a small team of scientific writing students from North Dakota State University at Fargo.

The cohort (n=29) was divided into two groups: Group A consisted of eighteen students and Group B included eleven students. Four other students participated in only one or two out of three tests and their data were excluded from the analysis.

Students' feedback activities could be either of the following two kinds. First, Ghent University students were able to contact their source text writers in Fargo and ask them for clarification of certain source text passages. Secondly, Ghent students themselves were organized in small teams of one translator, one reviser and one reviewer. Each student was also registered in three teams and therefore played each role once during the peer feedback activities for three different translation tasks in a period of three weeks, participating in the translation of three different texts or text passages.

To enhance comparability of the test data, three slightly modified versions of a fragment adapted from Colfer Eoin's children's book *Artemis Fowl: The Lost Colony* (see Appendix B) were translated in the Pre-, Mid- and Post-tests. This text allowed for testing the students' formal linguistic and meaning-related translation problem solving skills and included a set of ten diverse translation difficulties that students had to address. Formal linguistic items included six phrases that required translation problem solving skills related to reference, punctuation, numerals, noun phrase structure and completeness, while four meaning-related items involved considerations about the proper use of modality, figures of speech, register and cultural reference. These items remained unchanged in the three tests.

Translation competence was solely measured in terms of the (in)correct translation of the ten pre-selected items. For each correctly translated item students received one point. All scores were first individually determined by two assessors (two authors) and then discussed with the purpose to find agreement on scores allowing for a difference of only one point between the two scores for one student.

6. Score Data

The data analysis focussed on how the scores of the students developed with respect to the different sets of evaluation items, i.e. formal linguistic items versus meaning-related items. The main question in our analysis was therefore to examine whether any learning differences were found between the two sets of items. If feedback activities help students think critically (Berg 1999), it is logical to expect them to become better at the meaning-related items.

6.1 Student Score Development for Formal Linguistic Items

Figure 1: Student score development over the three tests: comparison of Pre-test to Mid-test (1T), Mid-test to Post-test (2T) and Post-test to Pre-test (TT) for six evaluation items. Letter F refers to formal linguistic translation competence. (n=29).

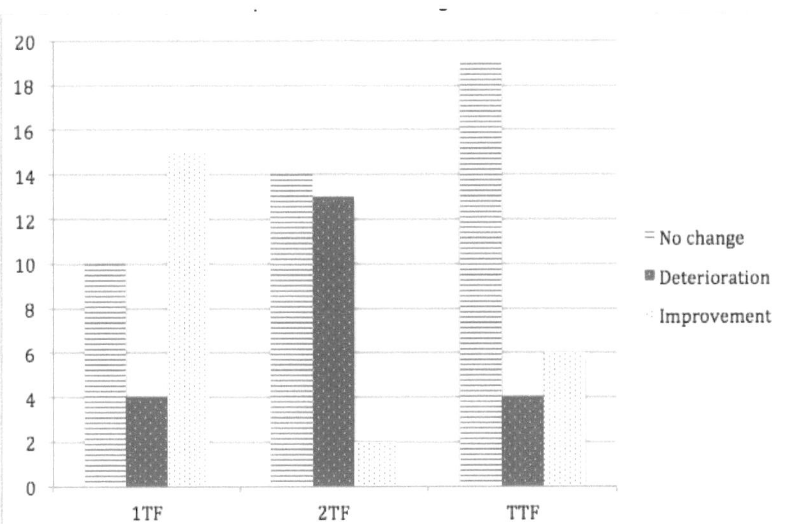

On the basis of the score development analysis using the six pre-selected formal linguistic evaluation items, the results visualised in Figure 1 emerged. They show that the pattern produced by taking only formal linguistic evaluation items highlights the increasingly dominant *No change* bar: the comparison between the Mid-test and the Pre-test (1TF) shows that 10 students (34.4%) received the same scores; however, their number grew when comparing the results of the Post-test to the Mid-test (2TF) (n=14, 48.27%) and was the highest (n=19, 65.5%) when comparing the Post-test to the Pre-test (TTF).

As far as improvement in the results is concerned, the most significant number of the students received better results in the Mid-test than in the Pre-test (1TF) (n=15, 51.72%). However, improvement decreased substantially in the Post-test (2TF) (n=2, 6.89%) and increased slightly when comparing the results in the Post-test to those in the Pre-test (TTF) (n=6, 20.68%).

In addition, score deterioration is also notable, especially when comparing the results in the Post-test to those in the Mid-test (2TF) (n=13, 44.82%). The comparison of the results in the Mid-test to those in the Pre-test (2TF) reveals that four students (13.79%) received lower scores in the Mid-test. The same number of students scored lower in the Post-test than in the Pre-test.

Figure 2: Groups A and B: Student score development over the three tests: comparison of Pre-test to Mid-test (1T), Mid-test to Post-test (2T) and Post-test to Pre-test (TT) for six evaluation items. Letters A and B represent Groups A and B respectively. Letter F refers to formal linguistic translation competence. (Group A: n =18, Group B: n=11).

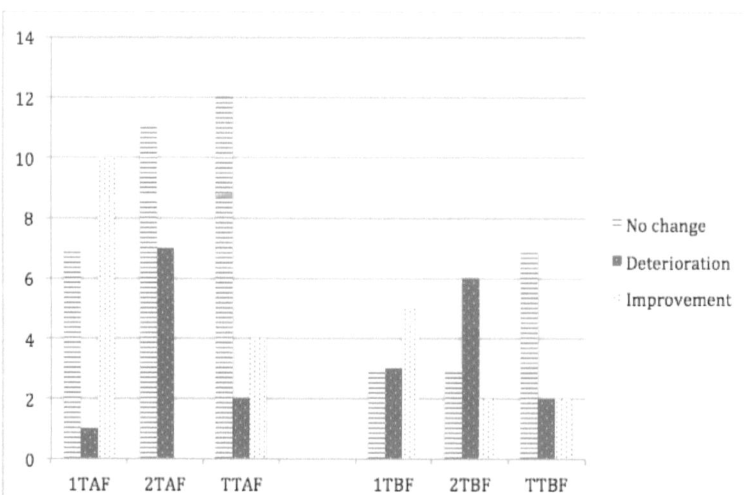

Figure 2 shows the separate score development patterns for both groups. Group A (left) reveals the same pattern as the entire cohort: the comparison between the Mid-test and Pre-test (1TAF) shows that more than half of the students scored higher in the Mid-test (n=10, 55.55%); however, this tendency was not retained when comparing the results of the Post-test to those of the Mid-test (2TAF): no students scored higher in the Post-test and more than one third of the students (n=7, 38.88%) scored lower than in the Mid-test. The comparison between the Post-test and the Pre-test (TTAF) shows that the situation changed again and there was a small number of students that improved upon their scores (n=4, 22.22%). However, the majority of the students did not see their results change (n=12, 66.66%) and the remaining 11.11% (n=2) received lower scores.

The situation in Group B is somewhat different. Even though Group B is smaller than Group A, the number of people whose results deteriorated in the Mid-test compared to the Pre-test (1TBF) is higher (n=3) than in Group A (n=1). The comparison between the Post-test and Mid-test (2TBF) shows that while there were some students who improved upon their results in the Post-test (n=2, 18.18%), more than half of the students (n=6, 54.54%) scored lower. The comparison between the Post-test and the Pre-test (TTBF) again reiterates the tendency seen in Group A: the most significant proportion of the students (n=7, 63.63%) received the same scores both in the Post-test and the Pre-test.

The analysis of the score development of formal linguistic evaluation items suggests a clear tendency of a steadily growing number of the students whose results remained unaffected. This is true of both individual groups and the entire cohort. While significant proportions of the students in both groups show improved results in the comparison between the Mid-test and Pre-test (1TAF and 1TBF) and worse results in the Post-test than in the Mid-test (2TAF and 2TBF), the highest numbers of the students ultimately received the same results in the Pre-test and the Post-test (TTAF and TTBF). This pattern implies that no lasting changes can be seen in the scores when evaluating the pre-selected formal linguistic items.

In terms of score development and the timing of peer feedback activities, it is interesting to observe again that whereas Group A shows a surge of improved scores in the Mid-test after engaging in the peer feedback activities (1TAF), the opposite is true of Group B (2TBF) as their scores received at the Post-test, after doing peer feedback activities, are worse than in the Mid-test. In spite of its overall better performance at all tests, Group B seems to score exceptionally badly at translating formal linguistic items, especially immediately after its peer feedback activities. We cannot account for these findings.

6.2 Student Score Development for Meaning-Related Items

Figure 3 presents the analysis of score development for meaning-related items. The results show that the majority of the students' scores (n=22, 75.86%) were either lower than (n=11) or the same as (n=11) in the Mid-test compared to the Pre-test (1TM). This tendency changes, however, when the results of the Post-test are compared to those of the Mid-test (2TM): the vast majority of the students scored the same (n=21, 72.41%), while equal proportions of the remaining students (27.6%, n=8) scored either higher or lower. The ultimate comparison of the Post-test with the Pre-test results (TTM) shows that the number of students who received higher (n=7, 24.13%) or lower (n=6, 20.68%) scores increased, but the most significant part of the students (n= 16, 55.17%) did not see their scores change.

Figure 3: Student score development over the three tests: comparison of Pre-test to Mid-test (1T), Mid-test to Post-test (2T) and Post-test to Pre-test (TT) for four evaluation items. Letter M refers to meaning-related translation competence. (Groups A and B: n=29).

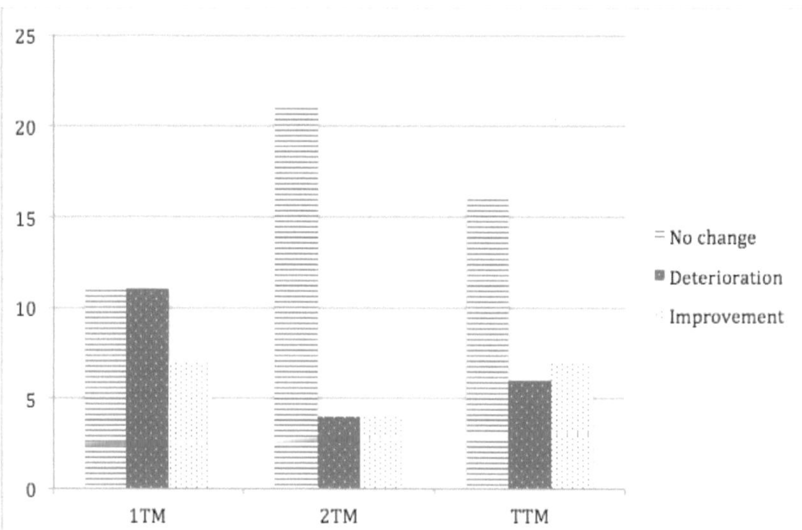

Figure 4: Student score development over the three tests: comparison of Pre-test to Mid-test (1T), Mid-test to Post-test (2T) and Post-test to Pre-test (TT) for four evaluation items. Letters A and B represent Groups A and B respectively. Letter M refers to meaning-related translation competence. (Group A: n= 18, Group B: n=11).

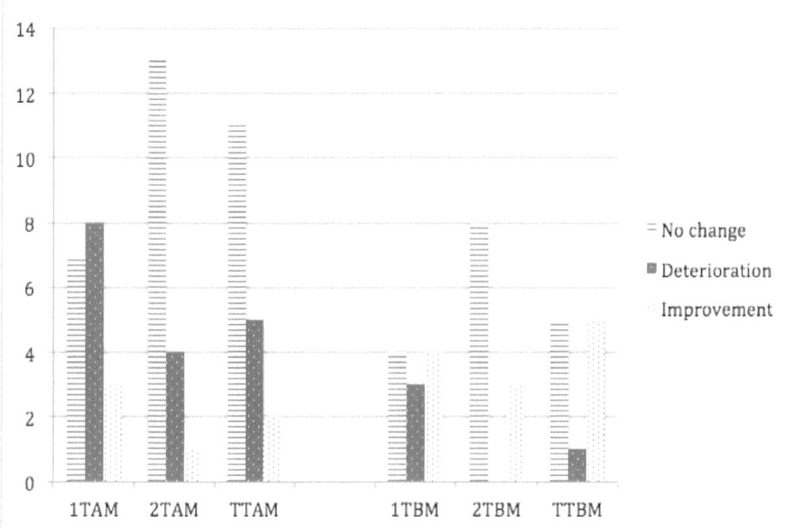

Figure 4 displays significantly different score development tendencies in Groups A and B. While in Group A half of the students (n=9) scored lower in the Mid-test than in the Pre-test (1TAM), in Group B this was the case for only three students (27.27%) (1TBM). The comparison between the results in the Post-test with those in the Mid-test (2TAM and 2TBM) indicates that the same proportions scored the same in both groups (72.72% in Group A and 72.22% in Group B); however, the remaining students in Group B (n=3, 27.27%) scored higher, while in Group A only one student did. The most remarkable difference between the two groups can be noted in the comparison between the Pre-test and the Post-test (TTAM and TTBM): while the majority of the students in Group A (n=16, 88.88%) scored either lower (n=5, 27.77%) or the same (n=11, 61.11%), in Group B almost half of the students scored higher (n=5, 45.45%) and only one student scored lower (9.09%).

This analysis shows that the score development for meaning-related items evaluation is much more substantial and positive in Group B. Crucially, this is the only domain in which the score development tendencies between the two groups are reversed. Specifically, in Group A, 50% of the students saw their results deteriorate in the Mid-test compared to the Pre-test after having done the peer feedback activities. In Group B, however, none of the students received worse results and nearly one third (27.27%) scored higher in the Post-test compared to the Mid-test, that is, immediately after their peer feedback activities.

A closer analysis of the score development over all the tests in Group B showed that the students' results improved in terms of almost all meaning-related items. Specifically, the scores on the translation of *It's [this blasted puberty]*, *give a bodyguard's once-over* and *work her way through* improved over the three tests; however, the translation of *a mane* [*of tight blonde curls*] deteriorated.

7. Discussion and Conclusion

The results presented above suggest no clear-cut trends in terms of score development patterns for formal linguistic and meaning-related evaluation items. Strikingly, the combination of the timing of peer feedback activities and types of evaluation items has resulted in substantially different score development tendencies in Groups A and B. Specifically, Group A performed best on the formal linguistic items and worst on the meaning-related items in the test that was conducted immediately after the peer feedback activities. In contrast, Group B scored best on the meaning-related items and worst on the formal linguistic items in the test organised after the peer feedback activities.

In addition, scores on formal linguistic items developed in a non-linear way regardless of the timing of peer feedback activities. The comparison of the score development with a focus on the formal linguistic evaluation items generated mixed tendencies: i.e. a relatively high number of students with improved results in the Mid-test compared to the Pre-test, a similarly high number of students with deteriorated or unchanged results in the Post-test compared to the Mid-test, and a dominant number of students with unchanged results in the Post-test compared to the Pre-test. Both groups displayed these score development tendencies regardless of when they engaged in peer feedback activities. This finding stands in contrast to the conclusions reported in the literature on the effects of peer feedback, but the limited number of students and items in the present study does not allow us to make any definitive claims.

Importantly, our experiment emphasised a number of elements that should be taken into account in future studies. First, the materials used in the tests and peer-to-peer activities should contain comparable stylistic and genre features so that students are assessed on the competences that they are asked to practise during peer feedback activities. This was not the case in the present study as the students practised popular science translation and the text used in the tests was an excerpt from a literary work.

The number of meaning-related pre-selected evaluation items is another point that needs to be considered. In our experiment, the balance of the ten pre-selected evaluation items was in favour of formal linguistic items (six versus four). In order to arrive at a clearer understanding of how peer feedback activities affect the generation and negotiation of meaning, future experiments should contain a more balanced number of form and meaning-related evaluation items.

References

Babych, B., Hartley, A., Kageura, K., Thomas, M., & Utiyama, M. (2012). "MNH-TT: a collaborative platform for translator training." Presented at *Translating and the Computer, 34,* London, UK.

Berg, E. C. (1999). "The effects of trained peer response on ESL students' revision types and writing quality." *Journal of Second Language Writing*, *8*(3), 215–241.

Desjardins, R. (2011). "Facebook me!: Initial insights in favour of using social networking as a tool for translator training." *Linguistica Antverpiensia, New Series–Themes in Translation Studies, 10,* 175–196.

EN 15038 (2006). *EN 15038:2006 Translation services—Service requirements.* Brussels: European Committee for Standardization.

Finn, G. M., & Garner, J. (2011). "Twelve tips for implementing a successful peer assessment. *Medical teacher*, *33*(6), 443–446.

Flynn, E. A. (1982). "Freedom, restraint and peer group interaction." Paper presented at the *Annual Meeting of the Conference on College Composition and Communication*, San Francisco, California, USA.

Gambier, Y. (2012). "Teaching translation / Training translators." In: Y. Gambier & L. van Doorslaer (eds.), *Handbook of Translation Studies, Volume 3*, 163–171. Amsterdam: J. Benjamins.

Gonzáles Davies, M. (2004). *Multiple Voices in the Translation Classroom.* Amsterdam: J. Benjamins.

Huertas Barros, E. (2011). "Collaborative learning in the translation classroom: preliminary survey results." *JoSTrans, 16*. Retrieved June 9, 2014, from http://www.jostrans.org/issue16/art_barros.php.

Humbley, J., Maylath, B., Mousten, B., Vandepitte, S. & Veisblat, L. (2005). "Learning localization through trans-Atlantic collaboration." In: George F. Hayhoe (ed.), *Professional Communication Conference Proceedings, 2005. IPCC 2005. IEEE International. Proceedings.* New York: IEEE. 578–595.

ISO 17100 (2015) ISO 17100:2015 *Translation services – Requirements for translation services.* Geneva: ISO.

Kenny, M. A. (2008). "Discussion, cooperation, collaboration: The impact of task structure on student interaction in a Web-based translation exercise module." *The Interpreter and Translator Trainer, 2*(2), 139–16.

Kiraly, D. (2001). "Towards a constructivist approach to translator education." *Quaderns: Revista de traducció*, 6, 50–53.

Leki, I. (1990). "Potential problems with peer responding in ESL writing classes." *CATESOL journal, 3*(1), 5–19.

Mangelsdorf, K., & Schlumberger, A. (1992). "ESL student response stances in a peer-review task." *Journal of Second Language Writing, 1*(3), 235–254.

Miao, Y., Badger, R., & Zhen, Y. (2006). "A comparative study of peer and teacher feedback in a Chinese EFL writing class." *Journal of Second Language Writing*, 15, 179–200.

Min, H. T. (2005). "Training students to become successful peer reviewers." *System*, *33*(2), 293–308.

Min, H. T. (2006). "The effects of trained peer review on EFL students' revision types and writing quality." *Journal of Second Language Writing, 15*(2), 118–141.

Muñoz Martín, R., Gervilla, E., Vargas-Quesada, B., Senso-Ruiz, J., Murillo-Melero, M., Castro-Prietro, M., Olvera-Lobo, M., Robinson, B., Raya, E., Lerma, J. (2007). "A professional approach to translator training (PATT)." *Meta* 52(3), 517–528.

O'Brien, S. (2011). "Collaborative translation." In: Y. Gambier & L. van Doorslaer (eds.), *Handbook of Translation Studies, Volume 2*, 17–20. Amsterdam: J. Benjamins.

Paulus, T. M. (1999). "The effect of peer and teacher feedback on student writing." *Journal of Second Language Writing*, 8(3), 265–289.

Pavlović, N. (2007). *Directionality in Collaborative Translation Processes. Ph.D. thesis.* Tarragona: Universitat Rovira i Virgili. Retrieved June 9, 2014, from http://www.tesisenxarxa.net/TDX-1210107-172129/

Risku, H. & Dickinson, A. (2009): "Translators as Networkers. The Role of Virtual Communities." *Hermes*, 42, 49–70.

Scardamalia, M. (2001). "Big change questions: Will educational institutions, within their present structures, be able to adapt sufficiently to meet the needs of the information age?" *Journal of Educational Change, 2*, 171–176.

Starke-Meyerring, D. (2008). "Cross-boundary knowledge making in globally networked learning environments." *SUNY Center for Online Collaborative Learning (COIL), Purchase, NY.*

Strijbos, J. W., & Sluijsmans, D. (2010). "Unravelling peer assessment: Methodological, functional, and conceptual developments." *Learning and Instruction, 20*(4), 265–269.

Swain, M., Brooks, L., and Tocalli-Beller, A. (2002). "Peer-peer dialogue as a means of second language learning." *Annual Review of Applied Linguistics,* 22, 171–185.

Tang, G. M., & Tithecott, J. (1999). "Peer response in ESL writing." *TESL Canada Journal*, 16, 20–38.

Tudge, J.R.H. (1990). "Vygotsky, the zone of proximal development, and peer collaboration: Implications for classroom practice." In L.C. Moll (Ed.), *Vygotsky and education: Instructional implications and applications of sociohistorical psychology* (pp. 155–172). Cambridge: Cambridge University Press.

Vandepitte, S., Mousten, B., Maylath, B., Isohella, S., Musacchio, M.T. & Palumbo, G. (2015). "Translation Competence Research Data in Multilateral International and Interprofessional Collaborative Learning. Chapter 9." Ying Cui and Wei Zhao (eds.), *Teaching Language Translation and Interpretation: Methods, Theories, and Trends.* Hershey, PA: IGI Global.

Van Steendam, E., Rijlaarsdam, G., Sercu, L., & Van den Bergh, H. (2010). "The effect of instruction type and dyadic or individual emulation on the quality of higher-order peer feedback in EFL." *Learning and Instruction, 20*(4), 316–327.

van Zundert, M., Sluijsmans, D., & Van Merriënboer, J. (2010). "Effective peer assessment processes: Research findings and future directions." *Learning and Instruction, 20*(4), 270–279.

Villamil, O. S., & De Guerrero, M. (1998). "Assessing the impact of peer revision on L2 writing." *Applied Linguistics*, 19(4), 491–514.

Vygotsky, L.S. (1978). *Mind in Society: The Development of Higher Psychological Processes.* Cambridge: Harvard University Press.

Vygotsky, L.S. (1986). *Thought and Language.* Cambridge, MA: The MIT Press.

Wells, G. (1999). *Dialogic Inquiry: Toward a Sociocultural Practice and Theory of Education.* Cambridge: Cambridge University Press.

Zili, D. (2009). "An Empirical Study on Campus Internet-based Peer Review and Interactive Translation." *Chinese Translators Journal*, 3, 44–49, 95–96.

Appendix A

Timeline	Week 1 day 1	Weeks 1-3			Week 4 Day 1	Weeks 4-6			Week 7
		Experiment Group: Group A				Experiment Group: Group B			
Tests	Pre-test				Mid-test				Post-test
Group A	Measurement of translation competences	Becoming familiar with and explicit application of student peer review and revision competences			Measurement of translation competences	No explicit application of student peer review and revision competences			Measurement of translation competences
		1. Translation of a text	2. Peer review and revision	3. Follow up of peer review and revision					
Group B	Measurement of translation competences	Becoming familiar with student peer review and revision competences No explicit application			Measurement of translation competences	Explicit application of student peer review and revision competences			Measurement of translation competences
						1. Translation of a text	2. Peer review and revision	3. Follow up of peer review and revision	

Appendix B

Test items are represented by the keywords in bold.

Pre-Test

Artemis rubbed his temples.
'**It's** this blasted puberty, Butler. Every time I see a pretty girl, I waste valuable mind space thinking about her. That girl at the restaurant for instance. I've glanced in her direction **a dozen** times in the past few minutes.'

Butler gave the pretty girl in question **an automatic bodyguard's once-over**.

She was twelve or thirteen, **did not appear** to be **armed** and had **a mane** of tight blonde curls. The girl was studiously **working** her way through a selection of **petits fours** while a male guardian, perhaps her father, read the paper.

Mid-Test

'**It's** this rotten puberty, Ron.'

Harry rubbed his temples.

'Every time I see a chick, I waste valuable mind space thinking about her. The girl at that cafeteria for instance. I've glanced in her direction **dozens** of times in the past few minutes.'

Ron first hesitated but then gave the chick in question **an automatic bodyguard's once-over**.

She was thirteen or fourteen, **did not appear** to be **armed** and had **a mane** of loose blonde curls. The girl was carefully **working** her way through a selection of **petits fours** while a male guardian, perhaps her grandfather, read the paper.

Post-Test

The girl was eleven or twelve and had **a mane** of tight black curls. She was diligently **working** her way through a selection of **petits fours** while a male guardian, perhaps her brother, read a magazine.

'Every time I see a pretty girl, I waste valuable mind space thinking about her. That babe at the bar for instance. **It's** this bloody puberty, Tim. I've been glancing in her direction **a dozen** times in the last few minutes.'

Nick rubbed his temples.

Tim gave the babe in question **an automatic bodyguard's once-over**. She **did not seem** to be **armed.**

Section II: Curriculum Design

Linda Dewolf

Crafting the Training and Testing of Interpreting Students towards Employability

Abstract: In July 2012, the Integration Decree contained an important reorganisation of the higher education landscape in Flanders. Following this, the integration of Erasmushogeschool (ehb) into the Faculty of Arts of the Vrije Universiteit Brussel (VUB) as from the 2013–14 academic year called for an 'academisation' of the core training curriculum for interpreting students. Attuning the curriculum meant adopting a research-oriented approach driven by a theoretical framework and implementing innovative pedagogical tools to comply with the general objectives and vision of the university whilst keeping the specific objectives geared towards professionalisation.

Despite the fact that Translation Studies research has been gaining momentum over the last years, little has been written about the changes induced by the integration process on didactics of interpreting.

This paper aims at depicting the present status of academisation and reports on the changes implied by the academisation process in terms of learning objectives, contents, benchmarking, requirements, pedagogical tasks and roles. It also reflects on how advances in technology are shaping interpreters' training within the faculty.

Within the education system in the Dutch-speaking community, testing criteria and tuition methods vary from sight translation, dialogue interpreting to role play. This study seeks to address the principles underpinning interpreting students' assessment based on learning outcomes. Interpreting requires, on the one hand, extensive practice under the supervision of trained professionals and, on the other hand, tuition in the theory and ethics of interpreting. Moreover, interpreting didactics present many challenges regarding tasks and rating consistency due to the many language combinations. Our research project focuses on curriculum design implemented in the physical or virtual classroom. A close analysis of course content and structure (matrix) reveals that students need to hone their skills in order to meet the demands of a rapidly evolving professional world.

Results from empirical research suggest that interpreting training needs to address new trends and to be tailored to the contemporary labour market. Blended courses, e-learning solutions and web-based coaching tools are paving the way for new developments in interpreters' education.

Key words: academisation, learning outcomes, T-profile, matrix, Bologna, professionalisation, craft, blended courses, employability, work placements.

1. Introduction

In Belgium, interpreting as an academic discipline is on the rise. Whereas in the mid-1980s, only three universities offered undergraduate training in Interpreting, today there are eight universities (UA Antwerp, Ghent University, KULeuven/KU-LAK, UMons, ULG Liège, UCL, ULB, VUB) which provide interpreting training courses at undergraduate and/or graduate level. Translation degrees were created in Belgium in the late 1950s in order to meet the ever-increasing demand for professional translators which could not be catered for by the existing degrees. The creation of the European Higher Education Area has created a new framework structure for degrees in Belgium, and interpreting has been no exception. This paper purports to describe the evolution, current status and foreseeable future of interpreting as a university discipline in Flanders. University curriculums are increasingly required to strike a balance between professionalisation and academisation, hence the need for practical programmes that could help university graduates enhance their employability skills. To build and provide the professional skills required by the market, interpreting training programmes – mainly at the MA level- are now seeking fresh insights from theoretical and empirical research.

The impetus for this research was to address key questions such as: which opportunities are offered new MA graduates to join the interpreting labour market? What special training needs to be given to student interpreters to help them enter the profession? What is the role that teachers play in this capacity-building process, and how do they go about it? How to maximise the effectiveness and meet with students' needs and desires?

This paper will therefore tackle the profile of the MA graduate, some salient features of the marketplace, the career prospects and finally, the challenges young graduate students will face in the near future.

2. State of the Art

Despite the fact that interpreting studies research has been gaining momentum over the last two decades, little has been written, and therefore is known, about the effects and impact of the Bologna process and academisation on the teaching context. This paper explores some of the collateral issues ranging from testing to learning objectives, training matrix design and contents.

3. Recent Changes in Content, Objectives, and Structure of Programmes

3.1 The Academic Component – Research Focus

The Vrije Universiteit Brussels (VUB) has, since 2013, been offering a Masters degree in Interpreting. The training of future interpreters now includes a theoretical component focused on interpreting studies. This paper outlines the some structure changes of the programme given in 2014–15 in the main language combinations and presents the findings of a literature study which also investigates future distance training facilities. Although widely recognised, the extent to which theory is affecting interpreting practice and how much students could take advantage of theoretical background and research experience has hardly been analysed in scholarly terms so far. The findings of this study have implications for the provision of future interpreter training programmes. Against this background, interpreter education in Flanders -particularly in Brussels, is an interesting topic from at least two angles: curriculum design and testing.

Within the Faculty of Applied Linguistics, research in interpreting is focused on improving the practice and the training of interpreters and translators; developing our understanding of the processes of interpretation and exploring the potential of translation technologies for students. Several sub-areas are currently explored and studied: community interpreting in hospital and prison settings, and cognitive analysis.

3.2 Curriculum Design – New Degree Structures

Almost sixteen years after the Bologna Declaration was completed in 2010, time has come to start looking at the question of how the Bologna Process has affected the development of interpreter training. The measures taken within the framework of the Bologna Process have harmonised the structure of degree programmes in the European Higher Education Area, for example, through the introduction of two-tiered (Bachelor and Master) programmes and of the ECTS credit-point system. Bologna has affected both the structure and contents of all types of higher education. The introduction of the two-tier system: Bachelor (3 years) and Master (1 year) degrees was a major challenge to all universities and institutions of higher education and replaced the former 'candidate/kandidaat' degree (after 2 years).

A Bachelor's degree is nowadays necessary to become an interpreter, especially for jobs within the government. The most important prerequisite is to be fluent in at least two languages by the end of a Bachelor's degree programme.

Currently targeted on five languages (Dutch, English, French, German, Italian, and Spanish), the interpreting programme trains students to be able to deal with any type of written production (commercial, legal, literary, political, technical…) and to transmit contents in an immediate fashion while respecting the context and the speaker's intent. The programme focuses on the discipline through a practical pedagogical approach. Students have to choose two foreign languages among English, French, Italian, German and Spanish. The programme is long-term higher education, meaning it is divided into two levels (cycles): the first cycle lasts 3 years (180 credits) and leads to a Bachelor's degree in translation/interpretation, and the second cycle is one year (60 credits) and leads to a Master's degree in translation or in interpretation.

The Bachelor relies on a versatile education that is organised around three areas: acquiring a perfect mastery of Dutch, reaching a deep understanding of two foreign languages, and acquiring general knowledge in fields related to the profession (law, economy, translatology, psycholinguistics, literature, philosophy, …). The third year of the Bachelor programme includes a one-term language immersion (Erasmus exchange programme) stay either in Belgium or abroad. Students also write a Bachelor dissertation.

As a consequence of the credit-system, the Master year of the interpreter's degree has become increasingly individualised. The Master in Interpretation aims at training professionals in the field of languages, who are able to translate specialists' speeches either simultaneously or consecutively. This is a demanding job, requiring specific personal skills: an impeccable knowledge of the native language as well as foreign languages, but also of the complexities of political, diplomatic, socio-economic, legal, technical or scientific contexts. It also demands solid general knowledge, considerable responsiveness, resistance to stress, and a personality that is open to international experiences. Students can choose among five languages: English, French, German, Dutch and Spanish. Two of these must be mastered perfectly. Classes are given by experienced professional interpreters or former practitioners who have a deep knowledge of the profession and its high demands. The programme also includes a compulsory professional internship, which gives students an actual opportunity to apply their new skills to the professional world. This professionally-oriented and research-based track prepares interpreters to work in a variety of fields. In their Master year students present a Master thesis, and the exam jury comprises several Faculty professors.

Being a craft on the one hand interpreting requires extensive practice under supervision, and on the other hand, being an academic field it is based on interpreting theories.

3.3 Learning Outcomes

During the first quarter of 2015 teachers were asked to brainstorm on a training matrix and work on clusters defining the learning outcomes, and ended up establishing a list of criteria. Practical problems related to the set-up of courses were discussed, such as how existing courses could be adapted to the needs and requirements of the training curriculum by adding new courses related to the introduction to interpreting in the 2015–16 academic programme. Language competence is a prerequisite, but it is not sufficient. The list of agreed descriptors comprises:

- *Language skills:*
  The student must be capable of expressing themselves appropriately in their mother tongue, demonstrating a rich vocabulary and appropriate use of register at C2 level of the Common European Framework of Reference for languages (CEFR). Students must demonstrate in their speech that they have an excellent understanding of each of their working languages at C2 level (as far as German, French, English and Dutch are concerned) or at least at C1 level (Italian, Spanish).
- *Specialised non-linguistic skills must be acquired through training and/or practice. Students should achieve the following knowledge outcomes:*
  *sufficient background knowledge, including terms, in the practised subject areas
  *knowledge and understanding of attitude and etiquette in various communicative settings
  *knowledge and understanding of interpreting research skills
  *knowledge and understanding of simultaneous interpreting techniques
  *awareness of the latest developments in interpreting theory and the professional practice
  *knowledge of best practices in terms of ethics
- *Students should achieve the following skills outcomes:*
  *ability to perform more advanced simultaneous interpreting skills
  *ability to make appropriate use of subject background knowledge / terms in interpreting
  *ability to prepare for and carry out interpreting assignments in a professional manner
  *ability to maintain concentration and interpret with accuracy while under significant psychological stress
  *ability to conduct research into interpreting studies

3.4 Testing

Another issue addressed in this section is how students are assessed in the interpreting examinations. About the evaluation criteria applied to interpreting students in their final exams (summative and/or formative assessment), there seemed to be a consensus among teachers in terms of the most suitable test for each skill. The evaluation of an interpreter's performance always depends on a large variety of factors but the template used is based on a review of existing sets of criteria, such as those proposed by Viezzi (1999) and the micro criteria suggested by Riccardi (2002). What is important is that students have a clear idea of the expectations and are told what exactly they will be assessed on, as well as the level at which they will be expected to perform at the different stages of the course (i.e. mid-term and final examinations). The following grid illustrates the set of assessment criteria used by the members of the examination panel so as to ensure inter-rater reliability.

Examination grid design

SCALE(*)	**1 clearly insufficient**	**2 insufficient**	**3 sufficient**	**4 good**	**5 very good**
Standard Dutch					
Completion of the sentences					
Grammar					
Omissions-additions					
Register					
Interpreting technique					
Knowledge of the foreign language					
Ability to auto-correct					
Booth behaviour					
Total					

(*) or N/A not applicable

In summary, the interpretation performance level is evaluated based on the command of two working languages, the ability to choose an appropriate expression, the familiarity with the cultural context of both languages, the knowledge of terminology in specialised fields, the observance of protocols applicable to different settings, and the mastery of modes applicable to these settings.

Academic publications and dissertations may outline different theoretical and methodological approaches and each system will weigh the various factors differently, but most assess roughly the same aspects of the students' performance. Whereas interpreting training has evolved from a professional training to an academic discipline, the most widely accepted approach to its assessment is focused on quality assessment. This set of criteria appears to be rather structured, yet it is obvious that they can still be scrutinised in the light of psychometric concepts of assessment, like validity and reliability, from other established disciplines, such as language testing and educational assessment. Along similar lines, Andrew Clifford (2005) suggests "the distinction between the quality-oriented assessment prevalent in translation and interpreting and the psychometric evaluation common in other disciplines". But how can this be achieved? According to Iglesias Fernandez (2011), "Some proposals put forward suggest the need for cross-fertilisation between second language acquisition (SLA) and testing theory (psychometrics), and Translation and Interpreting Studies. Reliable and valid measures for language assessment are already in place in SLA, and Interpreting scholars". Examples range from the use of portfolios, as feedback instruments, to rubrics (i.e. holistic and systematic grading systems), which would replace the point-adding/point-deducting system. This suggests that more research be done on interpreting testing, of which the first task is to develop a theoretical framework to provide guidance for testing practice built-in a robust academic programme with both a pedagogical and a vocational purpose.

4. Working Towards Graduate Employability

4.1 Work Placements for Students in Interpreting

To what extent are work placements useful? Do they really help students to develop workplace competence? Interpreting students may be called upon to work as volunteers for NGOs. The student offers his or her services free of charge and, in exchange, gains valuable experience and professional cross-fertilisation. Interpreting students may overlook the fact that there are many possibilities and openings for interpreters outside the field of conference interpreting in the so-called 'community interpreting'.

4.2 New Job Opportunities in Interpreting

Career prospects in the field of interpreting and translation are good, particularly in cities like Brussels where there is a constant need for linguistically qualified employees. For conference interpreters Brussels offers many opportunities. Apart from permanent or free-lance employment at the European institutions or NATO HQ, conference interpreters are also in demand in courts, social services, written press, radio, television, publishing companies, advertising agencies, international commercial and financial companies, organisations that promote foreign trade in Belgium and abroad. The Council of State, the federal police, embassies and consulates, scientific and cultural organisations… usually offer occasional employment to translators and interpreters.

4.3 Matching Training to Job Requirements – Job Profile Descriptions

To find an answer to our questions, we gathered data from typical job profiles edited by the Selection bureau of the Belgian Federal Government (SELOR). The standards are organized in four areas: translation/interpretation services provision, quality of the translation work, teamwork and self-assessment, and professional development. Taking these criteria into account, we were interested in observing to what extend students are aware of these job requirements. The analysis yielded some interesting results, especially as far as how interpreters are recruited, what their background and education is and how they can be supported in terms of training courses. Whereas in past interpreters learned languages by immersion or exposure, now most jobs require at least a Bachelor's degree. The following table outlines common requirements to become an interpreter.

	Common Requirements
Degree Level	A degree is not always required, but some institutions may prefer an applicant who holds a Bachelor's/Master's degree with formal coursework in interpreting.
Degree Field	Interpreting, foreign language or a related field.
Licensure and Certification	No license is required; voluntary certifications are available.
Experience	Experience working in interpreting or in a related field is required by most employers.
Key Skills	Strong verbal communication skills, fluency in at least two languages. Listening skills and cultural sensitivity are also required.

Positions are T-shaped. The vertical stem of the T is: an in-depth specialized knowledge in one or two fields. The horizontal crossbar refers to the complementary skills of communication (including negotiation), the ability to apply knowledge across disciplines, empathy (including the ability to see from other perspectives), and an understanding of fields outside your area of expertise.

4.4 Attuning the Curriculum to the Needs and Requirements of the Professional World

In this section I will address some of the recent dynamic shifts that occurred in the profession and the implications they have for future interpreters. Interpreting, and therefore teaching interpreting, has become increasingly influenced by technologies and media. Towards the end of the twentieth century the Internet made it possible for individuals and institutions involved in interpreting to exchange widely. Remote and video technologies have come into play and open up new possibilities. Research is challenged when we consider the various aspects and issues in relation to remote interpreting, from linguistic, sociological, physiological and environmental perspectives.

To cope with reduced contact hours and shortfall of interpreting booths in conference rooms, interpreting students and their trainers may need to explore new training solutions offered by various ICT tools (speech tools and speech repositories) and possibly resort to 'digital classrooms'. Access to interpreting has opened the door to the use of technology in university settings. There is a growing demand to shift the paradigm from traditional "brick and mortar" classrooms to online models.

Interpreting students express the need for adequate self-study opportunities and learning resources which would allow them to learn about and practice interpreting. "Yet, students do not always have access to suitable training materials" (Sandrelli 2007: 1). Students will need to show their ability to keep up with technology in an evolving marketplace.

5. Concluding Remarks

One of the major outcomes concluding the present stage of this study is that the delivery of university courses for interpreting skills training highlights many new issues pertaining to its hybridity. Since interpreting has established itself as an academic discipline, assessment has evolved and reflects the dichotomy between the professional conceptualisation of assessment criteria and those of the specialised courses in universities. This difference in approach points to a gap between academic theorising and the profession in the real word.

In the framework of growing internationalisation, interpreter training has become a very dynamic area in academic training and research. Researchers have also started showing interest in studying remote interpreting (RI) technology as it may open up new ways for training practices (Kiraly 2003). Hybrid communication forms such as real time text messaging, chat rooms, and live captioning have shaped a new reality for interpreters. As technology advances, tomorrow's interpreters need to be prepared for the challenges ahead. Further research in this area may include detailed information to better ascertain student interpreters' technology awareness and real needs in order to design new tools and improve existing ones. This project would concern the design, implementation and evaluation of a blended training course for interpreter trainers. Research in remote interpreting deserves a fine-grained analysis of the relations between the student interpreter and space, both conceptual and physical. The studies described above give rise to several questions about how training programmes should respond to new technological developments which impinge on the work of interpreters. For example, how students can be prepared for video interpreting is a question that has not been tackled often enough. It remains one of the under-researched areas in interpreting studies.

In his doctoral dissertation, Marc Orlando (2015) propounds the view that promoting cross-fertilisation of translation and interpreting practice, training and research makes for closer interaction between research, practice and training for both translation and interpreting.

To conclude, reinforcing the scientific potential was an important milestone in achieving the so-called 'academisation' of programmes. The changes introduced in the curriculum did (interpreting theories) not only affect the core of the MA-programme, but also teaching staff. In the literature on this subject, the term 'academic drift' was used to describe the tendency of non- university institutions to orient their activities in ways that bring them closer to the university image. It offers a theoretical explanation of the dynamics of academisation processes. 'Academic drift' refers to a long term process induced by educational systems' dynamics whereby vocationally and professionally oriented post-secondary education institutions strive to become like universities by incorporating university structures and emulating their values, norms, symbols and practices. Based on a typology inspired by Guy Neave's analysis of academic drift, six different, though related academisation processes can be distinguished: at student level (student drift), staff level (staff drift), programme level (programme drift), institutional level (institutional drift), sector level (sector drift), and governmental level (policy drift). First, the 'drift in curricular emphasis' resulted in an accentuation of abstract theoretical knowledge and eventually in a gradual reduction in the emphasis attached to practical work. Second, the academic drift encompassed a research dimension. The notion of 'research drift' was originally coined by Svein Kyvik and Benedetto Lepori (Kyvik and Lepori 2010, p. 9) as a descriptor of the transition from vocational training and teaching at the bachelor's level to research-led and research-informed professional education at the master's level. Finally, our current Interpreting programme presents an integrated and cohesive structure within the Vrije Universiteit Brussels suggesting that both horizontally and vertically, a convergence of the vocational and academic dimensions has taken place.

References

Clifford, Andrew (2005): "Putting the exam to the test: Psychometric validation and interpreter certification." *Interpreting*, Vol.7.1 :7–131.

Iglesias Fernandez, Emilia (2011): "Under Examination. Do All Interpreting Examiners Use The Same Criteria?" *The Linguist*, 50(2):12–13.

Kiraly, Don (2003): "From Teacher-Centred to Learning-Centred Classrooms in Translator Education: Control, Chaos or Collaboration?" In *Innovation and E-learning in Translator Training*, Anthony Pym, Carmina Fallada, José Ramón Biau, and Jill Orenstein (eds.), Universitat Rovira i Virgili, Tarragona: Intercultural Studies Group: 27–31.

Kyvik, Svein and Lepori, Benedetto (*eds.*), (2010): *The Research Mission* of *Higher Education Institutes Outside the University Sector*, Dordrecht: Springer, 77–96.

Neave, Guy (1979): "Academic drift: some views from Europe", *Studies in Higher Education,* vol. 6, No. 2.

Orlando, Marc (2015): *The training of translators and interpreters in the 21st century. At the crossroad of practice, research and pedagogy*. Unpublished doctoral dissertation, Monash University.

Riccardi, Alessandra (2002): "Evaluation in interpretation. Macrocriteria and microcriteria", in Hung, Eva (Ed.), *Teaching translation and interpreting 4: Building Bridges*, Amsterdam, John Benjamins, 115–126.

Sandrelli, Annalisa (2007): "Designing CAIT (Computer -Assisted Interpreter Training) Tools: Black Box." In Heidrun Gerzymisch-Arbogast & Sandra Nauert (eds.) *Challenges of Multidimensional Translation*. Proceedings of the Marie Curie Euroconferences Saarbrücken 2–6 May 2005.

Viezzi, Maurizio (2002) "Aspetti della qualità nell'interpretazione" in Falbo C. *et al.* (a cura di), *Interpretazione simultanea e consecutiva, Problemi teoretici e metodologie didattiche,* 140–145.

Don Kiraly

Beyond the Static Competence Impasse in Translator Education

Abstract: The translator's 'competence' has been a key topic of interest and debate in translator education for many years now. A number of two-dimensional translator competence models have been published and referred to in numerous other publications; and far beyond the field of Translation Studies, 'competency-based teaching' seems to have become the key catchword of education in the new millennium. While acknowledging the potential value of these models for contributing to the understanding of the translator's skills and capabilities as static virtual entities, this article will propose adding a third dimension: time, which will be shown to be necessary for illustrating and better understanding the dynamic nature of competence development.

Curriculum development work within the context of the European Graduate Placement Scheme provided a special opportunity for developing and applying a three-dimensional multi-vortex model on the basis of an emergentist pedagogical epistemology.

Keywords: translator competence, emergence, curriculum development, modularised curricula, compartmentalisation of knowledge.

1. Introduction

In this article[1] I will present an approach to the conceptualisation of 'translator competence development' that was developed within the context of a European Union sponsored project[2] created to establish an international platform for work placements in the language mediation domain. The originators of the project – which was entitled the European Graduate Placement Scheme (EGPS) – including the author of this chapter, believed that it was essential within the scope of the project to focus both on the actual day-to-day practice of work placements,

1 A significantly revised and expanded version of this article will appear in a volume edited by the author entitled *Towards Authentic Experiential Learning in Translator Education* to be published by Mainz University Press.

2 The European Graduate Placement Scheme. This EU project ran from 2012–2015. The University of Mainz was represented in the project by the Division of English Linguistics and Translation Studies. The other university partners were: the Universitat Autonomá of Barcelona, the Pedagogical University of Cracow, and Salford University in the UK.

as well as on theoretical considerations that might help justify and explain the incorporation of work placements into Translation Studies curricula. In the end, the competence development model in fact proved to be a key outcome of the project, serving to initiate, accompany and promote ongoing reflection – not only among the educators involved in designing and carrying out the project, but also among students at the participating universities as well as managers and work placement mentors in the companies that agreed to hire them – on the nature of learning processes and the role of the university in fostering those processes.

A key feature of the competence and curricular modelling work done in the course of this project was an underlying post-positivist *emergentist* epistemology that has become a major contender for displacing the effete objectivist epistemological paradigm underlying modern education and that dates back to the Enlightenment period. Space constraints will not allow even a minimal discussion here of emergence or emergentist epistemology, but scholarship on the topic is readily available (see, for example: Doll 1993, Davis & Sumara 2007)[3]. In a nutshell, emergentist epistemology rejects the reductionism, determinism and positivism underlying the conventional conduit or transmissionist view of knowledge and learning that has long been the mainstay of educational practice. Instead, from an emergentist perspective (based on complexity theory), a learning system is seen as dynamic, self-generating and self-perpetuating. This shift in perspective should become clearer over the course of this paper.

2. The Status Quo: A Modularised, Reductionist Building-Block Approach to Curriculum

In today's Bologna-influenced translation-studies curricula, skills and knowledge to be acquired are commonly represented with geometrical shapes or containers that are labelled with learning outcomes to represent the achievement of predefined educational outcomes and objectives – which may or may not be aligned with the demands of the market.

3 See also Risku (1998, 2002) and Kiraly (2012, 2013 and forthcoming) for a discussion of issues related to emergence in Translation Studies competence development.

Figure 1: A Linear Curriculum Model for Translator Education (MA in Translation Studies at the FTSK[4], 2015).

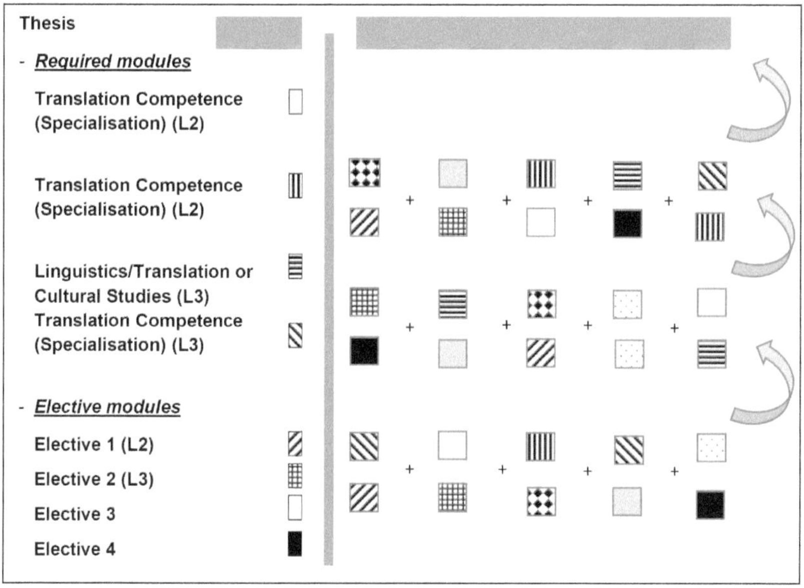

Figure 1 is my own depiction of the current curricular framework of the MA in Translation programme at the university where I teach. In this system, each module comprises either three or four courses that students' select from lists approved for inclusion within the respective modules on the basis of their personal preferences and the availability of the courses in a given semester. There is no room for progression in terms of difficulty, complexity, depth of topics – or pedagogical approach. The panoply of courses offered becomes little more than a patchwork quilt of content to be accumulated in a sequence that is based more on the chance of getting into the classes one wants to take and fitting them into one's schedule than anything else.

In discussing the so-called modularisation of translator education programmes as a result of the Bologna Agreement, Kelly notes the self-evident advantages of this approach to curriculum designers:

4 *Fachbereich Translation, Sprach- und Kulturwissenschat* (School of Translation and Interpreting, Linguistics and Cultural Studies at the Johannes Gutenberg University of Mainz, Germany).

> "Such a structure can afford a particular programme considerable flexibility, and of course allows the overall competence to be acquired to be sub-divided into smaller, more manageable, more easily assessable, gradable units" (Kelly 2007: 137).

But at the same time, she also acknowledges the risks that such modularisation brings with it: "The danger of this compartmentalization is, however, that from the students' point of view it can be difficult to establish relations between the different component parts" (Kelly 2007: 137).

She goes on to underline a key motivation underlying the creation of the alternative curriculum model that I am proposing in this chapter:

> [...] the rigid application of the list of competences and, perhaps more so, their assignation to particular departments at universities with inflexible bureaucratized systems have given rise to a sadly impermeable set of separate compartments of knowledge which are rarely approached from the coordinated networking perspective which is so necessary for full development of translation competence. (ibid 138)

We will see in the next section how this compartmentalisation of knowledge is also reflected in current models of translator competence, which depict the translator's skills and capabilities as the largely isolated contents of separate containers with only the vaguest of links between them. In our view, this is not only a problem of the relevance and clarity of the models. We believe it also reflects a potential lack of pedagogical coherence in terms of how institutions and teachers – but also students – structure the acquisition of knowledge and skills in preparation for the workplace.

3. Translator Competence and Competencies[5] Revisited

When we set out within the scope of the EGPS project to discern a suitable role for work placements within translator education programmes, it was clear that both a theoretical and a practical perspective on the nature of the skills and knowledge that translators are likely to need in order to perform competently in the workplace were necessary. This would then need to be followed up with a model of the eminently dynamic process of translator competence development. But in all of the existing graphic models of translator competence that we have come across (for example: Pacte (2005:610), EMT (2009:4) and Göpferich (2008:155),

---

5 'Competence' is used here in referring to general abilities to perform to standards (as in 'translator competence') and 'competency' is used to refer to more particular, atomistic abilities, like the competencies (or sub-competences) that comprise translator competence.

translator competence is represented as a static, two-dimensional image of a meta-competence divided into competencies. The models depict the learning outcomes and the competencies to be acquired by the end of the educational process and how this expert knowledge can be applied in the translation process to perform translatory actions (cf. Cnyrim, Hagemann & Neu 2013). But so far, they have not attempted to depict suitable or effective alternative paths for acquiring or developing the appropriate skills and knowledge.

A closer look at the influential PACTE model (Pacte 2005) shows that the different translation competences are depicted graphically as being essentially of equal volume and presumably weighting. Answers to questions from this perspective of this model concerning the nature or mechanism of competence acquisition, appropriate learner and teacher input in the competence acquisition process, and the need and modalities for a differentiated critical assessment of the respective competence levels over time remain elusive. Taking another look at our curriculum boxes, it is also clear that in Translation Studies, we currently even lack a consensus understanding of the content of the boxes. The contents vary from institution to institution (and of course even from module to module and from course to course!) often depending on the historical development of Translation Studies within a country or a local educational environment – as well as on each lecturer's professional translation experience and interpretation of the relevant curricular constraints and educational objectives.

From an educational philosophy perspective, curricular box models can be seen to reflect an underlying empirico-deductive epistemology. They invite us to understand the contents of curricular boxes as being both operationalisable (clearly definable and measurable), and acquirable by learners in a neat, step-by-step, cumulative and essentially linear manner. Curriculum planning – and not only in translator education – has conventionally been understood as a process of defining – by dissecting a macrocompetence into its composite parts and specifying learning outcomes and competence levels – the specific skills and knowledge needed at subsequent stages of education, and of organizing the transmission of that knowledge and those skills to the minds of learners, whose task it is to accumulate them in preparation for later use in real-world contexts. Stuart Campbell (1998) has concisely summed up this view as follows:

> Translation competence can be separated into relatively independent components, and those components can be used as building blocks in curriculum design… Translation is a matter of intervention in the development of the various components of translation competence. (Campbell 1998: 163).

4. A Case for (Further) Pragmatic Abduction in the Study of Translator Competence

In our view, there can be no question at this still incipient stage in research on 'translator competence' that overall translator competence and its component competencies are essentially heuristics with fuzzy boundaries that have been and can be used successfully to better comprehend and to operationalize the tremendously complex process of translation and the knowledge & skills needed to engage with it professionally. Nor do we believe that these conceptualisations are any less useful for having (virtually) no empirical basis because, from our post-positivist perspective, they clearly comprise socially constructed knowledge. In the absence of any objective proof for the ontological existence of any particular translatory sub-competences, plausible ones proposed by trustworthy stakeholders and recognized experts on translation matters can surely be used as heuristics to define what academics, students, educational administrators and professional organizations understand or believe to be the features, components, aspects or qualifications that translators must have in order to function expertly and professionally. If we can discern plausible and justifiable constellations of translatory sub-competences, we can use them as highly productive tools for designing both curricula and learning opportunities.

Space does not allow us to undertake here a review of the many definitions and models, both graphic and verbal, that have been proposed abductively to depict translation competence[6]. In lieu of a consensus view of which particular competencies are subsumed within the translator's macro-competence, the models presented in this article reflect the view of translator competence that has been depicted by Kelly (2002 & 2007). Kelly's model has been chosen as a suitable heuristic because we believe 1) it reflects a careful, well-balanced analysis of a number of other models; 2) it is clear, precise and comprehensive; and 3) her cogent discussion of its features suggests that her model is imbued with a high degree of ecological validity. In a nutshell, Kelly (2002 & 2007) describes translation competence[7] as comprising seven competencies: 1) communicative and textual competence in at least two languages and cultures; 2) professional instrumental competence;

6 The reader is referred to Kelly 2002 and 2007 for references to publications presenting many of these models.

7 Which I have referred to elsewhere as *translator competence*, that is the multi-facetted array of knowledge and skills needed by a professional translator. I have used *translation competence* to refer to the narrower set of skills and knowledge needed to undertake a translation per se.

3. (inter)cultural competence; 4. thematic competence; 5. interpersonal competence; 6. psycho-physiological competence; and 7. strategic competence, including skills and knowledge of how to organize one's work, resolve problems and evaluate one's own work. It is this strategic sub-competence that Kelly sees as the most important one, which links the various competencies to each other.

At this point, having selected a plausible initial set of competencies that can conveniently serve the modularised curricula dictated across Europe by the Bologna Agreement, it was essential to link the competencies to be developed to both the target meta-competence (translator competence) and to our underlying emergent epistemology. One model that finds support from a number of domains and has also been applied by Chesterman (2000) in the context of the study of intuition and rationality in translation is the model of skills acquisition developed by Hubert and Stuart Dreyfus (Dreyfus 2004), which will be introduced in the next section.

5. A fresh (Emergentist) Look at the Dreyfus Model of Skill Acquisition

It was in the 1980s that the brothers Hubert and Stuart Dreyfus – the former a professor of philosophy and the latter a professor of engineering, both at the University of California, Berkeley (USA) – introduced their now classic "Five-stage model of adult skill acquisition" (Dreyfus 2004).

In this article, they discuss findings by researchers in a number of skill acquisition domains (piloting, chess and language acquisition), winding up with a verbal model of instructed skill acquisition that proceeds in four stages, that represent steps on a teaching/learning continuum from non-situational, fragmented, and analytical to situational, holistic, and intuitive.

The five stages in the Dreyfus model are: novice, advanced beginner, competent, proficient and expert. The novice learner is exposed to context-free features of the subject matter to be learned and is provided with rules for determining how to react to those features. The advanced beginner has acquired some experience developing an understanding of the relevant context, but learning continues to be carried out in an analytic way, as the student follows instructions and is given examples. The competence stage comes after considerable experience dealing with recurrent patterns in relevant situations. Then comes the proficiency stage, where the learners is exposed to a wide variety of holistic situations and uses maxims to determine appropriate actions. And finally, at the expert stage, the individual no longer needs analytical tools like rules or maxims to link the situation at hand to specific actions. The learner's repertoire of experienced situations is so large that each specific situation encountered dictates an intuitively appropriate action.

The Dreyfus' generic model of skill acquisition of course makes no mention of the particular competencies that have been identified and studied in Translation Studies, but these competencies do appear to lend themselves particularly well to educational discourse and design given the current competence orientation that is almost pervasive throughout Western education today.

6. Chesterman's Application of the Dreyfus Model

In his chapter on competence development in Memes of Translation, Chesterman (2002) draws on the Dreyfus' theory of competence acquisition to explain how translators might acquire translator competence. He lists teaching techniques comprising: exercises with strategies, exercises on accountability, exercises on the communication norm, exercises on the relation norm and exercises on expectancy norms. He lists a panoply of topics that should be covered in the curriculum and even specifies the stage at which they should be dealt with. All of the exercises he suggests are created, contrived, applied and controlled by the teacher. There is no indication at all that authentic, autonomous or collaborative experience of the real work of translators in the workplace is of any relevance in Chesterman's curriculum or classroom. As Williams (2000) has suggested with reference to Chesterman's description of his recommended teaching approach:

> […] the widespread use of the passive voice in the description of the relationship between trainer and trainee ('students can be asked to …", 'students should be given') indicates a largely teacher-centred classroom, which may impede his goal of attaining the emancipation of the trainees.

We feel that Chesterman (2000) offers a plethora of invaluable insights into both curricular and didactic features than we can also subscribe to – sometimes, at the right time and in the right place. Where we part ways, is not so much in terms of what needs to be learned as how it can be learned and when it can best be learned. Whereas conventional (and even innovative) teacher-centred instruction is grounded in a reductionist, rationalist, Cartesian conduit-like view of learning, our emergentist view allows us to interpret the Dreyfus competence acquisition model as emphasizing the transition from conscious, contrived and simple learning (as understood in terms of complexity theory) to the subconscious, authentic and complex in a dynamic, largely unpredictable and uncontrollable but clearly emancipatory, embodied, enactive and empowering process.

7. Towards the Dynamic Modelling of Translator Competence Development

In designing our model of translator competence development (Figure 2), we first incorporated the competencies identified by Kelly in the form of individual sub-vortices, which, like the overall vortex itself, are intended to reflect the notion of perpetual dynamic change and growth over time. The emphasis in the Dreyfus model is on the progression from rule-based to autonomous learning and from conscious awareness of problem solving to intuitive action. The competency vortices swirling up from the bottom of the figure eventually merge into a single super-competence over time in line with the implication of the Dreyfus' model to the effect that in expertise, action in response to challenges comes largely in response to intuitions. The implications for translator education are significant: rather than having a smorgasbord of courses to be sampled in modules spread over a course of study, the model suggests that there can be a progression in terms of learning and also presumably with respect to teaching strategies over the course of a programme of studies, as students move along the continuum from novice to competent or even proficient or expert translator.

Figure 2: A Multi-Vortex Model of Translator Competence Development.

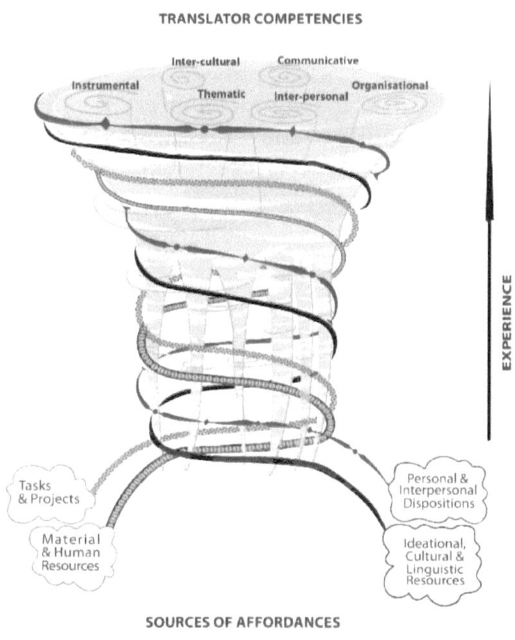

Together, these factors depict an evolutionary shift from building-block style curricula and uniform conduit-type teaching to progressively more autonomous learning over the course of a student's programme of studies and beyond. The underlying emergent worldview is, in my view, an integral component of the model.

From the perspective illustrated by this model, expertise development is an autopoietic process, that is: a self-perpetuating, self-regulating one supported by affordances or features of the environment (including more knowledgeable others, learning resources, activities, team members, tasks, etc.) that can guide experience and can potentially lead to learning. The affordances are represented as bands interwoven around the vortex, suggesting that a learner's level of expertise at any given moment is co-determined by the specific tasks and activities they engage in and learn from, their personal and interpersonal disposition for translating, their disposition for learning, the human and material resources available and drawn upon and a plethora of other affordances of the learning environment. Instructional intervention can indeed play a major role in this process, but from this viewpoint, learning is clearly the largely unpredictable and unprogrammable result of a complex interplay of processes and not merely or even significantly the direct result of transmissionist teaching.

The model also suggests that learners themselves must be proactive seekers of knowledge far more than being merely passive recipients of teachers' wisdom. Emergent processes proceed apace and not as the direct effect of one or more specific causes or stimuli (like instruction, for example). Teachers can also be seen as key agents and participants in the establishment and maintenance of conditions under which learners can perform the real work of professional translators and thereby develop professional expertise. The adoption of a view of translator competence as an emergent process is clearly an innovative step towards improving and refining collaborative, learner-centred approaches to translator education. In no way does this model obviate the social constructivist approach developed in Kiraly 2000. Instead, it is clearly intended to be seen as a refinement of that earlier approach.

Figure 3: Zooming in on the Learning Vortex: Emergent Workplace.

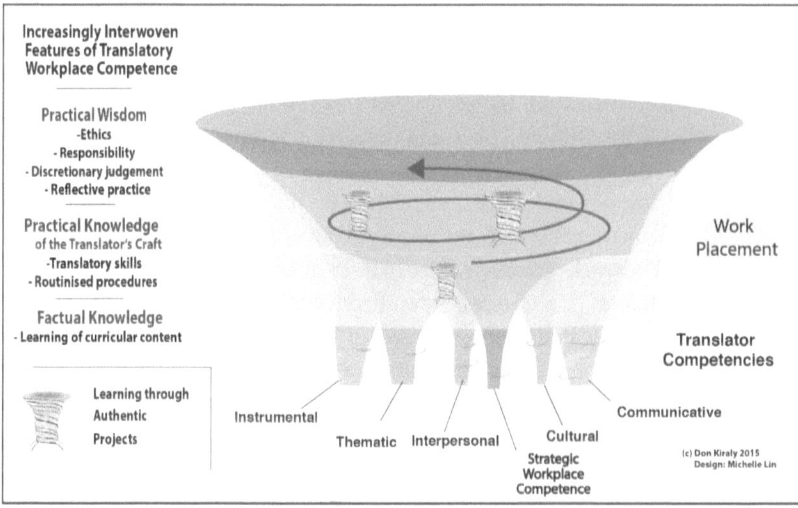

8. Competence and the Work Placement

Figure 3 represents a zoomed-in view of part of the emergent competence model near the end of the student's programme of post-graduate studies. It is at this stage that the EGPS project envisaged requiring students to undertake a work placement in a translation company. In this model, the work placement, where students finally have the opportunity to be fully incorporated into the day-to-day work of the professional translator and/or project manager, is the venue for the rapid expansion of what I call 'strategic workplace competence', which overlaps considerably with Kelly's concept of 'strategic competence'.

The model in Figure 3 depicts my current understanding of a plausible role for a work placement within the development of strategic workplace competence and that is to provide the unique affordances of a professional working environment to facilitate the merging of (institutionally) expedient competencies. In my view, it is specifically the experience of undertaking actual work in the workplace that allows the learner to move beyond the fragmented competences imposed by the classical curriculum and to merge them into a unified translator meta-competence. Unlike highly specialised classes that purport to cover specific sub-sets of subject matter or of discrete skills, the professional work done in the workplace can be seen to be comprised of multi-phase and multi-dimensional authentic projects, through which disparate knowledge and skills evolve in a largely spontaneous and indeed chaotic fashion as the placement student progresses from one project to the next. Although some critics argue that that this leads to an 'apprenticisation' of translator education[8], I believe that authentic practical experience within the protected learner environment of the higher education institution is a key to this progression of knowledge and skills because it allows the student's personal network of competence to be validated in a real life scenario.

By changing the way we look at competence, we may be able to change attitudes towards work placements as well as towards the overall educational process itself. No longer does the work placement have to be seen as an optional extra-curricular supplement added on to a university-level education in Translation Studies, but instead as a vital integrated component in the process of merging the competencies developed in the institutional setting into an all-encompassing translator meta-competence. And no longer does the Translation Studies curriculum need to be depicted as a smorgasbord of courses, undifferentiated in terms of sequencing or pedagogical approach. The model we propose in fact can bring much-needed structure into the curriculum, not in terms of rigid pre-specified boxes filled with content to be acquired, but in the sense of promoting the self-organization of skills and knowledge from the simple to the complex and from teacher-centred instruction to highly autonomous learning.

References

Campbell, S. (1998), *Translation into the Second Language.* London and New York: Longman.

Chesterman, A. (2000), *Memes of Translation.* Amsterdam / Philadelphiar: John Benjamins.

Cnyrim, A., Hagemann S. & J. Neu (2013), "Towards a Framework of Reference for Translation Competence". In: D. Kiraly, S. Hansen-Schirra & K. Maksymski (eds.). *New Prospects and Perspectives for Educating Language Mediators. Translationswissenschaft 10.* Tübingen: Narr, 9–34.

Davis, B. & D. Sumara (2007), "Complexity Science and Education: Reconceptualizing the Teacher's Role in Learning", *Interchange* 38, no. 1: 53–67.

Doll, W. E. (1993), *A Postmodern Perspective on Curriculum.* New York: Teachers College Press.

8 See, for example, Schopp (2013).

Dreyfus, S. (2004), "The five-stage model of adult skill acquisition", *Bulletin of Science, Technology & Society*, Vol. 24, No. 3, 177–181.

EMT Expert Group (2009), "Competences for Professional Translators, Experts in Multilingual and Multimedia Communication", http://ec.europa.eu/dgs/translation/programmes/emt/key_documents/emt_competences_translators_en.pdf (Accessed on 1 March 2015).

Göpferich, S. (2008), *Translationsprozessforschung.* Tübingen: Gunter Narr.

Göpferich, S. (2011), "From multidisciplinarity to transdisciplinarity: The investigation of competence development as a case in point", *MikaEL 3. Kääntämisen ja tulkkauksen tutkimuksen symposiumin verkkojulkaisu. Electronic proceedings of the KäTu symposium on translation and interpreting studies*, Nr. 5: 1–24.

Hagemann, S. & J. Neu (2013), „Vernetzte Translationslehre". In: *Projekte und Projektionen in der translatorischen Kompetenzentwicklung.* (eds.) S. Hansen-Schirra & D. Kiraly. FTSK: Publikationen des Fachbereichs Translations-, Sprach- und Kulturwissenschaft der Johannes Gutenberg-Universität Mainz, Reihe A, 61. Frankfurt am Main: Lang, 189–209.

Kelly, D. (2002), "Un modelo de competencia traductora: bases para el diseño curricular," *Puentes: Hacia Nuevas Investigativas en la Mediación Intercultural*: 9–20.

Kelly, D. (2007), "Translator competence contextualized, translator training in the framework of higher education reform: In search of alignment in curricular design", In: *Across Boundaries: International Perspectives on Translation Studies*: 128–142.

Kiraly, D. (2000), *A Social Constructivist Approach to Translator Education.* Manchester: St. Jerome.

Kiraly, D. (2013), 'Towards A View of Translator Competence as an Emergent Phenomenon: Thinking Outside the Box(es) in Translator Education," in Kiraly, D., S. Hansen-Schirra, & K. Maksymski (eds.), *New Prospects and Perspectives for Educating Language Mediators.* Translationswissenschaft, Vol. 10. 197–224.

Kiraly, D., S. Hansen-Schirra & K. Maksymski (eds) (2013), *New Prospects and Perspectives for Educating Language Mediators.* Tübingen: Narr Verlag.

PACTE (2005), "Investigating Translation Competence: Conceptual and Methodological Issues" *Meta* 50(2): 609–619.

Risku, H. (2002), "Situatedness in Translation Studies", *Cognitive Systems Research* Nr. 3: 523–533.

Schön, D. (1987), *Educating the Reflective Practitioner.* San Francisco: Jossey-Bass Publishers.

Schopp, J. F. (2013), „Auf halbem Weg…? Authentische Übersetzungsaufträge und professioneller Translationsprozess aus translationsdidaktischer Sicht“, *Alles hängt mit allem zusammen – Translatologische Interpendenzen. Festschrift für P.A. Schmitt*, A. K. Ende, S. Herold & A. Weiland (eds.), Berlin, Franke und Timme: 225–241.

Williams, J. (2000) *Theories of Translation.* Basingstoke & New York: Palgrave Macmillan.

Gys-Walt van Egdom

On "General" and Specialised Texts in the Translation Training Programme: Conjectures, Assumptions, Refutations and Implications

Abstract: Some painstaking attempts have been made to redirect the linguistic currents in Translation Studies. In one of his studies, Jean Delisle prevents linguistic theory from passing over into silence. In *L'Analyse du discours comme méthode de traduction* (1980/1984), he spins a thread for the inquiry into the usefulness of Critical Discourse Analysis (henceforth CDA) in translation training. In his study, he tears down the strongholds of the linguistic turn and introduces the inevitable notion of "context". Considering that, without exception, source texts as well as target texts are inextricably enmeshed in the cobweb of socio-cultural contexts, Delisle advises teachers and institutes to critically assess the texts that are (to be) subjected to interpretation or/and translation in the context of translation training. According to him, teachers should stick to "general pragmatic texts" in the initial phases of formation; they can be readily interpreted by students and allow the problems most proper to translation to take centre of stage. Thirty years later, this view is still widely shared: in most translation programmes, not only of vocational schools but also of academic institutions, specialised texts are introduced only in the final year of the BA-programme or even in the MA-year.

In this contribution, we will return to the assumptions that lie at the basis of a shared belief in the purposefulness of using general texts and we will try to cast new light on text selection procedures in translation training. We will do so in the company of Anthony Pym (1992/2010), who was the first not only to bestow attention upon these assumptions, but also to raise arguments against the "integration" of CDA theory in Translation Studies. In him we can find an ally against forces that prove to be extremely conservative. However, we contend that his critique appears too meagre a foundation for new and firm principles for text selection. To provide more foundation, we will cast a glance at some developments in the sociology of translation.

Keywords: translator training, text selection, specialised translation, curricular design, general texts, Critical Discourse Analysis, zero degree of specialisation, Jean Delisle, Anthony Pym, Sociology of Translation.

1. Introduction

Having addressed the issue of text selection and the need for curricular redesigning in *Translation and Text Transfer* (1992a/2010), Anthony Pym, at the time a teacher at the University of Las Palmas, was intent on dealing a blow to his colleagues of the Escuela Universitaria de Traductores e Intérpretes in Barcelona. Nuenzig and his colleagues had worked out a text difficulty profile (1985) that was to change the landscape of translation didactics. The profile was to form the backbone of academic translation programmes, as it aimed to make text selection processes dependent upon student progression. To disparage the profile, Pym had already launched the four-pronged attack that we will discuss later on. In the final chapter of his book, on the relevance of translation theory for the broad field of translator trainers and students, he would cap his critique by indulging in a remarkable metaphor:

> the tendency to exclude special text genres from the domain of translation theory leads to the assumption that one must first deal only with […] "general texts". From the perspective of a generality organized in terms of translation, there are no such beasts. One might as well go to a zoo and look for a cage marked "animal" (1992a: 188/2010: 190).

With this striking image, Pym put the finger on a problem that had vexed translation trainers for decades and that continued to exercise the minds of the theorists of the Barcelona translation school. What constitutes the "communality" of general texts? What distinguishes them from "non-general" texts? After Pym's publication, one would say, no other conclusion could be reached: just like the Linnaeic taxonomy holds no place for the "animal" within the *regnum animale,* a translation-specific text typology could no longer integrate what was called a "general text".

A quarter of a century later, text selection processes in translator training have hardly undergone sweeping improvements. In the 1980s and 1990s, training institutes still grappled with the burdens of the past: minds were set on redesigning the curriculum so as to foster the development not so much of foreign-language competence but, rather, of translation competence. It seems somewhat logical that they have not been prompted to action straight after Pym's publication. Yet it is surprising that presently so few translation institutes have granted specialisation a prominent place in the curriculum.

In this article, we will take a stab at explaining the lasting dominance of "general texts" in our training programmes and we will reassess the assumptions that lie at the basis of the shared belief in those texts. With this objective in mind, we will first provide a synthesis of early translation training practices. Later on, we will try to probe the depths of *L'Analyse du discours comme méthode de traduction* (Delisle 1980). A great many scholars had already drawn attention to text selection in a didactic setting, but Delisle was the first to address the issue in a systematic way. In his study, Delisle, whose thoughts were in line with those of the Barcelona school, hoped to mark a clean break with past practices in translation didactics by redirecting their course in a way that training practices would get attuned to the needs of translators. In the third section, Pym will enter the scene: we will discuss the four arguments advanced to counter the widely-held view that "general texts" are best suited for translation exercises for developing translation competence. Toward the end of this article, we will also challenge this view. To strengthen our position, we will acquaint the reader with the potential impact of recent "field-theoretical" developments on text selection.

2. Early Training Practices

The scope of this article requires a balance between comprehensiveness and focus. In other words, we need to work our way through the sweep of the history of translation didactics, and to focus, at the same time, on elements most relevant for attaining firm ground for a fruitful continuation of the discussion on text selection. However, the landscape of translation didactics is rich in resources and relevant resources are too scattered to be picked up in a simple article. Extending the ecological analogy, it might suffice to say that we are forced to farm out the responsibility of providing a "full" overview of the unwieldy landscape; we must strive to give an account of the texts that, after sifting through countless texts, seem to sum up the debate on text selection.

Before we plunge headfirst into those texts, we will offer an impression of the oldest of didactic habits in translator education. With the benefit of insights in various branches of Translation Studies, we have perhaps become so enlightened that those habits have dimmed in our memory. With the development of translation training programmes, shortly after World War II, we witnessed an influx of not only researchers but also of teaching personnel from contiguous domains, mainly philology and linguistics. As a consequence of what the philosopher John Dewey once called an "occupational psychosis", teaching staff was not sufficiently qualified to provide proper training and supervision to translation students. Most of the staff-members were lacking experience in the field of translation. What is more, quite a number of training programmes were still part and parcel of foreign language programmes. This meant that translation, having and being its own end, was often turned into a mere means.

In the 1980s, the training programmes had changed for the better, but they were in no way geared to the needs of the market. Awareness of the communicative function of a target text had yet to penetrate the consciousness of the academic staff. So Hönig and Kußmaul held up a mirror to them, stating that:

> die Studenten übersetzen einen Text, die sie nicht verstehen, für einen Adressaten, den sie nicht kennen. Und das Produkt ihrer Bemühungen wird nicht selten von einem Dozenten

> beurteilt, der weder praktische Erfahrungen als Übersetzer noch theoretische Kenntnisse in der Übersetzungswissenschaft besitzt (1982: 28).

Their statement could hardly be misunderstood. However, the mirror that is held up by the German theorists showed some cracks that could prevent us from confronting the true problem. What is lacking in the description is the set of criteria from which these classroom malpractices had issued forth. What Hönig and Kußmaul fail to mention is that, prior to "didactisation", short shrift was given to selection criteria. In more traditional veins, the text of choice of the teacher was most likely a text that he/she had stumbled upon in the cultural section of newspapers, in magazines and so on. Slipshod selection could only lead to ineffective and misleading class exercises – even in the cases in which students would have been able to identify the function of a prospective target text.

3. Jean Delisle and the Tectonics of the 1980s

Beneath the surface the ideas that would cause a tectonic shift of the 1980s were smouldering. Some ideas would initiate inquiries into text selection criteria and prompt a debate – albeit not a lively one – on the future of translation didactics. Jean Delisle was one of the first scholars to bestow considerable attention upon these criteria. In the preface of *L'Analyse du discours comme méthode de traduction,* he admitted that progress had been made, but he also noted that hitherto hardly anyone had dared to bear the consequences of made progress:

> [Bien qu'il] semble [...] acquis que la traduction puisse faire l'objet d'un enseignement *sui generis,* [...] son entrée [...] en tant que discipline autonome a soulevé de nombreux problèmes épistémologiques et méthodologiques (1984: 15).

As the saying goes: habits die hard. Consequently, the theorist took up the gauntlet to beat old habits. His approach diverged markedly from that of contemporaries who had their minds set on tearing down all linguistic strongholds. Like early functionalists, Delisle was still strongly drawn to linguistics – contrastive linguistics, sociolinguistics, stylistics. However, instead of siding with the functionalists, he decided to pick up some dominant notions in CDA, in order to expose the major flaws of prevalent practices (cf. *ibid.*: 60–61).

From the late 1970s onward, it seemed safe to maintain, in some circles, that CDA formed the single touchstone for reliable text analysis. The theory had been applied to all sorts of texts, addressing a wide range of research topics (text convention, power relation, sociological profiling). Yet it was still to make its first appearance in Translation Studies. Delisle was determined to salvage some of the old models that had been brought to bear on translation problems from criticism by moving from meaning at sentence-level toward textual significance and by seasoning the notion of text with an indispensable pinch of context:

> Le théoricien et le didacticien de la traduction ne peuvent donc pas limiter leur analyse du phénomène [...] aux seules composantes linguistiques des textes, il leur faut absolument déborder sur la pragmatique afin d'inclure dans l'analyse du processus de la traduction les compléments cognitifs et situationnels [...] dans les signes linguistique (*ibid.*: 23–24).

Soon his work would be hailed by many colleagues. This is not surprising as he had made a reasonable effort to establish – albeit few – criteria for text selection. Stated most generally, his contribution lies in the consideration given to interpretive value. Teachers and training institutes, he maintained, must kick the habit of focussing on equivalence, not because there is no such thing as equivalence, but mainly because the term diverts attention away from the situation and the (re)creational activity inherent to translation (*ibid.* 1984: 11: 43: 58). This brings us to his main criterion for text selection: to qualify as proper teaching material, he argues, a source text should sharpen our awareness of the distinction between meaning and sense. Precedence is given to "sense", as something that emerges out of and is altered through language use[1]. To increase awareness, it is recommended that pragmatic texts of a "general nature" be used in training, and specifically in the initiation phase (*ibid.*: 14: 17: 45).

> Ces écrits regroupent, à titre d'exemple, les articles de presse, la correspondance générale, les brochures explicatives non techniques, la documentation touristique, les rapports et documents officiels, bref, tout texte général traitant de pollution, santé physique, consommation, drogue, loisirs, économie, sports et autres domaines d'activités analogues (*ibid.*: 24).

It seems that Delisle followed the conventional wisdom that, due to the fact that they are in line with the interests of students, these texts are straightforward and accessible. He goes to some lengths to claim that the reading ease of these texts allows translator trainers to heighten relevant aspects of translation. The ability to tap into "real" processes is connected with a correct interpretative focus which, in turn, relies on an excellent command of the four landmarks of language use (*les paliers du maniement de langage*). Only when he gets to grips with writing convention, lexical exegesis, stylistic load and textual organicity, will the aspiring translator acknowledge the difficulties of re-expression in a target situation and will he accomplish his task by adopting the appropriate strategy (*ibid.*: 98–128).

1 Delisle makes it abundantly clear that Translation Studies must deal with *parole*, a series of uttered statements, not with *langue*, a closed formal system (1984: 23–24, 59).

The recommendations of Delisle and like-minded scholars impacted methodological and curricular decisions in a profound way. However, Delisle's call to action only did cause a real shift in the plate tectonics of translation didactics, because translation training was gradually freeing itself from the restrictions once imposed by linguistics and philology. The fact that the recommendations have been turned into peremptory norms has no more to do with the merits of his arguments than it has with compatibility with the prevalent norms of new translation institutes.

In the curricula, courses were developed that were more attuned to the needs of the translators. Learning outcomes were established before they trickled down to all layers of the curriculum. The stages in the formation of fully-fledged professionals took on greater importance: pedagogical progression – e.g. providing students with general principles and metalinguistic tools (*ibid.*: 17) – would prevail in earlier stages, while specialisation took pride of place in the final years or in post-graduate programmes (cf. Figure 1[2]). By the end of the 1980s, the contours of the modern curricula appeared indelible.

Figure 1: Specialisation in Translation Training Programme.

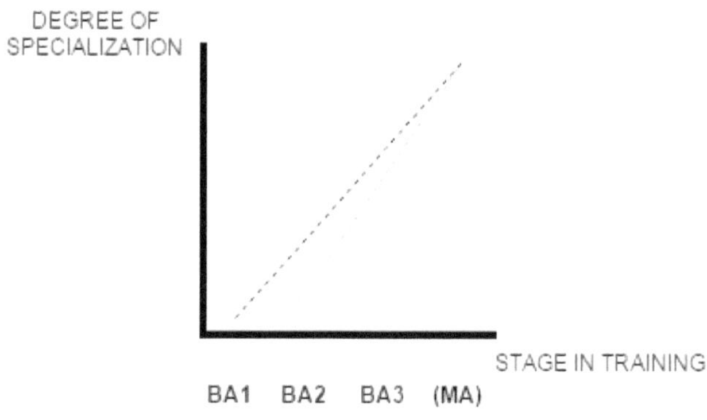

In the years following his debut, Delisle would continue along established lines (cf. 1993). He remained intent on ridding translation theory of the knee-jerk assumptions that had left us all mired in error for so long. Unfortunately,

2 Note the distinction in Figure 1 between programmes that indroduce translation as a subject/exercise in BA1 and programmes that do not confront students with translation until some underpinning for language proficiency and translation strategies has been provided.

he seemed oblivious to the demand for "authentic" translation assignments[3]. Wrapped up in the need for a "traduction raisonnée", he forgot all about the importance of text selection criteria. This meant that, to him, text selection would ultimately remain a subjective activity. Granted, source material is to be selected in the light of "difficulties" that prevent students from attaining their goal (i.e. obtaining translation competence), but, in the end, "l'enseignant est obligé à se fier à son intuition et à son expérience [...] pour choisir les textes les plus pertinents" (1980: 24).

4. Anthony Pym and the General Text

In 1992, when translation programmes were embracing Delisle's thoughts on didactics, Anthony Pym aired the complaint that translation didactics had done little but flounder analytically. The situation was all the more dramatic, since many had come to believe that translation training had indeed become meaningful and realistic. "General" pragmatic texts, often taken as points of departure in a swift movement toward translation competence, were, as Pym shows, nothing but workarounds – kept in place to provide the illusion of a rational orientation.

In that year, Delisle's work was put under scrutiny. In "Limits and Frustrations of Discourse Analysis in Translation Theory" (1992b), Pym discarded the masks of not only Delisle, but also of Hatim and Mason [1997]. He exposed the falsity of their critical discursive approach to translation. Hatim and Mason, who had a correct understanding of CDA, were not able to retain more than a nebulous notion of translation: when trying to pinpoint translation, the image of it appeared distorted due to equifunctionalist tendencies (*ibid.*: 228). Delisle did stay close to translation, yet his commitment to CDA was half-hearted: his stance was readily accessible without there being "any reference to discourse at all' (*ibid.*). We tend to agree with Pym: Delisle had only misused a modish term (*ibid.*). The "didacticien" had done little more than turning the attention toward near extra-textual surroundings.

In *Translation and Text Transfer* (1992a/2010), Pym furthered his critique by targeting the meaningfulness of certain exercises in training programmes. He set out to debunk the tenets that sustained not only the framework for text selection of the Barcelona school, but also that of Jean Delisle. Four claims that are left

3 Commonly acknowledged as the first to demand attention for "authenticity" is Christiane Nord, who advocated that real assignments be used in the classroom (1988). Her ideas were picked up by Donald Kiraly and later interwoven with his own socio-constructivist ideas (2000).

implicit in *L'Analyse du discours comme méthode de traduction* are interrogated, as they provided a case for the revision of conventional notions of difficulty. The four claims are summed up below:

- Subject matter: "general" texts are held to be easier to translate than "specialized" texts;
- Social location: communication between a non-specialist sender and a general public is believed to be easier than communication between specialists;
- Register: "Everyday" language is supposed to be easier to render than "technical" or "literary" language
- Distance: "cultural and temporal proximity" presents less problems than does extreme cultural and temporal distance. (1992a: 122/2010: 128).

None of these claims seem nonsensical: we can come up with examples of problematic communication that may serve as proof here (the lawyer who makes an effort to "translate" the plaintiff's demands to a client, the plumber who speaks of a missing part in the sewage system, etc.). Understandably, we cannot easily dismiss the four claims as unfounded. In point of fact, they appear all the more reasonable when we cast a glance at the market situation: "[...] specialized translations are deemed the most valuable in terms of the supply-and-demand economy [...], [for that reason] it is assumed that these same texts must be the most difficult from the pedagogical point of view" (1992a: 121/2010: 126). Why are specialised texts so high in demand, if not for the discursive complexity of these text types?

As stated, Pym challenged the validity of these assumptions, in spite of the above. In an acerbic critique, he focused the attention on the text's sense of belonging, on the extent to which they are bound to their situation. This approach would allow him to defend a broader notion of "translation difficulties", one that lays stress on the "relative ability [...] to escape embeddedness" (1992a:122/2010: 127). "General" texts, Pym rebutted, demand a reinvigorated attention, since they often contain words that pose particular problems to the translator. Contrary to real terms, which often have become standardised, those words, which at times can even be likened to terms, are inextricably tied to the situation in which they are uttered. A translator always has to take into consideration the nuances collected from the countless situations in which words have been expressed in the past and be ready to negotiate nuances when words are to be rendered in the target text (1992a: 123/2010: 128). To make his point, Pym referred to Delisle's reading of an article on breast reconstruction, in which the untranslatability of a lexical item ("sense of loss") is brought to the fore (1992a: 123 /2010: 128–129; cf. Delisle 1984: 66–135). What makes the three words come out garbled in interpretation is the very fact that they do not constitute a term.

Pym did not linger on subject matter, social location and register in the remaining pages of his critique, as his interest was piqued by the untranslatability of distant texts. This is unfortunate given the paramount role of those themes to CDA. However, we do not fault him for his omission: Pym seems to believe that objections to particular claims could only be quibbles, as objections would only acknowledge the existence of "general" texts (cf. 1992a: 124/2010: 129). Having read his critique, we can conclusively state that Pym was the first to successfully cut against the grain of common sense and of contemporary scholarly thought. By so doing, he has proved that the position of Delisle was ultimately untenable. In implicit terms, he called for a radical revision of text selection criteria and probably for a restructuring of the curriculum of translation institutes.

5. Translation Sociology and the Pivotal Status of the General Text

More than twenty years have passed since the publication of Pym's critique. The statement that "general" texts do not exist has not remained unnoticed. In her *Handbook for Translator Trainers* (2014), Dorothy Kelly sides with Pym, adamantly opposing the introduction of "general" texts in translation training: "[t]he concept of 'general' translation is particularly unhelpful, as it is essentially a non-category" (*ibid.*:123). Still, consent about the status of "general" texts has not proved sufficient to change the landscape of translation didactics. Taking a close look at existing translation programmes, we can only conclude that but a few institutes have acted upon their convictions. In their BA-years, aspiring translators continue to be exposed only to what Delisle would call "general" texts.

Why do we still use "general" texts? We believe that the "general" text has remained in place because we have failed to recognize what Pym has put at stake. We readily accept that there is no such thing as a "general" text. For that very reason, we merely pay attention to the degree of specialisation of text types and (in some cases) to the socio-cultural distance between interlocutors. Understandably, we go in search of text types that are deemed highly translatable, so as not to discourage our students. By so doing, we inadvertently revert to old habits: we unknowingly close the eyes to Pym's fundamental thrust – his introduction of a broader notion of text difficulty. As a result, we tend to make little account of the zero-degree of specialisation. That zero-degree of specialisation, we note, tends to coincide with what was once called "generality".

What can we do to promote realism in the classroom? Should we jettison the "general" once more? We have been distracted by petty details such as nomenclature for way too long. Key in our quest for "authenticity", we claim, is a solid ground for understanding the difference between ordinary and specialised communication. Therefore, we will return to Pym's fundamental thrust and see if his main arguments can be strengthened retroactively by insights that have been generated in the years separating us from *Translation and Text Transfer.*

References that immediately impose themselves apropos discursive difficulty are the recent applications of Field theory to translation[4]. The first three great claims that Pym rendered problematic (concerning subject, location and register) are indirectly criticised in "The Pivotal Status of Translator Habitus" (Simeoni 1998), a paper that played a decisive part in the emergence of translation sociology. In this text, Daniel Simeoni ventures an expedition into open and well-delineated "fields" of translation. In one sequence, he clarifies his point apropos of field delineation, noting that:

> "in [a socially open] environment, influences are so entangled on account of the fuzziness of field borders and the relationships within, that the larger social constituency can hardly be called a "field" or, at least, it should be viewed as a much more complex and messy system " (*ibid.*: 17–18).

Without knowing it, Simeoni refuted all "commonsensical" claims that Pym had touched upon. He stated that it is easier to identify the respective rules of specialised communication and to adhere to them, than it is with "everyday" discourse. He also maintained that this has everything to do with the presence of fuzzy and incompatible rules (*ibid.*). These insights are crucial not only in our critical interrogation of text/translation difficulties but also in our quest for selection criteria.

6. Conclusion

On the basis of insights that have trickled down from the plains of translation sociology, we can assert that there is ample reason to promote specialised texts in translation education. In point of fact, texts pertaining to "everyday" discourse are exceptionally difficult to dislodge: they remain tied to a wide variety of rules. The opaqueness of underlying rules makes "general" texts extremely difficult to translate. Our enriched understanding of text difficulty should make it easier to opt for specialised texts: teachers should not confront aspiring translators with texts that are *too* difficult – certainly not at an early stage. But text difficulty is not the only cogent argument for the use of specialized texts, since this only relates to the translation competence of students. We suggest that by promoting

4 Field theory tries to explain how translational interaction is regulated (cf. Inghilleri (ed.), 2005).

exercises with specialised texts, we can also tend the needs of teaching personnel. Evaluating translation is a difficult and arduous task. The problems of evaluating will only grow worse as long as specialised texts are excluded in the earlier stages, because it is precisely at those stages that students cannot cope with there being grey zones. When we decide to introduce specialised texts, with their inherent and rigid regulation, earlier, it will become easier to come to an objective evaluation.

To conclude, we would like to add a few remarks. We argue in favour of the Introduction of specialised texts at earlier stages of translator training, but we do not wish to do away with the "general" pragmatic texts altogether. They too could occupy a space in the curriculum. For it may well be that "general" texts are non-existent or fuzzy, we cannot deny that affinity with the subject can be a motivating factor and that "general" texts are therefore likely to encourage young students to keep engaging in the translation activity. In other words, the lesson to be fully endorsed is not that the balance is to be tipped, but rather that an equilibrium needs to be found.

References

Delisle, Jean: *L'analyse du discours comme méthode de traduction: théorie et pratique.* Ottawa: Presses de l'Université d'Ottawa, 1980/1984.

Delisle, Jean, *La traduction raisonnée: Manuel d'initiation à la traduction professionnelle de l 'anglais vers le français.* Ottawa: Presses de l'Université d'Ottawa, 1993.

Hönig, Hans & Kußmaul, Paul: *Strategie der Übersetzung. Ein Lehr- und Arbeitsbuch.* Tübingen: Narr, 1982.

Inghilleri, Moira (ed.), "Bourdieu and the Sociology of Translation and Interpreting" . *The Translator* 11(2) [Special issue], 2005.

Kelly, Dorothy: *A Handbook for Translator Trainers.* Oxon-New York [NY]: Routledge [second ed.], 2014.

Kiraly, Donald: *A Social Constructivist Approach to Translator Education. Empowerment from Theory to Practice.* Manchester: St. Jerome, 2000.

Nord, Christiane: *Textanalyse und Übersetzen: Theoretische Grundlagen, Methode und didaktische Anwendung einer übersetzungsrelevanten Textanalyse.* Heidelberg: Groos, 1988.

Nuenzig, Wilhelm: *Informe del proyecto global en la formación de traductores e intérpretes.* Barcelona: Universidad Autónoma de Barcelona, 1985.

Pym, Anthony: *Translation and Text Transfer: An Essay on the Principles of Intercultural Communication.* Peter Lang: Frankfurt a. M. *et al.*, 1992a.

Pym, Anthony: "Limits and Frustrations of Discourse Analysis in Translation Theory". *Revista de Filologia de la Universidad de La Laguna* 11, 1992b, pp. 227–239.

Pym, Anthony: "Translation and Text Transfer: An Essay on the Principles of Intercultural Communication." Tarragona: Intercultural Studies Group [revised ed.], 2010.

Simeoni, Daniel: "The Pivotal Status of the Translator's Habitus". *Target* 10(1), 1998, pp. 1–39.

Hildegard Vermeiren

L'interprétation à l'ère des tic

Abstract: During the last decade, the use of ICT has expanded enormously. The improved quality of sound, image and internet connection, combined with lighter hardware offers unprecedented opportunities. Interpreters and interpreting agencies alike therefore feel compelled to make use of new technologies.

Incorporating ICT in interpreting training can be challenging though: many institutes still focus on traditional interpreting techniques and enormous budgets are needed. As a result, a gap could emerge between the institutes that pay attention to ICT in interpreting and the ones that do not.

Starting from the actual practice at Ghent University, we construct a framework of the different forms of ICT that ideally should be included in a contemporary interpreter training course. The three pillars are: ICT for research, for education and for a professional context. In that third context, we distinguish software for documentation, terminology management, mobile communication, video conferencing and speech recognition.

Furthermore, on an educational-psychological level we assume that students will need to develop self-efficiency for using ICT. The best framework to develop such a competence seems to be social constructivist.

On the basis of a concrete example of mobile interpreting (bidule interpreting) we will illustrate an exercise with a view to self-efficacy.

Keywords: ICT, digital divide, interpreting, interpreter training, social constructivism, empowerment, self-efficacy, documentation.

Un « tsunami » : telle est la métaphore utilisée par Drechsel (2013b) pour parler de la vague de changements technologiques qui déferle sur les traducteurs et interprètes. Il y a déjà une vingtaine d'années, O'Hagan (1996) et O'Hagan & Ashworth (2002) faisaient le point sur les nouvelles technologies et mesuraient leur impact sur l'industrie de la traduction et l'interprétation. Leurs ouvrages à la fois clairvoyants et attentifs aux détails techniques nous parlent d'un futur dominé par la télétraduction et la télé-interprétation, ainsi que par des formes hybrides telles que la « transterprétation » (O'Hagan & Ashworth, 2002: 14). Dans ce nouveau contexte, les auteurs prévoient que les compétences de traduction ou d'interprétation ne suffiront plus (2002: 29) mais que les traducteurs et interprètes devront également maîtriser la culture numérique, connaître le matériel, les logiciels et être capables de les employer efficacement. Drechsel (2013a ; 2013b) signale toutefois que si les traducteurs ont rapidement intégré les nouvelles technologies, la culture numérique des interprètes accuse un net retard et qu'il est donc indispensable d'y accorder plus d'attention pendant la formation.

1. Les traducteurs et interprètes à l'ère des TIC

Compte tenu du caractère asynchronique et facilement numérisable de leur travail (le passage d'un produit fini à un autre produit fini), les traducteurs ont d'emblée pu profiter des TIC (notamment les bases de données, le traitement de texte, les logiciels de traduction et les mémoires de traduction) et de la communication numérique écrite. Mais ils ont également été contraints de les adopter en raison de la technicité croissante des traductions demandées, telles que les pages web, la localisation, etc. (Drechsel, 2013b).

Le travail de l'interprète, par contre, est synchronique et plus difficile à numériser. Le « tsunami » a déferlé sur les interprètes avec un retard de deux décennies, lorsque le son et l'image des TIC avaient atteint une qualité satisfaisante. Depuis, la légèreté du nouveau matériel informatique et les TIC sans fil n'ont fait qu'accroître leur succès.

À l'heure actuelle, tous les interprètes doivent s'adapter aux nouvelles tendances et aux exigences particulières de leurs clients. Même si l'interprète contrôle lui-même en grande partie le pôle « information » de son travail (sa recherche de textes en langue source, de textes parallèles, son utilisation de bases de données, de dictionnaires et de glossaires électroniques), le pôle « communication » dépend souvent du budget et des préférences du commanditaire.

Il suffit de jeter un coup d'œil sur les pages web d'une agence d'interprétation de conférence telle que Duvall (http://duvall.be/fr/) pour avoir une idée des solutions technologiques disponibles. Hormis les traditionnelles cabines sur le site, l'agence propose des services d'interprétation en visioconférence ou à distance. Duvall utilise pour cela la technologie fournie par la firme américaine LifeSize. La plate-forme LifeSize permet de constituer des réseaux de visioconférence mobile (« *on-the-go* ») entre tous les ordinateurs (de bureau, portables ordiphones) d'une firme ou entreprise et de ses filiales partout dans le monde.

Mais il existe d'autres perspectives que la visioconférence. Les interprètes pourraient aussi être confrontés à des formes hybrides d'interprétation telles que la 'transterprétation', qui combine le chat, l'audio et la vidéo, ou l'interprétation reliée à un système de reconnaissance vocale (O'Hagan & Ashworth, 2002: 14–15; 47).

2. Le défi des TIC dans la formation des interprètes

Ces avancées technologiques doivent être intégrées dans la formation des interprètes. Néanmoins, de nombreux obstacles se posent. En effet, pour se familiariser avec les TIC, les étudiants en interprétation ne peuvent, à l'instar des traducteurs, utiliser les labos classiques équipés d'ordinateurs. Ils ont besoin d'un matériel différent qui leur permette à la fois de travailler pour leurs clients (microphones ambulants, bidules, équipement de visioconférence) et d'utiliser leurs ressources personnelles.

Cependant, au sein des facultés universitaires, l'intégration des TIC dans le cursus des interprètes est lente et se heurte régulièrement à l'indifférence voire à la résistance des étudiants mais aussi des professeurs. Ces derniers considèrent souvent que les TIC destinés aux interprètes sont périphériques par rapport aux priorités du cursus que constituent les « modes » (interprétation consécutive, simultanée, traduction à vue, chuchotage).

Le plus grand obstacle est néanmoins le côté budgétaire. Les facultés disposent d'un budget limité pour s'équiper en ordinateurs, matériel fixe et mobile ainsi que logiciels. Elles veulent investir dans du solide. De plus, dans le cas des interprètes il faut un matériel professionnel à cent pour cent. Comme le nombre d'étudiants en interprétation est en général restreint, l'investissement *per capita* est élevé. Lorsque la faculté décide d'investir, c'est pour le long terme et il n'est donc pas question de suivre l'évolution technologique pas à pas. Les étudiants, pour leur part, ne disposent souvent que d'un budget limité et n'ont pas les moyens de se procurer tout ce matériel.

Un dernier obstacle est d'ordre humain. Les professeurs d'interprétation n'ont pas fait d'études d'informatique et sont donc de simples utilisateurs, même s'ils sont passionnés par les TIC. Il faut donc avoir recours à l'expertise de techniciens de l'université pour résoudre de nombreuses questions. Si l'assistance technique fait défaut, le matériel perd sa fiabilité et l'utilisation des TIC se complique. Il est donc préférable d'avoir une solution de dépannage à portée de main.

Drechsel (2004) a constaté qu'il y avait des différences considérables quant à l'intégration des TIC dans le cursus de cinq universités allemandes. Au niveau mondial, la disparité est encore plus grande (Berber Irabien, 2010).

3. Les TIC dans le cursus

Au sein d'une formation d'interprètes, il faudra décider quelle place on souhaite accorder aux TIC. À l'Université de Gand, les TIC constituent une facette de chaque cours du master en interprétation, Les étudiants se familiarisent surtout avec le travail mobile. Cela signifie que les TIC n'occupent pas une place prépondérante. Le cours de déontologie, adressé à ces mêmes étudiants, aborde brièvement les défis posés par la visioconférence dans le contexte médical. Les étudiants du post-graduat en interprétation de conférence, par contre, ont un cours spécifique intitulé « Techniques et Technologies ». L'objectif pédagogique visé est de former les futurs interprètes à opter pour la technique et la technologie la plus efficace dans des circonstances données. Or, pour disposer de cette capacité de jugement, il faut avoir acquis une certaine expérience. C'est ce dernier aspect qui nous intéresse ici.

Quand on se demande quelles TIC doivent être intégrées dans une formation d'interprètes (au niveau universitaire), on distingue trois grands axes, selon les relations sociales dans lesquelles ces TIC sont employées: la communication entre chercheurs, la communication entre l'enseignant et son élève, la communication entre l'interprète professionnel et son public.

4. Les TIC pour la recherche en interprétation

Vu qu'il s'agit d'une formation académique, les étudiants ont besoin de matériel pour leur cours et pour leurs travaux de recherche. Cette **documentation** ou **information** académique est accessible à travers les TIC. La première adresse à consulter est celle de la bibliothèque numérique de l'université. Dans le monde académique, les systèmes d'archivage électronique sont devenus aussi importants que l'endroit physique appelé « bibliothèque ». Ensuite il y a les bibliothèques numériques thématiques pour la traduction et l'interprétation. Depuis des années, les étudiants en interprétation de conférence peuvent trouver des documents sur le site de Gile (http://www.cirinandgile.com/). Ceux qui parlent l'espagnol peuvent consulter la base de données BITRA élaborée par l'Université d'Alicante. Bientôt, les étudiants d'interprétation de liaison pourront également consulter une bibliothèque thématique en construction au sein de l'organisation ENPSIT (European Network for Public Service Interpreting and Translation). D'autres bases de données peuvent s'avérer utiles, comme Google Scholar. À partir du portail Open Doar (http://www.opendoar.org/) on a accès à d'autres bibliothèques pluridisciplinaires telles que SHERPA, HAL et DIALNET.

5. Les TIC pédagogiques

La communication entre l'enseignant et ses élèves a suivi l'évolution des TIC. Nous pensons ici aux didacticiels pour l'entraînement individuel, appelés « *Computer Assisted Interpreter Training* » (CAIT) en anglais. Une pédagogie basée sur le virtuel exige toutefois une infrastructure informatique dont beaucoup de départements ne disposent pas, et les efforts dans ce sens se limitent souvent à des fragments audio ou vidéo que les professeurs enregistrent pour leurs étudiants. Plusieurs universités disposent d'une bibliothèque institutionnelle d'exercices. Sandrelli & de Manuel Jerez (2007) en expliquent les différentes modalités et envisagent également la possibilité de disposer d'exercices complètement virtuels. À Gand, la pédagogie en face-à-face a toujours la priorité, même s'il existe quelques collections de fragments vidéo.

Le Directorat Général Interprétation (SCIC) a eu la générosité de construire une bibliothèque contenant des discours en plusieurs langues (https://webgate.ec.europa.eu/sr/user/login) pour permettre aux futurs interprètes de s'entraîner.

D'autres TIC ont été lancées sur le marché. Un exemple de ces nouveaux didacticiels est LiveScribe, qui est lié au logiciel LiveScribe Desktop. Il s'agit d'un *smartpen* (une « plume intelligente » munie d'un microphone) qui permet de prendre des notes (et de les numériser), d'enregistrer des fichiers audio et de transférer le tout par wifi ou câble vers un ordinateur. Le prix de cet outil, entre 170 et 250 euros, est assez prohibitif. Il est dès lors peu probable qu'un département en fasse l'acquisition pour ses étudiants.

6. Les TIC professionnelles

Kalina (2009: 39) note que la cabine d'interprétation est devenue un lieu de travail hautement numérisé. En fait, l'équipement fixe de la cabine n'est qu'une partie de ce bilan. Deux TIC se rapportent à la documentation et à l'information, deux autres à la communication et la cinquième est la reconnaissance vocale. Ce sont les trois dernières qui nous intéressent ici. Nous ne parlerons pas de l'interprétation automatique.

- **Logiciels de documentation:** il s'agit avant tout du Web comme réservoir de sources primaires (textes en langue source et en langue cible, parallèles ou comparables) et secondaires (dictionnaires électroniques, glossaires) sur le sujet traité. Dû au caractère de processus du travail de l'interprète, celui-ci a besoin du Web pendant la phase sa préparation 'ad hoc' (Gile 2009: 140–141). Ce qui est nouveau, c'est que l'interprète peut maintenant, en théorie, prolonger son travail de documentation n'importe où grâce à son portable. L'étudiant doit donc être formé au travail de préparation à domicile et pendant son travail en cabine.
- **Logiciels de gestion terminologique**: il s'agit de logiciels spécifiques tant pour la gestion terminologique à l'avance (Gile 2009: 142) que pendant le processus

d'interprétation. Le succès et l'utilité de ces logiciels dépendent de leur capacité d'adaptation à la mobilité du travail de l'interprète. Les plus connus sont InterpretBank et Interplex. Rütten (2014a; 2014b) cite également Lookup, Terminus, Glossary Assistant et Interpreters'Help, parmi lesquels certains sont conçus pour les ordinateurs, d'autres (également) pour les ordiphones. Ce qui est nouveau, ici aussi, c'est que l'interprète peut emporter soit des glossaires papier, soit son portable en fonction de son contexte de travail. L'interprète doit donc être formé au travail de préparation terminologique à domicile et à la gestion terminologique en cours de travail.

- **Matériel numérique pour la communication en face-à-face**: il s'agit de l'équipement appelé « valise d'interprétation » (ou « bidule » en Belgique) composé d'un microphone-émetteur et d'une dizaine (ou plus) de casques circum-auraux ou supra-auraux, reliés à des récepteurs individuels. Cet équipement, très flexible, permet de travailler de façon mobile, dans de petites réunions, ateliers, rencontres ou visites. Cette nouvelle visibilité de l'interprète signifie souvent qu'il doit être polyvalent : travailler en bi-directionnel, en simultanée et en consécutive dans une même réunion. Actuellement, de nombreuses entreprises disposent déjà de leur propre « valise », ce qui leur évite souvent de devoir louer des cabines d'interprétation. L'interprète doit être formé à travailler avec ce matériel.
- **Logiciels pour la cabine**: l'équipement dans les cabines est entièrement numérique: les postes, la connexion au Web et les écrans reliés aux circuits vidéo. Peuvent s'y ajouter un matériel spécifique pour visioconférence comme le polycom ou d'autres logiciels basés sur le protocole *Voix sur IP*. Le commanditaire peut avoir son propre équipement de visioconférence ou louer une salle équipée. Il existe des « *remote interpreting hubs* » où les interprètes travaillent dans des cabines loin de leurs clients. L'interprète peut encore travailler depuis son domicile. Les avantages et inconvénients de la visioconférence et de l'interprétation à distance ont été étudiés (Mouzourakis,2000; Selhi, 2000 ; Korak : 2012). Tout semble indiquer que ce mode de travail sera important à l'avenir. Mouzourakis (2000) considérait le portable comme « encombrant », mais, selon Drechsel (2013a ; 2013b), la tablette est un outil pratique en cabine. Il est clair que l'évolution pousse de plus en plus les interprètes à avoir leur propre matériel (fixe et mobile). L'interprète doit être formé à travailler avec ces différents outils en plus de son portable.
- **Logiciels de reconnaissance vocale**: ce logiciel est moins connu, mais ambitieux. Il permet notamment de transformer le langage oral de l'interprète en langage écrit et de le projeter sur un écran ou de le traiter. O'Hagan & Ashworth

(2002:47) et ultérieurement Tripepi Winteringham (2010: 92–95) signalent que ces transcriptions en direct peuvent constituer une base pour une traduction automatique postérieure (Aiken, 2011). Là aussi, c'est l'interprète qui doit avoir son propre logiciel et le mettre à disposition de son commanditaire. Un interprète a donc tout intérêt à avoir suivi une formation en reconnaissance vocale.

7. Principes pédagogiques

Comme nous l'avons déjà dit, une formation en interprétation doit intégrer les TIC. Cependant, on peut aborder cette matière par différentes approches pédagogiques: lecture personnelle du syllabus, cours magistral par le professeur, ateliers... Ce qui veut dire qu'on met l'accent sur les connaissances, sur les compétences ou encore bien plus. À Gand, le cours de « Techniques et Technologie » opte pour une pédagogie de l'**auto-efficacité**.

La notion socio-cognitive d'**auto-efficacité** a été développée par Bandura (1986). Cette notion va plus loin que la conscience de ses propres compétences, mais concerne le degré auquel on estime pouvoir accomplir une activité spécifique avec des compétences acquises. Bandura (1986: 399–407) précise que quatre sources mènent à l'auto-efficacité: les réussites obtenues dans le passé, les expériences d'autrui, la persuasion verbale (par exemple par un parent, un enseignant) et les états physiologiques (les affects comme le stress, la joie). La confiance qu'on a d'atteindre un certain résultat (dans un domaine spécifique) crée une sensation d'efficacité et de pouvoir. En fait, l'auto-efficacité commence à se forger au sein de la famille et doit se poursuivre pendant la trajectoire scolaire, où les jeunes doivent puiser continuellement dans les quatre sources mentionnées par Bandura (1986: 415–417). Ce sont donc les pratiques pédagogiques des professeurs qui stimulent entre autres cette auto-efficacité et cette foi en ses capacités, en plus de la compétence spécifique de savoir maintenir cette auto-efficacité tout au long de la vie (1986: 423). Bandura (1986:430) estime que cette compétence permet aux individus de s'engager dans des tâches plus exigeantes, de les réaliser avec plus de motivation et de se reprendre plus vite après un échec. Dans cet article, nous voulons montrer que l'apprentissage des TIC cadre parfaitement dans cette optique.

Ensuite, lorsque nous pensons « pédagogie », nous tendons évidemment vers le constructivisme social. Kiraly (2000: 36–45) esquisse ce que le constructivisme social serait pour les traducteurs. Il défend un apprentissage coopératif (plutôt que compétitif), dans une interaction en face-à-face, en petits groupes en interdépendance positive, et dans des situations réelles. Cette pédagogie n'est pas centrée sur la transmission de savoir par le professeur, mais sur les étudiants qui acquièrent eux-mêmes l'expérience qui leur permettra plus tard d'agir avec confiance dans un champ ou une spécialisation. Les notions sociologiques d' « appropriation » et d' « autonomisation » (*empowerment*) utilisées par Kiraly (2000: 18) s'apparentent donc à la notion cognitive d'**auto-efficacité**. Il s'agit d'un procès interactif dans lequel le professeur n'impose pas ses propres idées mais travaille à partir des idées et des opinions des étudiants (Kiraly 2000: 39).

Le but du cours de « Techniques et Technologies » est de stimuler les étudiants à réaliser personnellement une activité avec succès, à regarder les autres faire de même, à recevoir l'évaluation des professeurs et des pairs quant au résultat obtenu, à ressentir certaines émotions ou sensations pendant l'activité et à utiliser plus tard cette expérience comme point de référence afin de développer la confiance en soi et de dépasser le défi de la première expérience. Cette pédagogie de l'auto-efficacité s'applique dans l'apprentissage combiné des techniques et de la technologie de l'interprétation.

8. Un exemple concret

Illustrons cela au moyen d'un exercice d'interprétation avec la « valise », une TIC qui mobilise une technique de communication particulière avec le public.

Le matériel se trouve dans une « valise de charge » contenant un émetteur main numérique (microphone sans fil), 12 casques supra-auraux et 12 récepteurs de poche rechargeables de la marque Sennheiser. Les étudiants connaissent plus ou moins ce matériel pour l'avoir utilisé dans les cours de master mais jamais en tant que clients. Ils savent donc que l'utilisateur du récepteur et de l'émetteur doivent ajuster leurs appareils pour qu'ils fonctionnent de façon optimale, par exemple, se trouver sur le même canal, régler le volume, parler près du micro (ou pas), s'éloigner de l'orateur.

Plan A: Le scénario habituel de l'exercice avec la « valise » est le suivant:
Les participants sont en général une dizaine d'étudiants en post-graduat qui suivent chacun deux ou trois langues étrangères. Les étudiants ne comprennent pas nécessairement toutes les langues (p. ex. le russe, l'italien), ce qui rend ces exercices particulièrement instructifs car il y a plus de coopération. Les participants vont jouer trois rôles: guide, interprète et public.

Les tâches sont les suivantes : chaque étudiant doit préparer dans l'une de ses langues étrangères ou en néerlandais une communication relative à une visite touristique. Chaque étudiant prépare un texte d'une dizaine de minutes sur un thème. Le professeur a du matériel de réserve (en 2–3 langues) au cas où plusieurs interprètes seraient malades et il n'y aurait pas assez de guides.

Le lieu visité est le campus de La Bijloke à Gand, qui se trouve à deux minutes de la faculté. C'est un ancien complexe hospitalier datant du 13ème siècle, mais qui a subi pas mal de transformations. On y trouve par exemple de vieux abris anti-aériens du 20ème siècle. Actuellement, c'est le campus de l'Académie des Beaux Arts et du Conservatoire de Gand. Les étudiants doivent se documenter sur le campus, ses bâtiments, ses architectes, les abris.

Quant au **moment et à la durée**, la visite a lieu pendant les heures de cours et dure deux heures. Le campus peut être visité dès huit heures du matin, l'heure à laquelle le cours est prévu.

Le point de départ est la réception du département où se trouve la « valise ». On effectue la distribution et le contrôle du matériel. Chaque participant reçoit un récepteur de poche et un casque supra-aural.

L'exercice consiste en une visite guidée avec interprétation simultanée vers le néerlandais ou une autre langue. Le microphone passe d'un interprète à l'autre, chaque fois qu'il y a un changement de guide. Chaque étudiant à l'occasion de faire le guide, l'interprète, le public et l'évaluateur et d'utiliser le microphone mobile et les récepteurs dans des conditions réelles. Le professeur sert d'accompagnateur et d'animateur.

À **la fin de la visite** suivent les évaluations et commentaires, et le matériel est remis dans la valise.

Le but de l' activité est de familiariser les étudiants avec l'usage de ce matériel, sous tous ses aspects. Mais il s'agit aussi de stimuler les futurs interprètes à l'auto-efficacité, de leur donner confiance dans une situation d'interprétation mobile avec la « valise ». Il s'agit d'éliminer leurs doutes et de les confronter aux possibilités et aux limites de ce matériel. En plus, il s'agit de construire ensemble une expérience agréable à se remémorer. Parallèlement, le but est de leur faire prendre conscience de la valeur du matériel.

Plan B

En 2014, un collègue s'est chargé de cet exercice pendant mon absence, mais, en raison de problèmes techniques, l'exercice n'a pu avoir lieu. Mes étudiants avaient donc été privés de cette expérience. J'ai alors dû appliquer un « plan de secours ». Je ne voulais pas retourner au Campus de La Bijloke, mais je devais trouver une alternative, réalisable entre 8.15-10.15 h. du matin.

L'exercice alternatif a été une visite dans un musée imaginaire situé dans la salle de cours habituelle. La « valise » a été utilisée dans un scénario de visite guidée simulée. Chaque étudiant avait préparé dans une langue étrangère ou en néerlandais un commentaire sur une œuvre d'art moderne de son choix. L'œuvre était projetée sur un grand écran dans la salle. Un étudiant jouait le guide du musée et présentait l'œuvre, un autre faisait l'interprète et le reste constituait le public. Le public avait reçu comme instruction de ne pas rester assis mais de se promener dans l'auditoire comme pendant une visite réelle au musée. Comptaient dans cette expérience, outre le fait de voir les autres faire cette même activité, les évaluations des autres étudiants et du professeur et puis les émotions comme l'amusement, la surprise, l'aisance dans ce rôle et la conscience que le public dépend de vous pour comprendre la langue du guide. L'exercice participait donc à l'auto-efficacité des étudiants.

Soulignons finalement la présence d'une dimension supplémentaire. Le plan A comme le plan B avaient comme but une visite sur un site (fictif ou réel) à valeur artistique. L'exercice implique non seulement des compétences cognitives mais aussi une dimension affective. Une activité à dimension esthétique suscite plus facilement des émotions, surtout si l'étudiant peut parler d'une œuvre qui l'a peut-être touché. L'exercice avec la « valise » permet de consacrer un cours d'interprétation à un thème esthétique, ce qui renforce l'émotion de l'expérience.

9. Conclusion

Les TIC sont omniprésentes et les clients s'attendent à ce que les interprètes les maîtrisent. Il peut s'agir en partie de l'infrastructure mise à disposition par le commanditaire lui-même mais également du matériel personnel dans lequel l'interprète doit investir (portable, tablette, logiciel terminologique, de visioconférence, de reconnaissance vocale).

Il va sans dire que les formations en interprétation doivent intégrer les TIC dans leur cursus. Pour cela, il faut d'abord investir dans les TIC (par exemple, avoir une « valise »), en parler explicitement et les intégrer de surcroît dans tous les cours, de façon plus ou moins prioritaire. En fonction de leur spécificité, on peut aborder les TIC par le biais d'un syllabus, d'une démonstration, d'une visite ou d'un exercice pratique en classe. Mais il faut aussi réfléchir sur l'effet pédagogique que l'on veut obtenir. L'apprentissage doit non seulement permettre à l'étudiant de connaître les TIC ou de savoir les utiliser mais doit aussi contribuer à son auto-efficacité. Cela suppose une pédagogie qui prête attention aux quatre sources d'auto-efficacité mentionnées par Bandura.

Nous avons illustré par un exemple comment mettre en pratique cet apprentissage. Il est clair que l'intégration des TIC dépend du cursus, du budget, de l'assistance technique et de l'intérêt que leur porte l'enseignant. Quant à l' auto-efficacité, il s'agit surtout de la stimuler et d'en parler.

Bibliographie

Aiken, M. (2011) "Transterpreting, Multilingual Electronic Meetings" *International Journal of Management and Information Systems* 13/1.

Bandura, A. (1986) *Social Foundations of Thought and Action: a Social-Cognitive Theory*. Englewood Cliffs: Prentice Hall.

Berber Irabien, D.C. (2010) *Information and Communication Technologies in Conference Interpreting. Thèse doctorale*. Tarragona: Universitat Rovira i Virgili.

Drechsel, A. (2004) *Computereinsatz beim Dolmetschen in Ausbildung und Praxis. Ein Beitrag zur Dolmetschdidaktik*. Thèse de licence. Leipzig: IALT.

Drechsel, A. (2013a) "Interpreter versus Technology. Reflections on a Difficult Relationship. Part 1". En ligne. http://aiic.net/page/6624/interpreters-versus-technology-reflections-on-a-difficult-relationship-part-1/lang/1 [14.5.2015].

Drechsel, A. (2013b) "Interpreter versus Technology. Reflections on a Difficult Relationship. Part 2". En ligne : http://aiic.net/page/6640/interpreters-versus-technology-reflections-on-a-difficult-relationship-part-2/lang/1 [14.5.2015].

Gile, D. (2009) *Basic Concepts and Models for Interpreter and Translator Training*. Amsterdam: John Benjamins.

Kalina, S. (2009) "Dolmetschen im Wandel – neue Technologien als Chance oder Risico." In: Baur, W. & S. Kalina, F. Mayer, J. Witzel (Ed.) *Übersetzen in die Zukunft. Herausforderungen der Globalisierung für Dolmetscher und Übersetzer. Tagungsband der Internationalen Fachkonferenz des Bundesverbande der Dolmetscher und Übersetzer. Berlin 11–13 September*. Berlin: BDÜ, pp. 393–401.

Kiraly, D. (2000) *A Social Constructivist Approach to Translator Education. Empowerment from Theory to Practice*. Manchester: St Jerome Publishers.

Korak, C.A. (2012) "Remote Interpreting via Skype- a Viable Alternative to in situ Interpreting?" *The Interpreter's Newsletter* 17, pp. 83–102.

Mouzourakis, P. (2000) "Interpretation Booths for the Third Millennium". *Communicate!* Mars-Avril 2000. En ligne : http://aiic.net/page/131/interpretation-booths-for-the-third-millennium/lang/1 [17.5.2015].

O'Hagan, M. (1996) *The Coming Industry of Teletranslation*. Clevedon: Multilingual Matters.

O'Hagan, M. & Ashworth, D. (2002) *Translation –Mediated Communication in a Digital World. Facing the Challenges of Globalization and Localization*. Clevedon: Multilingual Matters.

Rütten, A. (2014a) "Booth-friendly Terminology Management for Interpreters. A Snapshot." En ligne: http://blog.sprachmanagement.net/?p=265 [15.5.2015].

Rütten, A. (2014b) "Booth-friendly Terminology Management Revisited- 2 Newcomers." En ligne: http://blog.sprachmanagement.net/?p=305 [15.5.2015].

Sandrelli, A. & de Manuel Jerez, J. (2007) "The Impact of Information and Communication Technology on Interpreter Training. State-of-the-Art and Future Prospects". *The Interpreter and Translator Trainer* 1 (2), pp. 269–303.

Selhi, T. (2000) "Interpretation on the Internet". *AIIC Communicate!*, Octobre 2000. En ligne: http://aiic.net/page/245 [15.5.2015].

Tripepi Winteringham, S. (2010) "The Usefulness of ICTS in Interpreting Practice". *The Interpreters' Newsletter* 15, pp. 87–99.

Section III: Specialised Domains and Issues of Translation and Interpreting

Marcos Aranda

The Influence of Machine Translation and Cat Tools on Creativity and Quality

Abstract: The translation business has undergone a huge transformation in recent decades. Information technology, translation memory software and the integration of machine translation technology in the last few years, has changed the way we work. This has affected both the way translators work and how much translation buyers are willing to pay for quality translation. The challenge facing the translation industry is to balance the three key factors in the process: quality, speed and price. Trainers should also reconsider academic strategies aimed at future translation professionals in order to adequately prepare them for this unstoppable evolution.

There is a perception that translation is slowly ceasing to be a service and has become a product dominated by the ability to upgrade technologically. We are already dealing with semi-automated translation, for which the translator only needs to "fill in the gaps" and edit the proposal generated by machine translation systems. The future will only accentuate this trend. There is a perception that quality and creativity are affected by this way of working. The pressure to deliver within increasingly tight deadlines and at shrinking prices may force us to prioritize content-transmission over stylistic or aesthetic considerations. This leads us to ask: does the use of machine translation and computer-assisted translation tools affect quality and creativity? Can we measure this influence? Is there an effective increase in productivity which justifies this new way of working? And, finally, are the effects on creativity and quality offset by the increase in productivity?

Conducting a quantitative experimental study should help us to answer these questions. This is a descriptive-contrastive research project based on observing and recording the procedures and solutions created by a number of professional translators who worked on the same specialized text and were divided into two groups (with and without automated pre-translation and computer-assisted translation tools). We will quantitatively analyse the performance of both groups in terms of quality, creativity and productivity. In the qualitative part, we will individually analyse a representative subject from each group to determine whether differences exist in the translation process and, if so, what those differences are.

Keywords: Machine Translation, Computer-Assisted Translation, quality, creativity, productivity, Translation Memory, post-editing, translation process, Information Technology, translation training.

1. Introduction

It is a quantitative study that analyses the differences between two ways of working: translating in the traditional manner, without any extra aid other than that provided by the most renowned word processing application, and translating in the more current way; a way expected to gain more momentum in the future (Bédard, 2000), whereby automated pre-translation is combined with post-editing techniques by means of a computer-assisted translation tool.

Two fundamental reasons have led me to choose this field of study: my own professional experience in the field of translation and the lack of studies which focus on the impact of this new technology on the translation process. Having been working as a professional translator for 14 years and managing a translation agency for 13, I have witnessed an unprecedented transformation driven by three trade factors: The decrease in price, the Increase in volume of work, and shorter deadlines (Wallis, 2006, p. 4).

This situation has been giving rise to the following dilemma: If speed and price are the priority, then quality is not possible. If speed and quality are the priority, then a good price cannot be reached. If quality at a good price is the priority, then speed must be sacrificed (Beninatto, 2010).

Figure 1: Q stands for Quality, P stands for Price and S stands for Speed.

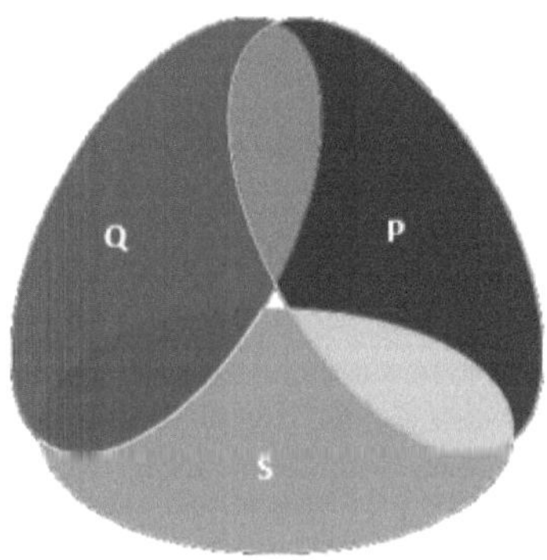

The dilemma posed by the resulting Euler's triangle has resulted in the emergence of automated or semi-automated translation with human post-editing using computer-assisted translation tools; in other words, CAT tools. These programs store previous translations in language pairs segmented by clauses and enable us to detect a total or partial match which is, in turn, used, rejected or amended by the translator. The problem with this work method resides in the fact that the business model which is being implemented means that the translator is not paid anything for 100% matches, but only for new content entered or changes made to partial matches. It is easy to see how this work procedure would have an impact on quality and creativity (Bédard, 2000).

It is precisely the lack of studies on the impact of this new technology on the translation process that spurred my interest in this relatively unexplored territory. Until a few years ago, in-depth studies only focused on user perception (Dillon & Fraser, 2006) (Wallis, 2006) (Merkel, 1998), the impact on productivity (Webb, 1998) (Circé, 2005) and final product quality (Mogensen, 2000) (Bédard, 1992), thereby confirming that despite the productivity advantages, there is still a negative perception of these tools which is reflected by a loss of quality. In spite of the rich research value of studies conducted, there is still an approach lacking which enables us to draw conclusions that can be directly applied in professional practice.

Hence the intention to conduct research on the influence of CAT tools on the translation process and their impact on quality and creativity, using professional translators in order to ensure maximum ecological validity, with the aim of answering the following questions:

- Does the use of MT and CAT tools affect quality and creativity?
- Can this influence be measured?
- Is there an effective increase in productivity that justifies this new way of working?
- And lastly, are the effects on creativity and quality offset by the increase in productivity?

In order to be able to answer these questions, I have chosen to conduct an experimental study on the effect technology has on the process by combining 2 fields of research: Translation technology and cognitive research on the translation process.

2. Research Framework

After considering the aforementioned questions, a theoretical framework has been defined where different phases are set out, based on the translation process models of Krings (2001), Kiraly (1995) and Hönig (1995), which differentiate between conscious and unconscious processes when it comes to understanding, searching for, evaluating and adopting a decision using macro- and micro-strategies.

If we look at the models to determine and evaluate translation quality, we come across many approaches with not a single consensus among them. For this reason, and from the perspective of professional practice, I have chosen to follow the ISO definition (1986), which states that quality is "The totality of features and characteristics of a company's product or service that bear on its ability to satisfy stated or implied needs".

Insofar as creativity in translation is concerned, I follow the most prevalent approach which states that the entire creative process involves innovation adapted to a certain context with phases including preparation, incubation, illumination and evaluation (Kussmaul, 1993).

Translating idioms without equivalents is one of the most demanding tasks a translator can face. Metaphors and idioms are abundant in financial texts (Panou, 2014, p. 12). Therefore, by choosing to focus on a financial text in this paper, it is essential to consider theories applicable to specialized texts. These are based on defined rhetorical and linguistic strategies given that they are intended for a specific audience and with a clear informative function. Obviously, they use specialized language and, in this specific case, the financial language is characterized by a large number of metaphors which, according to Alcaraz (2004), determine their high number of anisomorphic elements and their consequent difficulty to translate.

This last point ultimately leads us to the theory of the metaphor and its application to translation. In particular, I have chosen to focus on Lakoff & Johnson (1980) and their classification of metaphors; Göpferich's approaches (2008) regarding greater cognitive performance when translating metaphors and the subsequent difficulty to produce the meta-text, as well as Toury's metaphor translation processes (1995).

If we focus on CAT tools and their impact on the process, quality and creativity, we need to find out what other authors have concluded on this topic. Bédard (2000) believes that they hinder the resolution of difficulties and that translation memories become "sentence salads". Heyn (1998, p. 135) considers that they lead to a loss of intra-textual coherence and quality and indefinitely foster the propagation and replication of errors.

3. Research Hypothesis

The previous theoretical framework and the conclusions drawn by authors who have studied CAT tools allow us to pose the following research hypotheses.

H1 There is a negative influence on creativity which derives from the use of automated pre-translation and CAT tools in comparison with the traditional method.

H2 There is a negative influence on quality which derives from the use of automated pre-translation and CAT tools in comparison with the traditional method.
H3 There is a positive difference in terms of productivity which derives from the use of automated pre-translation and CAT tools in comparison with the traditional method.
H4 The difference in terms of productivity offsets the potential differences in creativity and quality.
H5 The translation process is affected by combining automated pre-translation with post-editing using CAT tools in comparison with the traditional method.

4. Methodology

In order to determine if the hypotheses presented are correct, I have chosen a mixed methodology based on a qualitative-quantitative approach. For this purpose, I have designed a contrastive experimental study with two subject groups: One with Machine Translation/Computer-Assisted Translation and another without Machine Translation/Computer-Assisted Translation. Data is collected by means of direct observation. The use of Think Aloud Protocols for data collection is disregarded for their lack of ecological validity as translators tend to tell researchers not what they think, but what they believe the researcher expects to hear (Jakobsen, 2003). With the aim of enhancing reliability of the study and the homogeneity of the sample, the subjects chosen are professional translators. Professional evaluators with between 5 and 10 years' experience were asked to assess quality and creativity.

Creativity is assessed following the Newmark (1988) model, which establishes a scale of 1 to 5 according to solutions for translation problems concerning metaphors in the source text. The evaluation instrument used by the creativity evaluator indicates the metaphoric element and the score assigned to each one. At the end, the average score or creativity index used is indicated in the quantitative part of the research.

The Rothe-Neves holistic model (2002) is used to assess quality. This model scores fluency, grammatical accuracy, orthographical accuracy, meaning, terminological coherence and suitability, adherence to instructions, design, style and overall score, on a scale from 1 to 5. The use of two identical scales enables us to compare the resulting quality index with the creativity one.

With the aim of researching the impact of Machine Translation and Computer-Assisted Translation on quality and creativity, I have created an experimental study in which ecological validity takes precedence. 10 professional translators were chosen and divided into 2 groups: 5 subjects carried out the test using machine translation/SDLX and 5 subjects were not allowed to use machine translation/ SDLX. All subjects are translation and interpreting graduates with Spanish as their native language and English as their second working language and the minimum professional experience is 3 years. One of their specializations had to be legal-financial translation and they were also expected to translate a minimum of 2,500 words daily. Half of the participants were chosen due to their knowledge of the computer-assisted translation tool, SDLX.

The test consists of translating a financial document from English to Spanish, drawn up from various articles from the Financial Times and intentionally edited for this research study. This was due to the fact that a translation test must not be excessively long but should contain all of the elements to be evaluated. Therefore, it was necessary to include a maximum number of metaphoric elements which had to be creatively conveyed in the target language. Consequently, 22 elements were selected for analysis. This ensures that each group will have 11 elements which will be scored according to creativity. This will enable statistical analysis and lead to more reliable results.

Figure 2: Translation test (all creativity elements are underlined).

Dubai World

After <u>peering into the abyss</u> of default in November, Dubai World has <u>come back from the brink</u>. Dubai World is a veritable <u>smorgasboard</u> of companies in fields of activity you don't want to <u>touch with a barge pole</u> during a major cyclical downturn. Nakheel was at the <u>acme</u> of property development <u>pushed to excess</u>, competing with God, nature and the Netherlands by constructing islands, which it hoped to sell to gormless rock stars and European football geniuses. The emirate will convert to equity almost $9bn of its claims on Dubai World and over $1bn owed by Nakheel, so <u>taking a back seat</u> to bank creditors. Bond prices <u>rallied</u> even though the plan is far from a <u>fait accompli</u>.

True, global and regional bank creditors, which had feared a <u>haircut</u> on their $14.2bn of debt, will not take an <u>upfront hit</u> on their principal. However, they will have to accept extended maturities. But the interest rate proposed could still <u>derail the plan</u>. Although not publicly disclosed, it is said to be <u>adrift</u> of current market rates.

Dubai will use the remaining $5.7bn of wealthier neighbour Abu Dhabi's $20bn <u>bail-out</u> package to fund part of its commitment. That leaves $3.8bn to find. Here, Dubai World's investment portfolio could <u>come in handy</u>.

In attempting to resolve Dubai World's debt <u>woes</u> in an equitable way, the emirate clearly <u>has an eye</u> on its longer-term refinancing needs. Yet the damage to its reputation has been done: banks will not <u>open their cheque books</u> again in a hurry. If Dubai is serious about regaining its credibility, it should not <u>push its luck</u> on borrowing rates.

> Sovereign defaults are not acts of God. If we continue to play the political game in a business-as-usual mode, there could be quite widespread sovereign debt restructuring throughout the advanced industrial world. If we grow up, we can avoid the worst.

In order to increase the ecological validity of the experiment, I chose to integrate the tests into a real selection process with the aim of forming a team of translators for a financial project. To ensure that all the candidates could carry out the test with equal environmental conditions, they were called to the offices of my translation company so as to complete the translation in an isolated, distraction-free environment, which is visible from outside as it is separated from the rest of the office by a glass wall. The CAT tool selected is SDLX 2007, the most commonly used CAT tool in the translation sector at the time of the experiment. The Automated Translation tool selected for pre-translation is Google Translate, the most reliable and cost-effective automated translation system on the market. The subjects are informed that the task consists of translating a financial text without a time limit. They may use an online dictionary of their choice and all the internet resources they wish.

By activating a secret combination of keys, an on-screen recording system, BB Flashback Pro, starts to secretly record both the activity happening on screen and the keyboard and mouse actions, and includes a still image of the subject carrying out the test without their knowledge. All translators are informed afterwards and asked to grant their authorisation for the use of these data for research purposes.

The tests are subject to the criteria of two professional evaluators with a specific profile. In both cases they are translation and interpreting graduates and Spanish native speakers with English as a second working language. The creativity evaluator will have 5 years' experience as a proofreader and the quality evaluator 10.

Once all the tests have been performed, we then proceed to systematize and analyse the data for the quantitative study. Firstly, the Word files are randomized and assigned a number, ensuring there is no trace that could identify the subject, before sending them to the evaluators along with the quality and creativity forms. They then evaluate the tests and determine the quality index and the creativity index, both on a scale of 1 to 5. The combined quality-creativity score is then obtained by merging both averages together. The duration of the tests is determined using the activity recording application. The averages of both groups are compared using the statistical analysis tool PASW Statistics 18.0, the most up-to-date version of the well-known SPSS application.

For the qualitative study, one subject is selected from each group to determine the median of the combined quality-creativity score for each of them. The activity file, recorded using the BB Flashback Pro application, is then collected from the 2 subjects. The activity parameters are defined as the number and duration of long pauses, the average duration of the pauses or the text production actions. Finally, a report is drawn up simultaneously for both subjects comparing times, procedures and solutions for each of the elements analysed.

5. Quantitative Analysis of the Results

Firstly, the average quality scores are analysed and compared between both groups. A higher average of 3.88 can be observed in the group performing the test without automated pre-translation or SDLX, whereas the group who used these resources scored an average of 3.26, supporting the hypothesis presented. If we consider each of the quality elements analysed, we can see that those who work without automated pre-translation or SDLX systematically obtain higher scores.

Statistically speaking, the correlation has a significance of 0.213, which only enables us to establish one trend. One of the factors that likely prevents a more significant result is the reduced sample size and also the reduced number of variables analysed (10 in this case).

Figure 3: Comparison of quality averages.

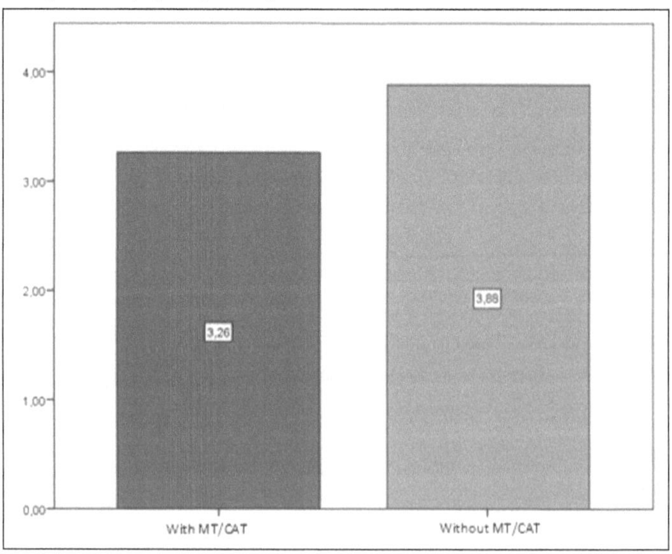

In terms of creativity, a higher average of 4.24 is again observed in the group performing the test without automated pre-translation or SDLX, whereas the group who used the aforementioned tools scored an average of 3.75. By analysing each of the metaphors, we can see that there is only one element on which the group performing the test using automated pre-translation and SDLX scores higher than the other group. In 4 other cases, both groups obtain the same average score. For the rest, the group without automated pre-translation or SDLX constantly scores higher. If we compare both groups, a statistical significance can be observed in the 0.034 correlation.

Figure 4: Comparison of creativity averages.

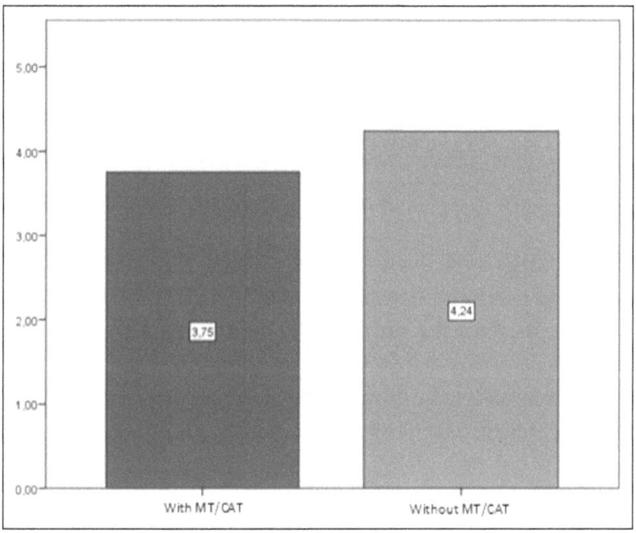

We have to take into account that, in spite of the reduced size of the 2 groups, the creativity analysis is based on 22 variables, whereas quality is based on 10, providing us with an appropriate number of results.

If we consider the previous results, the combined quality-creativity score will provide an additional advantage for the subjects who carried out the translation without the computer assistance subject to analysis. An average of 4.06 without automated pre-translation and SDLX compared with 3.50 in the group using these tools. 0.086 is not strictly a statistically significant correlation; however, we can infer that there is a favourable trend towards the traditional work method, likewise in the quality score, yet more noticeable in this case.

Figure 5: Comparison of combined quality-creativity scores.

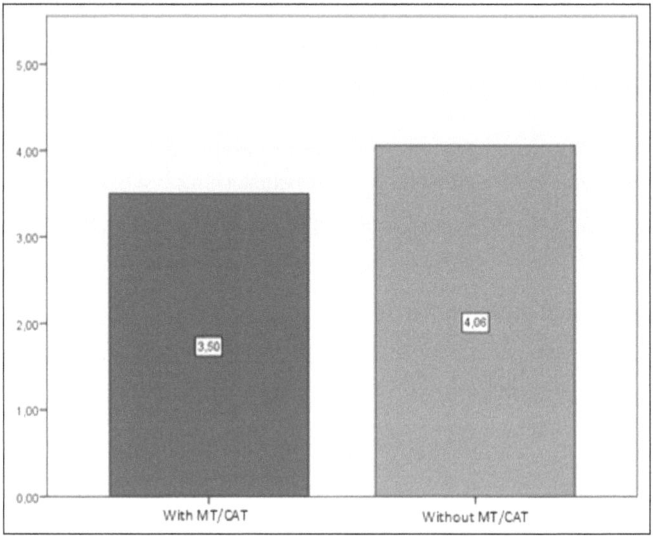

The most astounding result, even if it was predicted by other studies using automated pre-translation and computer-assisted translation tools, concerns the duration of the tests, thus the productivity gain derived from the use of these technologies.

The average duration for the group using automated pre-translation and SDLX is 49.14 minutes compared to 75.19 minutes for the group who took the test using these resources.

Figure 6: Comparison of test durations.

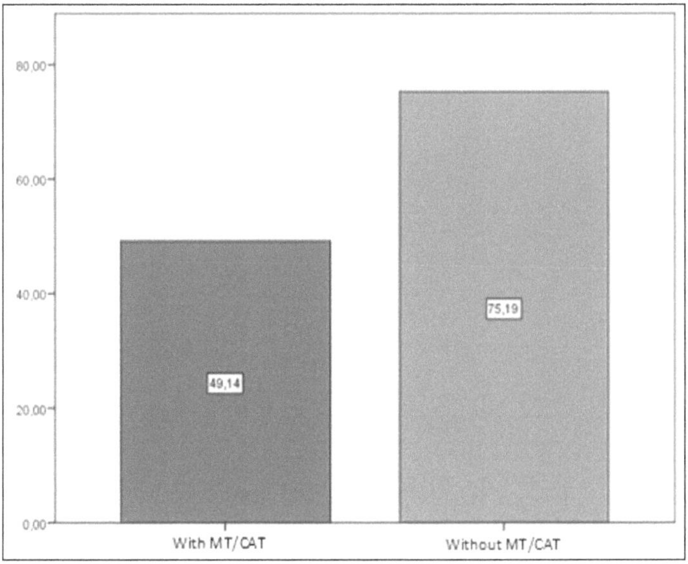

Here we can undoubtedly observe a comparison of averages with a statistical significance of 0.023, which is conclusive when applied to this sample. Even before analysing this activity record, this information could have been predicted by observing how the subjects using computer aids finished the test long before the subjects in the other group.

6. Conclusions

With regard to quality, our opinion is that, even though the result is not extrapolative or statistically significant, the trend individually set by the quality indicators shows that translating using the traditional method results in higher-quality texts. With regard to creativity, a statistically significant difference of averages is recorded in favour of translation using traditional methods. The combined quality-creativity score, without being statistically significant, substantiates the same trend which is unfavourable to the use of automated pre-translation using SDLX.

However, the greatest difference in terms of productivity, where the contrast of averages is statistically significant, leads us to question whether the loss of quality and creativity is indeed offset. If we analyse the percentage decrease in creativity (-11%) and in quality (-16%) or the combined quality-creativity score (-13%), the negative percentage result is a lot less than the positive difference in productivity achieved using automated pre-translation with CAT tools (34%).

Figure 7: Comparison of analysed parameters.

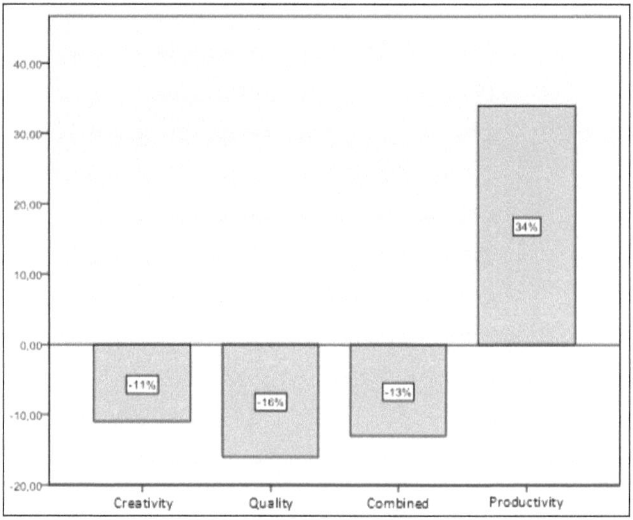

It can be stated that the loss of creativity/quality caused by using this new technology in translation is offset by the increase in productivity gained. Under no circumstances do we aim to justify the loss of quality and creativity but, in this case, the difference is indeed justified because the final result of the documents translated using automated pre-translation and SDLX continues to offer adequate quality in line with the ISO definition stated above.

It seems that the future will be dominated by automated pre-translation with post-editing using CAT tools. The trend is unstoppable, making it necessary to further analyse the effects on all aspects of translation with the aim of being able to establish the training needs of both current and future translators. The apparent negative perception of these tools must be overcome in order to guarantee new generations of translators who evolve with the times without feeling that their professional worth is undermined. It will be necessary to adopt new attitudes, apply changes to syllabuses, place a greater emphasis on learning proofreading and post-editing techniques, as well as promoting other skills that will be defined in the future.

References

Alcaráz, E. (2004). "Anisomorfismo y lexicografía técnica." *Las Palabras del Traductor* (pp. 201–220). Brussels: Esletra.

Bédard, C. (1992). "La prétraduction automatique, outil de productivité et d'évolution professionnelle." *Meta XXXVII(4)*, 738–760.

Bédard, C. (2000). "Translation memory seeks sentence-oriented translator…" *Traduire 186*, 41–49.

Beninatto, R. (2010, 12 12). *Localization Industry 411*. Retrieved 12 23, 2010, from http://www.l10n411.com/2010/12/what-i-expect-to-see-in-2011.html

Circé, K. (2005). *Traduction automatique, mémoire de traduction ou traduction humaine? Proposition d'une approche pour déterminer la meilleure méthode à adopter, selon le texte.* Ottawa: University of Ottawa.

Dillon, S., & Fraser, J. (2006). "Translators and TM: An investigation of translators' perceptions of translation memory." *Machine Translation 20(2)*, 67–79.

Göpferich, S. (2008). *Translationsprozessforschung: Stand, Methoden, Perspektiven.* Tübingen: Günter Narr.

Heyn, M. (1998). "Translation Memories: Insights and Prospects." In L. Bowker e.a. (eds.), *Unity in Diversity? Current Trends in Translation Studies* (pp. 123–136). Manchester: St. Jerome.

Hönig, H. G. (1995). *Konstruktives Übersetzen.* Tübingen: Stauffenburg.

ISO. (1986). *Quality vocabulary.* Geneva: International Organisation for Standardization.

Jakobsen, A. L. (2003). "Effects of think aloud on translation speed, revision, and segmentation." In F. Alves, & e.a., *Triangulating translation: perspectives in process oriented research* (pp. 69–95). Amsterdam: John Benjamins.

Kiraly, D. (1995). *Pathways to translation, pedagogy and process.* Kent, Ohio: The Kent State University Press.

Krings, H. (2001). *Repairing Texts: Empirical Investigations of Machine Translation Post-Editing Processes.* Kent: Kent State University.

Kussmaul, P. (1993). "Empirische Grundlagen einer Übersetzungsdidaktik: Kreativität im Übersetzungsprozeß." In J. Holz-Mänttäri, & C. Nord, *Traducere navem* (pp. 275–286). Tampere: Universitätsbibliothek.

Lakoff, G., & Johnson, M. (1980). *Metaphors We Live By.* Chicago: The University of Chicago Press.

Merkel, M. (1998). "Consistency and Variation in Technical Translation: A Study of Translators' Attitudes." In L. Bowker e.a. (eds.), *Unity in Diversity? Current Trends in Translation Studies* (pp. 137–149). Manchester: St. Jerome.

Mogensen, E. (2000). "Orwellian Linguistics: How using computer-aided translation tools impacts the target language." *Language International (12)5*, 28–31.

Newmark, P. (1988). *A Textbook of Translation*. Hertfordshire: Prentice Hall.

Panou, D. (2014). *Idiom Translation in the Financial Press: A Corpus-Based Study*. Newcastle upon Tyne: Cambridge Scholars Publishing.

Rothe-Neves, R. (2002). "Translation Quality Assessment for Research Purposes: An Empirical Approach." *Cadernos de Tradução X*, 113–131.

Toury, G. (1995). *Descriptive Translation Studies and beyond*. Amsterdam: John Benjamins.

Wallis, J. (2006). *Interactive Translation vs Pre-translation in the Context of Translation Memory Systems: Investigating the effects of translation method on productivity, quality and translator satisfaction*. Ottawa: University of Ottawa.

Webb, L. (1998). *Advantages and Disadvantages of Translation Memory: A Cost-benefit Analysis*. Monterey: Monterey Institute of International Studies.

Łukasz Bogucki

Rendering Otherness in Film – Techniques for Translating Multilingual Audiovisual Material

Abstract: A pertinent area of audiovisual translation (AVT) research is rendering films (and other audiovisual material) where more than one language is used. The other languages are typically deployed to introduce characters which do not belong: foreigners or possibly aliens, in the case of sci-fi productions. In line with Relevance Theory, the audience are forced to make additional cognitive effort (process an utterance in a tongue they may or may not speak), to be offset by extra benefits (experiencing the verisimilitude of a multilingual world).

The foreign utterances may or may not be translated into the dominant language of the given audiovisual production; occasionally a diegetic interpreter may be used, such as the Chinese cook in *Blade Runner* or Juan Antonio in *Vicky Cristina Barcelona*. The rendition (or lack thereof) of these utterances when producing a foreign language version of the material depends on the method of audiovisual translation (subtitling, dubbing, voice-over or others), as well as the translator's decision filtered by applicable constraints. The issue takes on a new meaning in the case of intralingual modes of AVT (respeaking, subtitles for the deaf and hard-of-hearing).

Using examples from audiovisual productions, I will examine the thorny issue of translating material with multilingual dialogues, setting out to construct a taxonomy of techniques based on why foreign utterances are used in the first place, and what resources are available to the audiovisual translator. I will focus on the skopos of the target text, as well as its intended (and occasionally inadvertent) reception.

Keywords: subtitling, dubbing, audiovisual translation, film, multilinguality, skopos, translation techniques, Relevance Theory, otherness, constraints.

1. Introduction – Multilinguality

Techniques for translating multilingual films have recently commanded the attention of a number of audiovisual translation researchers (Bogucki 2013, Díaz-Cintas 2011, Heiss 2004, Parini 2015, Sepielak 2014); films where more than one language is used have also become the empirical material for other AVT-centred discussions (see Maszerowska *et al.* 2014 for a comprehensive discussion of audio description based on Tarantino's *Inglourious Basterds*). There are movies (e.g. *Lost in Translation*, *The Interpreter* and *Babel*) whose plots centre round the very notion of language plurality and disparity. Film being the director's view of the world (whether fictitious or real, historical or contemporary), it bears a linguistic resemblance to post-Babel reality, where individuals speak a variety of tongues, sharing them, learning them or resorting to the assistance of translators/interpreters. This multilinguality is part and parcel of film diegesis. For the viewers' convenience (and also to account for the film's setting), there is usually a dominant language and the use of the other(s) is either incidental or more prominent. In the aforementioned *Inglourious Basterds*, Italian is used in only one (though memorable) scene, but French and German are nearly as important as English. They are used as a plot device (in the opening scene Colonel Landa talking with the farmer LaPadite lapses into English to avoid being understood by the Jewish family hiding under the floorboards) or merely to add a semblance of naturalness in scenes with Nazi officers (including Adolf Hitler) and French civilians. In another scene spies are disclosed by a Nazi major thanks to an odd German accent that one of them has; this particular plot development would have been impossible to show had the German language not been used in the movie. However, expedience may take precedence over verisimilitude. The Polish TV series *Fala Zbrodni* talks about Russian mafia (played by Russian actors speaking their mother tongue) operating in Poland and pursued by Polish police (played by Polish actors also speaking their native language); many dialogues involve characters speaking Polish and Russian respectively (with most, but not all Russian utterances subtitled for the benefit of the Polish audience) and yet manage to establish communication without resorting to an interpreter.

This paper looks into the complex phenomenon of multilinguality in film and rendition thereof, making recourse to concepts and ideas established in Translation Studies and used in theoretical discussions on audiovisual translation over the years, in order to explain and systematise the rationale behind introducing foreign languages in movies and the choices available at the film translator's disposal.

2. The Translation Studies Background

Multilinguality in film may be interpreted from the perspective of two approaches that have influenced Translation Studies to a considerable extent. Relevance Theory (Sperber and Wilson 1986), applied to translation by Gutt (2000) and subsequently to audiovisual translation by Bogucki (2004), has it that ostensive-inferential communication, whereby participants draw inferences about their interlocutors engaging in purposeful exchanges, is geared at conveying relevant information. Gutt (2000) argues that the same applies to translation, a particular case of secondary communication, while Bogucki (2004) draws on these assumptions concluding that the multifarious constraints on subtitling result in the subtitler translating only what is relevant. Since greater cognitive effort is supposed to be offset by extra benefits, introducing more than one language in a filmic message, therefore putting the audience to extended effort, must be intentional and bring about additional meaning. The common rationale behind introducing multilinguality in film is to create a semblance of the real world, whereby instant communication does not always take place and some characters do not belong (see also section 3 below).

The notion of inferential communication as understood within the framework of Relevance Theory is observable in scenes with code-switching in multilingual films. A character may begin a conversation in their second language, for instance, and then swap into their mother tongue, as a consequence of learning or assuming that the interlocutor can comprehend it, perhaps also due to being carried away emotionally, etc. It may also be possible for a character to pose a question in one language and receive an answer in another, or even to have a longer dialogue where the two parties speak two different languages (cf. the example of *Fala Zbrodni* discussed above). In real-life inferential communication, when the sender of a message discovers that the addressee speaks a language other than the one he or she chose to begin the conversation with, the two parties either agree to use a shared linguistic code or, where possible, decide to continue the conversation with the help of an interpreter; in the world of film, however, naturalness may have to be sacrificed due to financial or logistic concerns.

Skopos theory (Reiss and Vermeer 1984) posits the purposeful nature of translation. It is the aim of the particular translation assignment that determines the translation process. In line with this seminal approach, it may be said that the choice of translational techniques in the case of filmic multilinguality depends on the purpose of the filmic message in general and the multilingual fragments in particular. It is the film translator's job to arrive at the skopos of the filmic message and make decisions accordingly. A common purpose of introducing multilinguality is presenting certain characters as culturally different from the others; this is discussed in the next section.

3. Rendering Otherness

From the point of view of Translation Studies, the inclusion of dialogue in an idiolect different from the main language of the movie may be treated as a manifestation of Otherness (see, for example, Bassnett 2005). From the point of view of subtitlers/dubbers it would appear that preservation of Otherness should result in deliberately leaving the foreign dialogue untranslated, if it is untranslated in the original version. Thus the translator is faced with a dilemma whether to follow the director's intention or to do his/her job, that is to get the message across. The director's (or more likely the scriptwriter's) intention is to portray a character as not belonging where s/he currently is and failing to establish communication with other characters; the audience are not told what the character is saying (unless they happen to speak that language), only that s/he is speaking a foreign tongue. The use of subtitles in the original version weakens the manifestation of the Other, but helps the audience understand the message.

A particularly interesting convention is deployed in the Ocean's trilogy, directed by Steven Soderbergh. One member of the gang speaks only Mandarin Chinese (his utterances are not translated); however, he easily establishes mutual comprehension with the other ten members. Clearly, despite the language difference, he belongs in the titular eleven. This is another example of expedience over verisimilitude (cf. section 1 above), but in this particular case it appears to be the director's friendly wink at his audience rather than cost-cutting or shoddy filmmaking.

As suggested above, reception of Otherness may vary depending on whether the audience are familiar with the language of the other(s) or not. Meryl Streep speaking German and Polish in *Sophie's Choice* will be seen differently by the original (English speaking) audience as opposed to German/Polish viewers watching the respective language version, who can attest to the actress' effort put into learning foreign phrases and assess how well it was done.

A peculiar manifestation of the Other in film is the use of artificial alien languages in sci-fi movies. As some aliens may apparently take human form, the language that they use may be the only feature distinguishing them from humans; this is the premise of *Men in Black*, where in one scene it is only when characters begin to converse in Arquillian at a dinner table that the audience realise they are extraterrestrials. Alien languages may be created specifically for the movie (e.g. Cityspeak in *Blade Runner*) or borrowed from books that the films are adaptations of (e.g. Tolkien's languages in *The Hobbit* and *The Lord of the Rings*). They may be relatively unimportant plot devices or creations whose popularity extends beyond the movie and endures (cf. Klingon in *Star Trek*, which has developed a fan base and a number of speakers). The reception of an alien language is different from that of a foreign natural language, as the chances of the audience speaking it are practically none (perhaps with the exception of Klingon, famous quotations from Tolkien and similar rare instances). Interestingly, the Elvish word *mellon* („friend") was left untranslated in *The Hobbit*, arguably because it was known to the audience from *The Lord of the Rings*, where it was used by Gandalf as a password to open a secret door – a peculiar case of twisted chronology, as *The Hobbit* in fact precedes *The Lord of the Rings*, despite being filmed a few years after it.

4. Techniques for Rendering Multilinguality

The following techniques may be deployed to account for the use of multilingual dialogue in foreign versions of movies. This is a working taxonomy and the application of a particular technique is dependent on a number of factors, viz. the director's intention, its interpretation, audience expectations, the translator's intention and available resources.

It should be noted here that in the case of translating multilingual films the traditional translational dichotomy of source vs. target text does not apply. What gets translated is actually a translation of the foreign language utterance provided in the original version; thus the process may be comparable to that of relay in interpreting. Assuming that the concept of translational loss is a valid one, the resulting language version may depart from the original to some extent. To account for the relative complexity of the process, the following abbreviations shall henceforth be used: FLU for foreign language utterance (in a language other than the main language of the movie), SLT for source language translation (a translation of the FLU into the main language of the movie, where applicable), and TLT for target language translation (a translation of the SLT by the film translator/subtitler/dubber).

By far the easiest choice is transference, whereby no translation is provided and the FLU is left intact. This appears to be the natural decision when there is no SLT; obviously, the film translator would have to understand the FLU in the first place and even if s/he could, translating the FLU would constitute a change in the intended effect and would place the target audience in a privileged position over the source audience.

A choice that fits naturally within the film diegesis is the use of a diegetic interpreter; for instance, the Chinese cook in *Blade Runner* translates the utterances in Cityspeak for the benefit of the protagonist (and indirectly the source language audience); the same is the case in Woody Allen's *Vicky Cristina Barcelona*, where Maria Elena's frequent lapses into Spanish are translated into English by Juan Antonio. Such situations pose no challenge for the film translator, as FLUs are simply ignored and the rest of the dialogue is translated as if the film were monolingual.

Imposed monolinguality is a third choice, particularly suitable in the case of dubbing. In the case of this technique, the viewers understand the message, as it is translated, but fail to spot Otherness, never being aware that the utterance was originally spoken in a tongue other than the main language of the movie.

Another possibility is the use of a language variety. In the Spanish version of the film *My Big Fat Greek Wedding*, the utterances of a Greek character spoken in heavily accented ungrammatical English were rendered as proper, but accented

Spanish. The use of a foreign accent as a translation technique has its limitations, as naturally it would not work in captioning, only in revoicing. A more versatile choice is dialect. The famous „Italian gatecrashers" scene in *Inglourious Basterds* was dubbed into Italian using Sicilian dialect (see Parini 2015 for a discussion). The translator's choice was in this case determined by the attempt to capture the humour of the scene, in which three American spies gatecrash a movie premiere by pretending to be an Italian film crew, though speaking very little Italian with a thick American accent at that. They are immediately disclosed by the polyglot SS colonel Hans Landa, whose Italian is impeccable and who ridicules them by addressing them in that language. The technique appears well-chosen and manages to preserve the otherness of the American characters.

Hybrid translation is a technique which may help alleviate the issue of the translation mode. As indicated above, certain translation techniques would not work in both revoicing and captioning. A solution is to translate parts of the filmic message using one mode and other parts using another. This was suggested for *Vicky Cristina Barcelona* by Díaz-Cintas (2011: 230), who thought that in the case of that particular film opting for subtitling instead of dubbing in some scenes would work better for the Spanish version, as some parts of the film are actually in Spanish. This technique has more theoretical than practical significance, though, as its use would violate the established conventions for the geographical distribution of audiovisual translation modes (Spain, for instance, is generally recognised as a dubbing country).

In countries which prefer captioning over revoicing, SLT typically becomes TLT. State-of-the-art subtitling software makes it easy to replace what is traditionally, yet in today's reality wrongly, referred to as a burnt-in caption. In the past, when subtitles were first chemically etched onto a roll of film and later burnt in by means of laser, a burnt-in caption which was a SLT had to remain intact and the corresponding TLT usually had to be positioned at the top of the screen, so both could be legible. The advantage of that over what is common practice today was that the audience could easily tell that a foreign language was being used. Nowadays spotting multilinguality may be difficult if the viewer pays little attention to the spoken dialogue, especially if s/he does not speak any of the languages used in the given film and relies only on the subtitles; if an American viewer is watching a Polish film with English subtitles, where parts of the dialogue are spoken in Russian or Czech, s/he may never realise that the film is in fact multilingual.

For the sake of comparison, the following techniques may be used in the case of subtitling for the deaf and the hard-of-hearing (SDH), according to Szarkowska *et al.* (2013). Note that hearing-impaired audiences cannot attest empirically whether a foreign language is being used in the aural-verbal channel; thus their perception of a multilingual movie is different and consequently the choice of translation techniques may be different. Note also that SDH is intralingual, therefore no translation of the dialogue into another language is provided.

The first choice in the case of SDH is vehicular matching, that is showing the hearing-impaired audience the transcribed version of the foreign utterance. Another choice is translation with explicit attribution, whereby the foreign language dialogue is translated, but there is indication (usually in square brackets before the subtitle) that a foreign language is being spoken. Colour coding may also be used; in SDH colours indicate characters, therefore the use of a particular colour points to a character speaking a different language. Another technique is explicit attribution, that is telling the audience that a foreign language is being used, but unlike in the case of the technique described above, failing to provide a translation. Finally, linguistic homogenisation is an option; thus the marking of a foreign language is avoided at all and a simple translation is provided.

5. Conclusions

The polysemiotic nature of film has to be taken into account when scrutinising multilinguality. Utterances in foreign languages are typically delivered through the aural-verbal channel of the filmic message (that is the dialogue), but may also be spotted in the visual-verbal channel (e.g. a close-up of a foreign language newspaper, neon sign, billboard, notice etc.). Cultural differences, regardless of the semiotic channel, make communication (and consequently translation) more challenging. Gestures may be interpreted differently depending on the culture (cf. the conventions for nodding or shaking the head) and information transmitted via the visual channel (and therefore not normally subject to translation) may be culture-specific; thus visual clues function as translational constraints (e.g. Helen Hunt's reaction to a car with the M. D. licence plate in her doorway in *As Good as it Gets*, understandable only if one is aware that the car must belong to a medical practitioner and therefore an accident must have taken place; see also Pedersen 2005). Moreover, if we assume that image and sound are languages in their own right, the discussion can be transferred onto a more abstract level and a possible conclusion may be that all films are multilingual by definition, even if all dialogue is spoken in the same language. Directors' trademarks (Tarantino's famous long take, Lynch's use of dreams, Scorsese's slow motion, Hitchcock's penchant for leading blond actresses and the number 13, etc.) may be markers of their „language" that they use to communicate with the audience, more or less versed in that „language". Bellantoni (2005) convincingly explains the meaning of particular colours in filmic messages and how they are skilfully utilised by directors.

The taxonomy of techniques for rendering multilinguality presented herein is tentative and, as stated above, the choice of technique depends on a number of factors. Assuming that the main language of the movie is English (which is, of course, not always the case), the secondary language(s) may be well-known (French, Italian, German etc.), less well-known (Estonian, Czech etc.), or artificial, either created especially for the given movie (e.g. Arquilian) or copied from a literary work that the movie is an adaptation of (e.g. Elvish). The audience may not be familiar with the secondary language, even if it is a well-known one (Mandarin Chinese in the case of an European audience); conversely, a little-known secondary language may be recognised by the audience (the case of Hungarian audiences spotting rude Hungarian words in Cityspeak).

The final remark is in fact a call for cooperation on establishing the grounds for a potential academic discipline. Audiovisual translation research would greatly benefit from contributions not only by translation scholars (who are by and large linguists and who tend to concentrate on linguistic aspects of translation), but also semioticians, communication scholars, specialists in film and culture studies. A thorough insight into the language of film and methods used in its research would broaden the scope of audiovisual Translation Studies and help to understand the specificity of translating filmic messages, including multilingual ones.

References

Bassnett, S. (2005). 'Translation, gender and otherness.' *Perspectives* Vol. 13 (2), 83–90.

Bellantoni, P. (2005). *If It's Purple, Someone's Gonna Die: the Power of Color in Visual Storytelling*. Burlington: Elsevier.

Bogucki, Ł. (2004). *A Relevance Framework for Constraints on Cinema Subtitling*. Łódź: Wydawnictwo Uniwersytetu Łódzkiego.

Bogucki, Ł. (2013). *Areas and Methods of Audiovisual Translation Research*. Frankfurt a. Main: Peter Lang.

Díaz-Cintas, J. (2011). "Dealing with multilingual films in audiovisual translation." In: Pöckl, W., Ohnheiser, I. and P. Sandrini (eds.), *Translation, Sprachvariation, Mehrsprachigkeit. Festschrift für Lew Zybatow zum 60. Geburtstag*. Frankfurt am Main: Peter Lang, 215–233.

Gutt, E.-A. (2000). *Translation and Relevance: Cognition and Context*, 2nd. ed. Manchester: St. Jerome.

Heiss, C. (2004). "Dubbing multilingual films: A new challenge?" *Meta*, 49(1), 208–220.

Maszerowska, A., Matamala, A. and P. Orero (2014). *Audio Description. New Perspectives Illustrated.* Amsterdam/Philadelphia: John Benjamins.

Parini, I. (2015). "Cultural and linguistic issues at play in the management of multilingual films in dubbing." In: Bogucki, Ł. and M. Deckert (eds.) *Accessing Audiovisual Translation.* Frankfurt a. Main: Peter Lang, 27–49.

Pedersen, J. (2005). "How is culture rendered in subtitles?" In: *MuTra 2005 – Challenges of Multidimensional Translation: Conference Proceedings.* Available online at: http://www.euroconferences.info/proceedings/2005_Proceedings/2005_Pedersen_Jan.pdf.

Reiss, K. and H. J. Vermeer (1984). *Grundlegung einer allgemeinen Translationstheorie.* Tübingen: Niemeyer.

Sepielak, K. (2014). "Translation techniques in voiced-over multilingual feature movies." In: Şerban, A. and R. Meylaerts (eds.) *Multilingualism at the cinema and on stage: A translation perspective.* Linguistica Antverpiensia 13, 251–272.

Sperber, D. and D. Wilson (1986). *Relevance: Communication and Cognition.* Oxford: Blackwell.

Szarkowska, A., Żbikowska, J. and I. Krejtz (2013). "Subtitling for the deaf and hard of hearing in multilingual films." *International Journal of Multilingualism* 10(3), 292–312.

Eleanor Cornelius

Exploring and Developing Legal Translation Competence: Learning from the Old Dogs

Abstract: The need for well-trained legal translators is increasing globally (Obenaus, 1995; Šarčević, 1997; 2000; Asensio, 2003; Llopis, 2007). This is also true for South Africa, where government received an instruction through a high court ruling in 2010 to publish legislation in the other official South African languages, not only in English. This development holds far-reaching implications for the training of legal translators. The present paper focuses on legal translation competence, and relies heavily on Chesterman's (1997) five levels of general translation competence. In a novice-expert paradigm, the aim of this paper is to determine the difference and extent of the perceived gap between experienced and inexperienced translators. Findings indicate that legal translator competence follows the same route of automatization as general translator competence; that both groups prefer faithful translation methods but for different reasons; that experienced translators are more aware of translation problems; that experienced translators consult sources more often and use a wider variety of sources; and that experienced translators are more aware of the need for accuracy and precision when translating legal texts.

Keywords: novice translator; expert translator; translator training; translation method; translation strategy; time on task; translation problems; doublets; triplets; quadruplets; word strings.

1. Introduction

Legal translation is a highly specialised form of translation and translators of legal texts are often confronted with unique challenges that require unique solutions. According to Cornelius (2010a), the difficulties presented by legal translation result from the specialised nature of the law, and from the complexity and peculiarity of legal language. Newmark (1981:47) views legal translation as a special case with tremendous limitations: "Legal documents require a special type of translation, basically because the translator is more restricted than in any other form." Moreover, mistranslation of legal texts may give rise to serious risks and consequences. Against this background and taking into account the notions of legal status and legal consequence, the primary aim of legal translation is to have available a set of parallel texts that make uniform interpretation and application in practice possible (Garzone, 2000:4).

Cornelius (2011) points out that the training of legal translators is not adequately addressed at institutions of higher learning in South Africa, with only a limited number of courses devoted to legal translation at very few institutions. This, in light of the prediction by some (Obenaus, 1995; Šarčević,1997; 2000; Asensio, 2003; Llopis, 2007) that the demand for competent translators will increase in future as a result of globalisation remains a serious indictment. According to Cornelius (2011), the demand for well-trained and qualified legal translators is also on the increase in South Africa in light of the instruction that national legislation should be made available in all eleven official languages. A huge gap is developing between retiring competent legal translators and the new generation who should take their place.

It is by now widely accepted that legal texts are often complex on all levels, confronting readers with comprehension problems, and translators with both comprehension and production problems. Chesterman (1997:92) refers to the space that exists between the source text (ST) and the translation (TT). In this space the translator brings about many changes – s/he solves problems, finds tentative solutions, revises aspects of the initial version and so forth. In this space there are problems that may be experienced differently by different translators. In order to reduce the number of terms used in translation research, Chesterman (2005:26) proposes "method" for a specific type of translation (free, literal, etc.). The term "strategy" he limits to cognitive, problem-solving procedures, whereas "techniques" refer to linguistic procedures, as "ways to manipulate textual phenomena". Important though is that techniques are routine procedures. The term "shift" Chesterman reserves for the result of a procedure.

The aim of this article is to determine the difference and extent of the perceived gap between experienced and inexperienced legal translators as regards (1) time on task; (2) choice of method; (3) the number and nature of particular translation problems they are confronted with resulting from the use of legal language; and (4) the translation strategies they resort to in order to solve particular problems posed by legal language. Techniques, strategies and methods can be taught and are therefore, in Chesterman's terms, "portable" (2005:25); these are useful conceptual tools in translator training. This means the new generation can model their behaviour on that of their predecessors. This kind of modelling may narrow the growing gap between the outgoing and the incoming corps of legal translators.

2. Legal translation competence

A survey of the literature reveals some variation as to the amount, nature and extent of legal knowledge required by translators. There are scholars who emphasise the importance of a solid foundation and training in law. Schwarz (1977:21) is unequivocal when he remarks: "As in all other fields of knowledge, the translation of a legal and administrative text depends on the translator's full understanding and comprehension of the subject matter in question." Šarčević (1997:91; 2000:5) and Rek-Harrop (2010:38) also believe that the legal translator must fully understand the legal ST, but the translator is not required to interpret such texts in a legal sense. Understanding of the ST is sufficient for producing a satisfactory translation. Interpretation should be done by legal professionals.

Schroth (1986:55-56), however, refers to the notion of legal effect, and warns that "… the legal translator must know how to achieve the same legal effect in the target language". Schroth therefore not only emphasises the importance of subject knowledge, but also the need to achieve similar legal effect in the TT.

The issue of the nature and extent of the legal competence of the translator is multifaceted and complex. It may well be wholly impossible to find such an ideal translator (Šarčević 1997:114). Schroth (1986:65) agrees: "Legal translation in practice usually involves the additional difficulty that neither the lawyers nor the professional translators combine the necessary qualifications in one person."

3. Translator Competence

As the debates on legal translator competence focus mostly on the role, nature and extent of legal training and legal knowledge, and less on a description of legal translator competence itself, it is necessary to turn to findings of studies on general translation competence. Chesterman (1997) refers to the work done by Dreyfus and Dreyfus (1986), describing the development of any skill in terms of five stages, from novice to expert. The process involves "gradual automatization" (Chesterman, 1997: 150) along a continuum, visually represented below as follows:

Whereas the novice's behaviour is "fully conscious, easily verbalised, and atomistic" (Chesterman, 1997: 147), the expert "gives priority to intuition" (ibid, 149).

The five stages of competence/expertise by Dreyfus and Dreyfus (1986) (in Chesterman, 1997: 147).

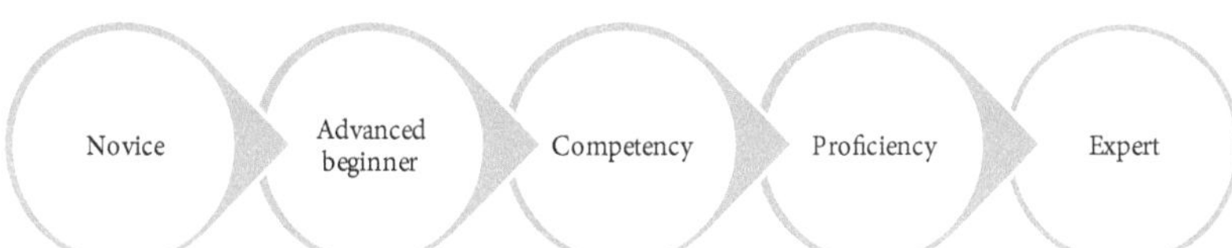

4. Sources of Complexity in Legal Texts

Cornelius (2010a; 2010b) lists a number of lexical and grammatical features that are sources of difficulty in legal texts. On word level these include archaic deictics; technical vocabulary; doublets, triplets, quadruplets and longer word strings; and morphological complexity. On syntactical level sources of complexity include extreme sentence length; sentence complexity; syntactic discontinuity; nominalisations; passive constructions; and whiz and complement deletion.

In this article, the focus is on doublets, triplets, quadruplets and longer word strings. These constructions typically present translators with particular problems, as expounded below. In this paper, the ways in which experienced and inexperienced translators deal with these constructions are investigated.

Doublets, Triplets, Quadruplets and Longer Word Strings as Problems for Translators

Doublets, triplets and quadruplets are two, three or four words, respectively, of the same category "having some semantic relationship", joined by *and* or *or* (Bhatia, 1993: 108), and word strings are lists of more than four closely related words of the same grammatical category. These constructions occur in legal texts mostly for historical reasons (Garner, 2002; Gibbons, 2003; McKenna, 2009). Examples, from Garner (2002:196), include doublets *bind and obligate; uncontroverted and uncontradicted; due and payable; null and void; do and perform;* and triplets *give, devise and bequeath; rest, residue and remainder*. An example of a quadruplet, from McKenna (2009:24), is *in lieu, in place, instead, and in substitution of.* It is not uncommon in legal texts to find word strings consisting of more than four items, also semantically related and of the same grammatical category.

Cao (2007:88) points out that this linguistic feature poses translation challenges. One problem is that the target language may not have "a string of corresponding words with similar meanings" (Cao, 2007:90). She points out that, in law, each of the words in a word string may convey a distinct legal meaning and it may create problems relating to legal effect should the translator combine two or more lexical items into one single word; either purposefully, in order to be more economical, or accidentally, such as when the translator is not aware of the importance of maintaining the nuanced semantic differences between items in a string of corresponding words.

Another problem is that more than one preposition may be required in the target language to collocate with particular lexical items in the word string. In such cases, apart from sorting out meanings, the translator also has to sort out prepositions. In "Any person who has **in** his possession or **under** his control or **at** his disposal ..."[1], each of the items in the triplet collocates with a unique preposition (*in, under, at*). In Afrikaans, "Iemand wat in besit of beheer is **van** of beskik **oor** ..."[2], the first two items collocate with the same preposition (*van*), whereas the last item collocates with a different preposition (*oor*).

5. Methodology

This study is guided by the following research question: What is the difference, and extent of the perceived gap, between experienced and inexperienced legal translators? In order to answer this question, this study incorporates four aspects of legal translator competence as outlined in the introduction.

Sample of Respondents

A purposive sample of ten respondents participated in the study in a novice-expert paradigm: five inexperienced and five experienced translators. For the purposes of this study, with its focus on legal translation, which is generally regarded as a difficult field of translation, respondents with five years or less experience as translators were regarded as inexperienced – they are either "novices" or "advanced beginners"; respondents with more than five years were regarded as experienced – they are either "proficient" or "expert". The transition from inexperienced to experienced takes place somewhere in the middle of the continuum (at the level of "competent"). The inexperienced and experienced groups have among them a total experience of 11 years and 165 years respectively. The L1's of all respondents are Afrikaans.

Materials

The ST is a typical legal text in English: a confidentiality agreement used by a major bank. Respondents were requested to translate, into Afrikaans, only one clause of 545 words under the heading "Confidentiality". The text is replete with complex lexical and syntactical constructions and is high in information density.

1 Section 4(1) of the Protection of Information Act 84 of 1982.

2 Section 4(1) of the *Wet op die Beveiliging van Inligting 84 van 1982.*

Procedure

Each respondent received a set of instructions, a translation brief, the full text and the extract to be translated, and a link to a questionnaire to be completed. Respondents were also requested to record the time they spent on the entire assignment, including time spent on reporting problems and decisions. Respondents were requested to describe, using MS Word's comment function, all the translation problems they experienced and to propose solutions to these problems. They were also requested to identify the sources they used. This Integrated Problem and Decision Reporting (IPDR) method proposed by Gile (2004) is frequently used in translation *training*. A distinct advantage of this method for *research* purposes is that observer effects are minimised (Hansen, 2006:7), although ecological validity may be reduced as translators generally do not have to record their decisions. After completing the translation task, the translators completed a questionnaire, eliciting biographical information, and information about their translation experience, translation training and the translation method they followed.

For the purposes of determining the quality and validating the classification of translators as either inexperienced or experienced, the translations were assessed by two expert professional translators, each with more than 35 years of experience as full-time translators of mostly legal texts. As Rothe-Neves (n.d.:118) explains: "The choice [...] is to skip the researcher's own subjectivity by letting translations be assessed by others. These referees [...] are not involved in the research process: they are not aware of the hypotheses to be investigated."

The evaluators were provided with an assessment rubric containing five categories: 1) accuracy, 2) vocabulary/terminology, 3) cohesion and coherence, 4) grammar, spelling and punctuation, and 5) research strategies (use of dictionaries or other sources).

6. Results and Discussion

Rating of Competence Levels of Respondents by Evaluators

The assessment by the two expert translation professionals resulted in an even distribution of experienced and inexperienced translators. Translators who scored below 50% were deemed inexperienced; those who scored more than 50% were regarded to be experienced. Five of the translators were inexperienced, with four on the level of advanced beginner and one at the bottom end of the competent range. Four of the five experienced translators were classified as proficient and one at the top end of the competent range.

Respondents were also asked to rate their own legal translation competence, based on their experience in and exposure to legal translation. Nine of the respondents' self-ratings corresponded with the results of the experts' evaluation. Only one respondent (R1) viewed herself as proficient and thus as experienced, whereas she scored below 40% for the translation task which classified her as an advanced beginner and thus an inexperienced legal translator.

COMPETENCE LEVELS OF RESPONDENTS

Time task on

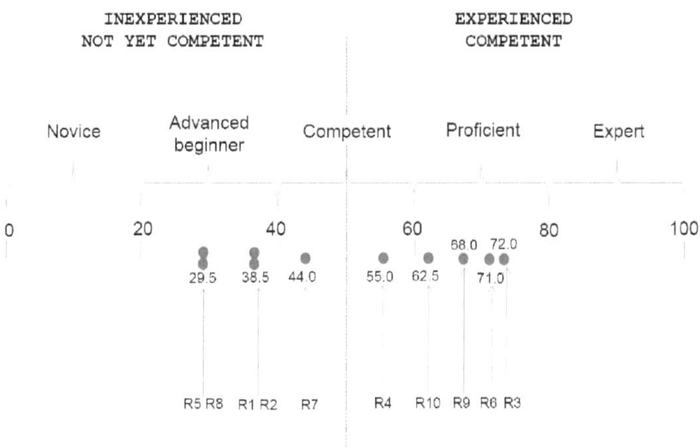

Time on Task

The amount of time spent can be taken as a measure of how difficult a particular task is (Sless, 1999:144; Nienaber, 2001:128). The inexperienced group took, on average, almost twice as long to complete the translation task compared to the experienced group. The inexperienced group spent on average 3 hours and 54 minutes on the task (almost four hours), whereas the experienced group spent 2 hours 8 minutes (almost two hours). Interestingly, the shortest time (1 hour 35 minutes) and the longest time (7 hours 35 minutes) were both logged by inexperienced translators.

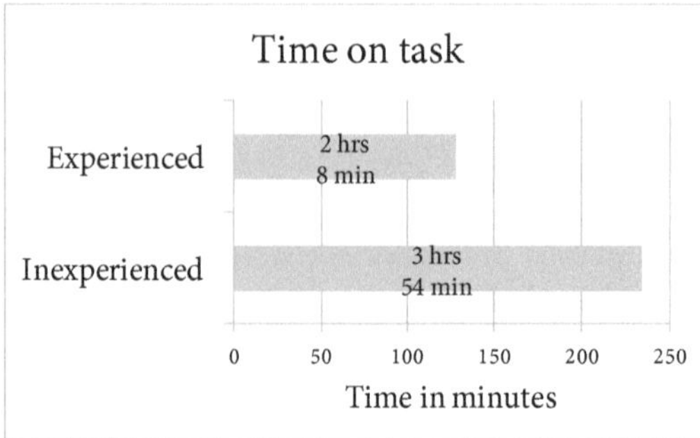

Choice of and Motivation for Translation Method

In terms of **choice of translation method**, 8 out of 10 respondents preferred a faithful approach. "Faithful" means that the TT will bear a strong resemblance to the ST, that there is strong literal adherence to the meaning of the ST and that the translator remains faithful to the intentions of the ST producer.

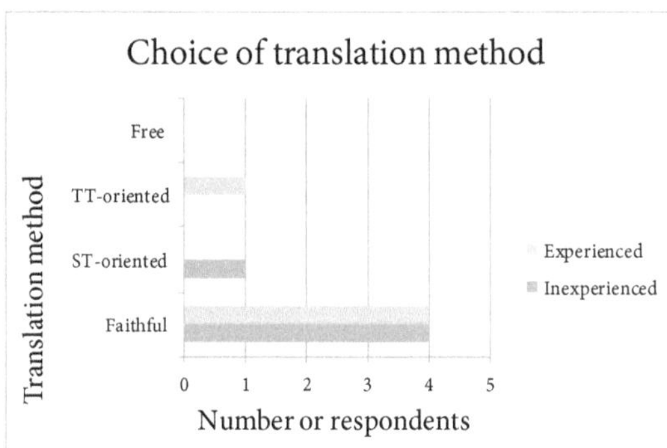

In terms of respondents' **motivation** for their choice of translation method, three experienced translators acknowledged the importance of legal consequence in determining translation method, as opposed to only one inexperienced translator. Respondents were free to elaborate on their choice of translation method.

Overall Number of Translation Problems

In terms of general translation competence, it has been found by Gerloff in 1988 and Jääskeläinen in 1999 (in Göpferich & Jääskeläinen, 2009:174) that experienced translators are more **aware of translation problems**, and that they are more tentative in producing translation equivalents, that they edit/revise more, and that they are more critical in their monitoring of their translation solutions. This increased awareness of translation problems is reflects the findings of this study.

The group of experienced translators reported almost twice as many translation problems (92) compared to the inexperienced group (48); two experienced translators indicated that they used TMs and as a result did not report "old" problems that they had managed to solve in earlier translations. Although this finding may relate to problems with the IPDR method, it is also possible that inexperienced translators are (1) simply not aware of the problems that they experience or "should" experience, or (2) that they are depleting their attentional resources with the translation task and that they do not have cognitive energy left to report problems and decisions. The total number of reported problems must also be interpreted with time spent on task. Even though the experienced translators worked twice as fast, they reported twice as many translation problems.

Number Of Translation Problems Caused by Doublets, Triplets, Quadruplets and Word Strings and Use of Sources

The experienced translators reported 15 problems compared to only six by the inexperienced translators. This finding points to a stronger awareness by the experienced group of the problems these constructions may cause during translation. They are therefore more cautious in their approach when translating constructions of this type.

The graph below shows the number and distribution of sources consulted by the two groups of translators, across the six sets of doublets, triplets and word strings.

The experienced translators consulted sources in twice as many instances (ten times) compared to the inexperienced group who consulted sources (five times). The experienced translators consulted mainly legal dictionaries, but also general dictionaries and TM glossaries. The inexperienced translators consulted mainly general dictionaries, with one instance where a legal dictionary was used. This reflects Gerloff's 1988 finding (in Göpferich & Jääskeläinen, 2009:175) that professionals use reference works more regularly compared to students (and bilinguals).

Rendering of Doublets, Triplets, Quadruplets and Word Strings in the Target Text

There were six occurrences of these type of constructions in the ST. Both groups opted for a strategy to render all ST items in the TT, except for one translator in one particular case. As this experienced translator did not report this particular construction (a doublet *disclose or divulge*) as a problem, it is not clear whether s/he consciously decided to use only one TT item (*bekendmaak*) instead of two, or whether this was an accidental omission. As the translator rendered all other similar constructions completely, this is possibly an accidental omission.

As all lexical items have been rendered (with no contraction of two items into one item), evidence is provided that both groups resorted to a literal, one-to-one translation strategy in the case of these constructions (Newmark 1995:69; Munday, 2001/2012:87).

The translations are shown below (first the ST, then the renditions of the inexperienced translators, followed by those of the experienced translators):

Example 1

ST:	*unlawful,*	*improper,*	*wrongful use*	*or*	*infringement*
TT:	*onwettige,*	*onbehoorlike,*	*onregmatige gebruik*	*of*	*skending*
	onwettige,	*onbehoorlike,*	*onregmatige gebruik*	*of*	*oortreding**
	onwettige,	*ongepaste*,*	*onregmatige gebruik*	*of*	*oortreding**
	onwettige,	*onvanpaste*,*	*wederregtelike gebruik*	*of*	*oortreding**
	onwettige,	*ongepasde*,*	*onregmatige gebruik*	*of*	*inbreuk*
	onwettige,	*onbehoorlike,*	*onregmatige gebruik*	*of*	*verbreking**
	onwettige,	*onbehoorlike,*	*onregmatige gebruik*	*of*	*skending*
	onwettige,	*onbehoorlike,*	*onregmatige gebruik*	*of*	*aantasting*
	onwettige,	*onregmatige,*	*verkeerde* gebruik*	*of*	*skending*
	wederregtelike,	*onbehoorlike,*	*onregmatige gebruik*	*of*	*inbreukmaking*

Although both groups are equally consistent (with an average consistency of 70%) in their use of translation equivalents, the inexperienced group shows greater variation across all items and made more errors (marked with an asterisk): six equivalents provided by the inexperienced group can be regarded as errors, as opposed to only two by the experienced group. Although the experienced group shows variation (60%) in the equivalents of *infringement*, there is only one occurrence of an error (*verbreking*). In the translation of *wrongful* one experienced translator committed an error. These errors can possibly be attributed to the use of general dictionaries, including the error made by the experienced translator.

Example 2

ST:	*an advisor or consultant to,*	*employee, servant or agent of*	*or subsidiary of*
TT:	*'n adviseur of konsultant tot,*	*werknemer, dienaar of agent van*	*of filiaal van*
	'n adviseur, konsultant,	*werknemer, diensbode, agent*	*of filiaal*
	raadgewer of raadpleger,	*werknemer, beampte, verteenwoordiger*	*of ondergeskikte*
	'n adviseur of konsultant,	*werknemer, diensnemer, agent*	*of plaasvervanger*
	'n adviseur of konsultant is vir,	*werknemer, beampte of agent van*	*of 'n filiaalmaatskappy*
	'n adviseur of konsultant vir,	*of 'n werknemer, amptenaar of agent,*	*of 'n filiaal van*
	'n adviseur of konsultant,	*werknemer, beampte, agent*	*of filiaal van*
	'n adviseur of konsultant,	*werknemer, amptenaar of agent*	*of filiaal van*
	'n raadgewer of konsultant,	*werknemer, beampte of agent*	*of filiaal van*
	'n adviseur of konsultant vir,	*werknemer, beampte of agent*	*of filiaal van*

Both groups of translators again rendered all items. More variation occurs in the inexperienced group's choices of equivalents. There was more variation with the rendering of *employee, servant or agent* compared to the experienced group. Where all inexperienced translators rendered *employee* as *werknemer* in the TT, they used four different equivalents for *servant*, namely *dienaar, diensbode, beampte* and *diensnemer*. The experienced translators varied between two equivalents: *amptenaar* and *beampte* for *servant*. As regards *subsidiary*, there was more variation in the inexperienced group: *filiaal, ondergeskikte* and *plaasvervanger;* the experienced group displayed no variation.

7. Conclusion

From this experiment a number of conclusions can be drawn, with particular consequences for the training of legal translators.

Legal translator competence seems to follow the same route of (gradual) automatization as general translator competence. This is evident from the faster recorded times logged by experienced translators. Even though experienced translators spent half the time on task than inexperienced translators, they recorded twice as many problems, thus pointing to them being able to free attentional resources to engage in more tasks. Trainers could track trainees' development along the competence continuum, as a record of their progress towards expert competence.

Both groups preferred a faithful method for the translation of a legal text, but for different reasons: inexperienced translators were more concerned about their inexperience (and this informs their choice of method) and experienced translators were more concerned about legal status and effect. Trainers are advised to warn trainees of the implications of these considerations for legal translation.

Experienced translators were more aware of translation problems as they reported twice as many translation problems. Trainers should focus the attention of trainees on particular problems caused by legal language; trainees should approach legal texts fully aware of the translation problems caused by particular legal constructions, such as doublets etc.

Experienced translators used sources more often and used a wider variety of sources to solve translation problems, where inexperienced translators turned to general dictionaries more often (experienced translators tended to do this as a last resort). Trainers are advised to point out the correlation between the use of specialised sources and translation quality.

In relation to the translation of doublets, triplets, quadruplets and longer word strings, the end products of experienced translators were more homogenous, compared to those of the inexperienced group that displayed more variation. This points to the accuracy and precision required by legal translation. Trainers are advised to point out the importance of accuracy and precision, and should foster an awareness of the translation problems created by these constructions.

References

Asensio, R.M. 2003. *Translating official documents*. Manchester: St. Jerome Publishing.

Bhatia, V.K. 1993. *Analysing genre: Language use in professional settings*. London: Longman.

Cao, D. 2007. *Translating law*. Clevedon: Multilingual Matters.

Chesterman, A. 1997. *Memes of translation: The spread of ideas in translation theory.* Amsterdam/Philadelphia: Johan Benjamins Publishing Company.

Chesterman, A. 2005. "Problems with strategies." In K. Károly and Ágota Fóris, eds, *New Trends in Translation Studies. In Honour of Kinga Klaudy.* Budapest: Akadémiai Kiadó. p. 17–28.)

Cornelius, E. 2010a. "n Verkenning van regsvertaling as 'n 'spesiale geval'". *Suid-Afrikaanse Tydskrif vir Taalonderrig*, **44**(1): 71–87.

Cornelius, E. 2010b. "Plain language as alternative textualisation." *Southern African Linguistics and Applied Language Studies* 2010, **28**(2): 171–183.

Cornelius, E. 2011. "The curious case of legal translation." *Literator*, **32**(1): 121–143.

Garner, B.A. 2002. *The elements of legal style*. Second edition. Oxford: Oxford University Press.

Garzone, G. 2000. *Legal translation and functionalist approaches: a contradiction in terms?* http://www.tradulex.org/Actes2000/Garzone.pdf Date of access: 28 Oct. 2009.

Gibbons J. 2003. *Forensic linguistics: An introduction to language in the justice system*. Oxford: Blackwell Publishing.

Gile, D. 2004. "Integrated problem and decision reporting as a translator training tool." *The Journal of Specialised Translation*, **2**: 2–20.

Göpferich, S. and Jääskeläinen, R. 2009. "Process research into the development of translation competence: where are we, and where do we need to go?" *Across Languages and Cultures* **10**(2): 169–191.

Hansen, G. 2006. "Retrospection methods in translator training and translation research." *Journal of Specialised Translation*, **5**(1): 2–41.

Llopis, M.A.O. 2007. "The untranslatability of law?" *European Journal of English Studies*, 11(1):17–28.

McKenna, D. 2009. "And the verdict is … many legal doublets are superfluous and unnecessary." *Proteus*, **XVIII**(2), Summer 2009: 24–26.

Munday, J. 2001/2012. *Introducing Translation Studies. Theories and applications.* London: Routledge.

Newmark, P. 1981. *Approaches to translation*. London: Pergamon.

Nienaber, A. 2001. "The accessibility and comprehensibility of South Africa's Bill of Rights: An empirical study." *De Jure*, **34**(1): 113–135.

Obenaus, G. 1995. "The legal translator as information broker." In Morris, M., ed. *Translation and the law*. Amsterdam: John Benjamins. p. 247–259.

Rek-Harrop, J.J. 2010. *Polish and English translation of jurilinguistic discourse: key aspects and problem areas in the translation of certain forms of legal contracts in terms of terminology transfer between two different legal systems: Polish and English*. http://www.harroptranslations. com/ Date of access: 13 Jul. 2010; and http://www.docstoc.com/docs/ DownloadDoc.aspx? doc_id=6337519&ref_ url= Date of access: 13 July 2010.

Republic of South Africa. *Child Care Act* 74 of 1983.

Republic of South Africa. *Protection of Information Act* 84 of 1982.

Republic of South Africa. *Consumer Affairs (Unfair Business Practices) Act* 71 of 1988.

Rothe-Neves, R. n.d. *Translation quality assessment for research purposes: an empirical approach*. Available from http://www.lingoturk.com/Sources/Rui-Cadernos10.pdf (113-1310). Accessed 19 May 2015.

Šarčević, S. 1997. *New approach to legal translation*. The Hague: Kluwer Law International.

Šarčević, S. 2000. "Legal translation and translation theory: a receiver-oriented approach." http://www.tradulex.org/Actes2000/sarcevic.pdf Date of access: 25 Nov. 2009.

Schroth, P.W. 1986. "Legal translation." *American Journal of Comparative Law (Supplement)*, **34**: 47–65.

Schwarz, H. 1977. "Legal and administrative language." *Babel*, **23**(1); 19–22.

Sless, D. 1999. "Designing and evaluating forms in large organizations." In: Zwaga, H.J., Boersema, T. & Hoonhout, H.C.M. (eds.). *Visual information for everyday use: design and research perspectives*. London & Philadelphia: Taylor & Francis: 135–153.

Test your document's readability. Available from https://support.office.com/en-us/article/Test-your-documents-readability-85b4969e-e80a-4777-8dd3-f7fc3c8b-3fd2. Accessed 18 May 2015.

Montserrat Franquesa Gòdia

Katalanische Übersetzungen der griechischen und lateinischen Klassikern unter der Franco-Diktatur[1]

Abstract: The translation of Greek and Latin classics in several European languages for publication in bilingual collections occurred simultaneously, just in the period between the two world wars. This was not by chance: at the end of World War I, the Loeb Classical Library in England, the collection of the Association Budé in France, and the collection of the Bernat Metge Foundation in Catalonia had common origins. Some of their goals show many similarities but also differences. This contribution analyses the origin and ideology of each and examines in detail the Catalan case: the collection of the Bernat Metge Foundation is included in a classicist movement that crossed all Europe in the first two decades of the twentieth century, leaving -however- the rest of Spain out of it. After the Spanish Civil War and despite the prohibition of the Catalan under Franco's Dictatorship, the versions of the bilingual collection Bernat Metge were a reference language model. Ancient Classics in translation incorporated in Catalan have produced a prestige and stronger language. Why?

Keywords: Catalan translation, history of translation, Franco's dictatorship, Bernat Metge Foundation.

1. Einleitung

Die Übersetzung der altgriechischen und lateinischen Autoren, in mehrere europäische Sprachen zur Veröffentlichung in einer zweisprachigen Sammlung, ist im 20. Jahrhundert zeitgleich aufgetreten, genau in der Zeit zwischen den beiden Weltkriegen. Dies kann kein Zufall sein. Ende des 19. Jahrhunderts begann in Deutschland in Bezug auf die klassische Philologie und Textkritik eine neue Epoche. Darüber hinaus wurden die Übersetzungen in den jeweiligen Sprachkreisen und Ländern anders bewertet. Auf Grund dieser neuen Bewertungen entstanden in Europa drei verschiedene Übersetzungsprojekte mit ähnlichen

---

1 Dieser Beitrag ist Teil der Forschungsgruppe Grup d'Estudi de la Traducció Catalana Contemporània (GETCC) (2014, SGR 285), von Agència de Gestió i Ajuts Universitaris der Landesregierung Generalitat de Catalunya erkannt und des Projektes «La traducción catalana contemporánea: censura y políticas editoriales género e ideología (1939–2000)», Referenznummer FFI2014-52989-C2-1-P, vom spanischen Ministerio de Economía y Competitividad gefördert.

Ausgangspunkten und Übersetzungskriterien, um alle Klassiker der Antike systematisch zu übersetzen. Aber die Entwicklung der katalanischen Übersetzungsreihe ist fest an die zu der Zeit ungünstigen politischen Lagen Spaniens gebunden und hat deshalb ein ganz anderes Verfahren erlebt. Die katalanischen Übersetzungen mussten dem Sprachverbot und der Zensur des Franco- Regimes (1939–1975) entgehen. Einige Jahre zuvor mussten sie bereits die Diktatur von Primo de Rivera (1923–1931) überwinden. Demzufolge spielen die Übersetzungen der Klassiker ins katalanische eine bedeutsame Rolle, da deren Existenz das Überleben der literarischen Zielsprache bedeutet. Bei der Analyse der katalanischen Versionen und ihrer Entstehungsgeschichte tauchen Elemente auf, welche das literarische System einer Zielsprache immer beeinflussen (Even-Zohar 1978:117).

2. Drei neue zweisprachige Übersetzungsreihen in Europa

Am Anfang des 20. Jahrhunderts erschienen die *Loeb Classical Library* in England, die Reihe der *Association Guillaume Budé* in Frankreich und die Sammlung *Fundació Bernat Metge* in Katalonien fast gleichzeitig. Unter sich zeigen sie viele Ähnlichkeiten. Die *Loeb Classical Library* wurde im Jahr 1912 von James Loeb, einem amerikanischen Bankier und Kunstsammler, gegründet. Die ersten Bände enthalten eine Einleitung *A Word About Its Purpose and Its Scope,* welche von dem Gründer verfasst wurden, um die Zwecke des Projektes zu erklären. Was er damit erreichen wollte war "to make the beauty and learning, the philosophy and wit of the great writers of ancient Greece and Rome once more accessible by means of translations" und um dazu noch die Beste Reihe für Originaltexte herauszugeben, "to place side by side with these translations the best critical texts of the original works is the object of the Loeb Classical Library" (Loeb 1912?: 5). Dabei war auch die Endsprache wichtig, nämlich die englische Version, denn der textkritische Apparat ist sehr knapp gehalten worden, so dass für eine wirklich wissenschaftliche Arbeit im Bereich der klassischen Philologie die deutsche Ausgaben schon heranzuziehen waren und noch heute sind. Ursprünglich wurden die Loeb-Bände in London hergestellt. Nach dem Tod von James Loeb im Jahre 1933 wurde der Verlag von Harvard University Press übernommen. Heutzutage umfasst die Reihe mehr als 500 Bände, die immer wieder gedruckt werden.[2]

---

2 http://www.hup.harvard.edu/features/loeb/history.html [15/05/2015]. Die Editions-Reihe Loeb der griechischen und lateinischen Autoren jeweils mit englischer Übersetzung war so gut vorbereitet, dass bereits im ersten Jahr nach der Gründung 20 Bände erscheinen konnten, mit Autoren wie Apollonius Rhodius, Catull und Tibull, Cicero und Euripides. In den vier Jahren des Krieges, zwischen 1914 und 1918, erschien

Anfang des Jahres 1917 haben Professoren des Collège de France, der Sorbonne, der École des Hautes-Études und anderer französischen Universitäten den Verband Guillaume Budé in Paris gegründet.[3] Unter der Schirmherrschaft dieses Verbandes begann erst im 1919 die Veröffentlichung einer Sammlung altgriechischen und lateinischen Klassiker, die bekannte *Collection des Universités de France*, mit der finanziellen Unterstützung von "des industriels français, amis des lettres classiques". Es handelte sich um "une tâche qu'ils regardent comme utile à notre pays" von dreihundert Gründungsunternehmern der "Société Les Belles Lettres pour le développement de la culture classique" (Mazon 1921: 4), heutzutage noch bekannt als *Société d'Édition Les-Belles-Lettres*. Nach dem 1. Weltkrieg waren deutsche Verlage die besten für Originaltexte, deshalb wollten die Franzosen "créer en France une veritable édition savante des textes anciens, afin de se soustraire à la domination allemande".[4] Die abgekürzt CUF genannte oder einfach *Collection Budé* betitelte Reihe umfasst textkritische Ausgaben griechischer und lateinischer Schriftsteller mit französischer Übersetzung. Der erste Band erschien 1920 mit der Edition des *Hippias minor* von Platon, herausgegeben von Maurice Croiset. Heutzutage zählt sie circa 750 Titel.

Genau im Jahr 1920 kam die französische Initiative nach Katalonien, wo der gute Ruf des Guillaume Budé Verbandes eine Gruppe von dort lebenden Intellektuellen, Professoren und Schriftellern ermutigte Mitglied des Budé Verbandes zu werden und damit eine katalanische Schwester zu gründen, *la soeur catalane*, eine zweisprachige Reihe altklassischen Autoren mit katalanischer Übersetzung. In Auftrag von dem damaligen Politiker und späteren Millionär, Francesc Cambó, reiste der Herausgeber Joan Estelrich mehrmals nach Paris, als Mitglied des katalanischen Budé-Sektion. So traf er u.a. den Altphilologe Paul Mazon. Sie vereinbarten Kooperationen wie z.B. die kostenlose Übertragung von den griechischen Buchstaben, um den Originaltext drucken lassen zu können, die damals in Katalonien unmöglich zu finden gewesen wären. Wenige Monate nach dem Treffen und nach mehreren Briefaustäuschen zwischen Joan Estelrich und Paul Mazon, schrieb Louis Havet, Professor an der Sorbonne und Collège de France, Latinist und Vizepräsident des Budévereins, in der französischen Presse: "un fait

---

einen stetigen Strom von 54 neuen Bänden, darunter Werke von Vergil, Ovid, Marcus Aurelius und Galen.

3 "Le nom de Guillaume Budé, le premier professeur de grec du Collège de France, pour bien marquer qu'ils entendaient relier leur effort à la tradition française de la Renaissance" schrieb Paul Mazon. In gleicher Weise wurde das katalanische Projekt zur Erinnerung an Bernat Metge genannt, Hellenist und Übersetzer im 15. Jahrhundert.

4 http://www.lesbelleslettres.com/info/?fa=historiquefull [15/05/2015].

interessant vient de se produire à Barcelone. Là s'est fondée une section catalane de notre Association Guillaume Budé".[5]

Die später so genannte *Fundació Bernat Metge* wurde im Jahr 1922 mit der finanziellen Unterstützung von Francesc Cambó, dem konservativen katalanischen Politiker und Minister in der spanischen Regierung von 1918 bis 1922 und ab 1919 Millionär und Kunstsammler in Barcelona gegründet, mit dem Zweck "completar l'edifici de la nostra Renaixença literària", sonst "Catalunya no obtindrà la seva executòria d'alta i profunda cultura" (Cambó 1926: 48).[6] Genau in der Zeit erlitt Katalonien die erste Diktatur des 20. Jahrhunderts, die Diktatur von general Miguel Primo de Rivera (1923–1931), wobei die katalanische Sprache und Kultur verboten wurde. Deshalb verließ Cambó die Politik und beschloss, sich der katalanischen Kultur zu widmen. Sein Projekt fand gleich Unterstützung seitens der katalanischen Bourgeoisie, vor allem von kleinen Unternehmern und reichen Familien, ansässig in der Hauptstadt Barcelona, die politisch und ideologisch mit Cambó einherging. Nach wenigen Monaten hatte der Verlag mehr als tausend Abonnenten, nicht nur im gesamten Katalonien sondern auch im Ausland. Die meisten kamen jedoch aus intellektuellen Kreisen der Stadt Barcelona. Auf dem Land abonnierten normalerweise Priester, Notare und Apotheker aus jeglichen Dörfern. Heutzutage ist die Abonnentenliste etwas anders, da es die Gesellschaft mittlerweile auch ist. Man kann die Bände z.B. in spezialisierten Buchhandlungen finden oder on-line kaufen.[7] Die Reihe zählt nun über 400 Titel, eine respektable Zahl im Vergleich mit *Loeb Classical Library* (500) und *Collection Budé* (750).

3. Übersetzungskriterien und Zielsprache

Die auffälligsten und interessantesten Punkte der katalanischen Reihe sind zum einen das Sprachniveau der Übersetzungen und zum anderen die Verwendung der Kriterien. Das Projekt hatte das Hauptziel, eine echte, hohe, literarische Sprache zu erreichen. Vom Anfang an hatte Herausgeber Joan Estelrich die Übersetzungskriterien nach den Kriterien von Association Budé zusammengefasst. Dieses

5 "Ein interessantes Ereignis ist gerade in Barcelona geschehen. Da ist eine katalanische Sektion unseres Verbandes gegründet worden" schrieb Louis Havet in *Le Temps* am 8. Juni 1923. Zwei Tage später, am 10. Juni, veröffentlichte die katalanische Zeitung *La Publicitat* den Artikel als Beispiel der ausgezeichneten Rezeption der Stiftung Bernat Metge im Ausland.

6 "Das Gebäude unserer literarischen Renaissance zu vervollständigen, sonst wird Katalonien seine Hochkultur nie erreichen".

7 http://www.bernatmetge.com [15/05/2015].

Manuskript wurde bei unserer Recherche entdeckt und erst danach veröffentlicht (Franquesa 2010: 213). Was lässt sich aus diesem Dokument ableiten? Die zwei wichtigsten Prinzipien in Bezug auf die Übersetzungsmethode sind, dass die Übersetzungen nie Wort für Wort, *verbum pro verbo*, sein müssen und dass man immer nur Prosa benutzen darf, auch wenn es sich dabei um alte Dichtung, Tragödie oder Komödie handelt, denn das katalanische hatte damals das Niveau einer Hochsprache noch nicht erreicht (Fundació Bernat Metge 1922: 12).

Um die Genauigkeit und Vollkommenheit der Sprache sicherzustellen, war Pompeu Fabra Korrektor.[8] Carles Riba, Poet und Hellenist, hatte die Verantwortung für die griechische Übersetzungen und Professor Joaquim Balcells, Latinist, für die Lateinische. Unter ihrer Aufsicht und Leitung wurden im Laufe von nur 15 Jahre 84 Titeln veröffentlicht. Das Projekt, das Francesc Cambó an Joan Estelrich beauftragte, hatte das erste Ziel, 10 Bände pro Jahr zu veröffentlichen. Dies erwies sich nicht realistisch, denn es war kaum durchführbar aufgrund der Übersetzerknappheit. Katalonien hatte damals nämlich noch kein Studium klassischer Philologie. Die Aus-und Fortbildung der Latinisten und Hellenisten wurde erst ab 1925 ein Ziel der Stiftung Bernat Metge. Noch heute organisiert man Seminare, orientiert an den besten ausgewählten Studenten der klassischen Philologie.

Im Vergleich mit der ersten Epoche wurden unter Francos Regime viel weniger Bände veröffentlicht (von 1923 bis 1938, 84 Titeln, von 1939 bis 1975, 110). Auch wenn es wenige waren, waren die Übersetzungen ins Katalanischen ein Referenzsprachmodell für die literarische Sprache. Es handelte sich um philologische Versionen, in denen das wichtigste nicht der Originaltext oder das textkritische Apparat war, sondern die Zielsprache (Fundació Bernat Metge 1922: 8). Das hatte natürlich bestimmte Konsequenzen: die katalanische Sprache wurde stärker gemacht, aber nicht alle Sprachregister konnten in gleicher Weise entwickelt werden.

4. Katalanische Übersetzungen im Schatten

Nach dem spanischen Bürgerkrieg und trotz des Verbots der katalanischen Sprache unter der Franco-Diktatur, konnte die Reihe *Bernat Metge* weiter veröffentlichen.

---

8 1912 veröffentlichte Pompeu Fabra ein bis heute verwendetes Standardwerk: *Die Grammatik der katalanischen Sprache*. Das *Institut d'Estudis Catalans* erklärte 1913 die in Pompeu Fabras Buch enthaltenen grammatischen Normen zum Standard. Später wurde er auch Vorsitzender des Instituts. Erst nach der Diktatur von Primo de Rivera (1932) erschien das erste *Diccionari general de la llengua catalana* (*Allgemeines Wörterbuch der katalanischen Sprache*), seit 1923 von Francesc Cambó gefördert.

Sie musste jedoch die strenge politische Zensur des Regimes überwinden. Wie war das möglich?

Im Juni 1938 war ein Band von Plutarch von Carles Riba übersetzt und zum Druck abgegeben worden; das Buch wurde dann aber nicht gedruckt. Nach dem Bürgerkriegsende, genau im Dezember 1939 hat der Sekretär von Francesc Cambó, Narcís de Carreras (denn Cambó war schon im Exil) den Franco Innenminister Serrano-Suñer geschrieben um Erlaubnis zu erbitten, die Reihe Bernat Metge fortsetzen zu dürfen. So lautete die Bitte:

> se digne conceder a Editorial Alpha, S.A. autorización para continuar su colección de clásicos griegos y latinos, con traducción catalana; para acabar su publicación, casi ya completa, de su Biblia en catalán; para continuar sus ediciones en castellano, catalán y lenguas extranjeras, como al inglés, y para iniciar inmediatamente una colección de textos griegos y latinos con traducción castellana[9]

Im Jahre 1940 und 1941 unternahm Sammlungsdirektor Joan Estelrich mehrere Reisen von Barcelona nach Madrid und unterhielt sich damit Professoren der CSIC,[10] was dem Ziel diente die Veröffentlichung des Plutarchs von Carles Riba zu gewährleisten. Es gelang ihm, erst im Jahr 1942, Francesc Cambó mitzuteilen, dass sie Erlaubnis zur Veröffentlichung erhalten hatten, aber mit der Bedingung, auch eine Reihe mit spanischer Übersetzung zu veröffentlichen.[11] So durfte Plutarchs Übersetzung von Carles Riba ohne Namen des Übersetzers veröffentlicht werden. Es wäre zu gefährlich gewesen, auch wenn Carles Riba noch im Exil war.

Unter Francos Regime sind verschiedene Phasen in der Bernat Metge Stiftung zu bemerken. In den 40. Jahre gab es Zensur und Papiermangel, die Übersetzer und Philologen waren im Exil. Deshalb konnten nur wenige Bände veröffentlicht werden. Nach seiner Rückkehr wurde Carles Riba Sammlungsdirektor bis zu seinem Tod im Jahr 1958. Im Jahr 1960 hat Frau Helena Cambó, Erbin des Verlags, als einzige Töchter von Francesc Cambó, 1947 in Argentinien gestorben, einen Bernat-Metge-Vorstand gegründet. Mitglied dieses Vorstandes wurden Professoren aus den verschiedenen Universitäten in Katalonien. Das ermöglichte die echte Wiederaufnahme des Verlags. Im Jahr 1962 wurde in Spanien ein neues

---

9 Erlaubnis um die Reihe beenden zu dürfen und auch eine Sammlung altklassiker Autoren auf Spanisch herauszugeben. Es ist doch klar, dass eine Reihe altklassiker Autoren nie beendet werden kann: die Ausrede wollte einfach die Zensur überwinden.

10 *Consejo Superior de Investigaciones Científicas*, eine Art von *National Research Council*, vom Franco-Regime gegründet.

11 Eine spanische Editionsreihe sollte aber nie herausgegeben werden.

Pressegesetz verordnet und erst ab dann gab es eine gewisse Pressefreiheit für Veröffentlichungen aller Art. Heutzutage gibt die Reihe Bernat Metge sechs Bände pro Jahr heraus, dank der Mitarbeit von Übersetzern, Forschern und Professoren aus allen Universitäten der katalanischen Ländern und Unterstützung der Landesregierung Kataloniens und des spanischen Kultusministeriums. Nach der Finsternis des Franquismus, welcher die katalanischen Versionen der Klassiker mit Geringschätzung erlaubte, aus welchen Gründen nur eine unregelmäßige Entwicklung der katalanischen Sprache und des literarischen Marktes zustande kam, erhob sich eine neue Epoche in der Übersetzungsgeschichte Kataloniens.

5. Zusammenfassung

Die Geburt der Sammlung katalanischer Übersetzungen der Klassiker in dem europäischen kulturellen Raum Anfang des 20. Jahrhunderts enthält ein bestimmtes Ereignis: die Entscheidung der katalanischen Intellektuellen der 20. Jahre, Mitglied des Vereins Budé zu werden. Dies zeigte der deutliche Wille, am kulturellen Leben Europas teilzunehmen. So eine Einstellung konnte in Spanien nicht vertreten sein, denn nur Katalonien und die Hauptstadt Barcelona gingen damals wegen der Industrialisierung und wirtschaftlicher Entwicklung mehrere kulturelle Schritte vorwärts.

Nach den Theorien von André Lefevere (Lefevere 1992) ist Übersetzung die Umschreibung oder Manipulation eines ursprünglichen Textes und alle Umschreibungen spiegeln eine bestimmte Ideologie und Ästhetik wider. Nach dieser Theorie und nach den Manipulationstheorien sind die Übersetzungen leichter von dem Sprachsystem zu akzeptieren, wenn sie nicht in Konflikt mit der dominanten Ideologie geraten. Da der Gründer Francesc Cambó eine konservative Ideologie verteidigte und für das Franco-Regime war, konnten die Übersetzungen der Klassikerreihe Bernat Metge erst im 1942 wiederveröffentlicht werden, auch wenn Katalanisch streng verboten wurde. Daher sollten sie im Hintergrund bleiben, nur im Kreis der Hochkultur und von ausgewählten Abonnenten gelesen werden. Festzuhalten ist dennoch, der Versuch einer Kultur, eine eigene Stimme zu erlangen, auch wenn sie von dem Staat nicht unterstützt wurde. Statt der Finanzierung und Unterstützung durch den Staat, gab es dann das private Kapital von Francesc Cambó (wie James Loeb), die privaten Investitionen der Abonnenten und vor allem die Bemühungen der Übersetzer. Der Erfolg beruht wahrscheinlich auf einem Akt des Widerstands seitens der Übersetzer und Korrektoren, die ihre Mitarbeit als eine Art Patriotismus verstanden haben, eine Art Wortarbeit um die eigene Sprache erhalten zu können. So kann festgestellt werden, dass Katalanisch durch Übersetzungen stärker gemacht wurde und das Land durch die alten Klassiker den

Status einer Hochkultur erreichen konnte. Und es bestätigt sich dadurch, dass die katalanische Sprache im Übersetzungsbereich der alten Klassikern endlich eine ganz normalisierte europäische Sprache ist.

Literatur

Bassnett-Mcguire, Susan. *Translation Studies*. London: Routledge, 1991.

Cambó, Francesc. "Paraules de Cambó als col·laboradors de la Fundació Bernat Metge". *Almanac de Catalunya*, 1926.

Estelrich, Joan. "La Fundació Bernat Metge". *Revue des Études Latines* IV, 1926, p. 187–194.

Even-Zohar, Itamar. "The position of translated literature within the literary polisistem". *Literature and translation. New perspectives in literary studies*. Leuven: J. S. Holmes, 1978.

Franquesa Gòdia, Montserrat. *La Fundació Bernat Metge, una obra de país (1923-1928)*. Barcelona: Publicacions de l'Abadia de Montserrat, 2013.

—. "Les primeres normes generals de traducció de la Fundació Bernat Metge" *Quaderns, Revista de traducció*, núm. 17, Bellaterra: Universitat Autònoma de Barcelona, 2010, p. 213–223.

Fundació Bernat Metge. *Una col·lecció catalana dels clàssics grecs i llatins*. Barcelona: Editorial Catalana, 1922.

Gallego Roca, Miguel. *Traducción y literatura: Los estudios literarios ante las obras traducidas*. Madrid: Júcar, 1994.

González, Arnau. *La tercera Catalunya (1936-1940),* Barcelona: Edicions de 1984, 2013.

Lefevere, André. *Translation, Rewriting, and the Manipulation of Literary Fame*. London: Routledge, 1992.

Loeb, James. *The Loeb Classical Library*. London: Heinemann, [1912?].

Manent, Albert. *De 1936 a 1975. Estudis sobre la guerra civil i el franquisme*, Barcelona: Publicacions de l'Abadia de Montserrat, 1999.

Mazon, Paul. "L'Association Guillaume Budé". *Le Flambeau, Revue des Questions Politiques et Littéraires*, 12 (Dezember 1921).

Sandys, John Edwin. *A History of classical scholarship*. New York-London: Hafner, 1967.

Steiner, George. *After Babel: Aspects of Language and Translation*. New York: Oxford University Press,1992.

Toury, Gideon. *Descriptive Translation Studies and Beyond*. Amsterdam: John Benjamins, 1995.

Tovar, Antonio. *Lingüística y filología clásica: su situación actual*. Madrid: Revista de Occidente, 1944.

Venuti, L. *The Translator's Invisibility*. London: Routledge, 1995.

Koen Kerremans

Variation in the Translation of Terms: Corpus-Driven Terminology Research

Abstract: In this article, we will argue that terminology resources are not able to fully cover the different 'linguistic options' found in texts referring to specialised knowledge. We will illustrate this point on the basis of a comparative study between a parallel corpus comprised of English EU source texts and their translations into French and Dutch, and a selection of terminological records from the EU's terminological database IATE. We will report on how the research was carried out, present the major qualitative and quantitative findings and reflect on how the research methodology – i.e. a corpus-driven approach applied to terminology research – is now taught in a terminology course which is part of the master programmes of translation and interpreting at Vrije Universiteit Brussel.

Keywords: corpus-driven approach, environmental domain, EU, IATE, parallel corpus, terminography workflow, terminology, terminology course, terminological variation, translation-oriented terminography.

1. Introduction

Terminology refers to the collection of lexical expressions that constitute a given subject field. Practical terminology research – also known as terminography – involves amongst others collecting, creating, organising and managing domain-specific vocabulary in one or several languages.

For translators working in any field of specialised translation (e.g. translations in technical, scientific, financial, legal or medical domains) it is important to acquire the necessary knowledge and practical skills to be able to carry out terminological research that leads to the creation of translation-oriented terminological products. Examples of such structured terminological 'products' are terminological glossaries, dictionaries, thesauri or databases for translators.

In this article, we will argue that such resources are not able to fully cover the different 'linguistic options' found in texts to refer to specialised knowledge in different cognitive, situational and linguistic contexts. We will illustrate this point on the basis of a comparative study between a parallel corpus comprised of English EU source texts and their translations into French and Dutch, and a selection of terminological records from the EU's terminological database IATE.[1] The case study will also be used to show how a contrastive, corpus-driven analysis can be incorporated in translation-oriented terminology research in order to create better-quality terminological resources for translators.

We will report on how the research was carried out, present the major qualitative and quantitative observations and reflect on how the research methodology – i.e. a corpus-driven approach applied to terminology research – is now taught within a terminology course which is part of the master programmes of translation and interpreting at Vrije Universiteit Brussel (VUB).

The article will be structured as follows. Section 2 is a summary of the research background, which will serve as a motivation for the research project presented in this article. In Section 3, we will briefly present how variation is dealt with in the IATE database. Section 4 will be devoted to a discussion of the comparative research. We will report on how it was carried out and present some qualitative and quantitative findings. In Section 5, we will discuss how the research methodology that was worked out for this project is now taught within the terminology course as part of the master programmes of translation and interpreting at Vrije Universiteit Brussel (cf. supra). A conclusion will be drawn in Section 6.

2. Research Background

Traditional terminological research is determined by a conviction that terms should be used unambiguously to refer to clearly delineated concepts in order to arrive at unambiguous communication. This prescriptive view was a guiding principle in many terminographical studies and dominated terminology theory for many years (Cabré 2003), resulting in the General Theory of Terminology or GTT (Wüster 1979; Felber 1984; Picht and Draskau 1985).

Terminological resources developed within the framework of the GTT are essentially normative. In a translation context, for instance, bi-/multilingual terminological resources are developed for the purpose of presenting harmonised (or standardised) solutions for given translation problems. This normative function defines specific design principles for bi-/multilingual terminological resources within the GTT framework. For instance, terminological databases are characterised by a concept-oriented structure. The concept, which is the starting point of the terminological analysis, is identified by means of an authorised term. Preferred terms and their equivalents in other languages appear in separate fields

1 Source: http://iate.europa.eu.

of the same terminological record in order to support translators in translating terms consistently, i.e. by means of the same translation equivalent. The number of terminological variants – i.e. different ways to refer to the same concept by means of terms – recorded in such resources is rather limited because variation is believed to undermine the normative function of the terminological resource.

In more recent years, the terminography workflow has been influenced by descriptive terminology studies focusing on linguistic, cognitive, cultural, sociocommunicative, pragmatic and/or functional aspects of terminology (Temmerman 2000; Cabré 2003; Collet 2004; Faber 2009). Such approaches to terminology have emphasised the importance of context in the interpretation, use and/or description of terminology. For a translator, who works within the confines of specialised discourse, for instance, it is important to know what linguistic options are available in languages for expressing specialised knowledge and to understand how these options can be used in specific communicative contexts.

As a result of these views, existing types of terminological resources – i.e. terminological dictionaries and databases – have been extended with new types of information, "taking into consideration factors that are relevant in the translation process, most of which had hitherto been paid no attention to by specialized lexicographers: text types and genres, use situation (for example, a translator of specialized texts also needs conceptual data), and culture" (Fuertes-Olivera 2011, 99).

Looking at terms and their translations from a descriptive point of view – i.e. by studying term occurrences and their translations in parallel, specialised texts – we argue that none of the aforementioned types of structured terminology resources is able to fully account for the diversity or wealth of linguistic options encountered in texts.

A first point supporting this view is the fact that terminological resources in general are limited to representing "the 'langue' or 'norm' level of language and not the individual actual text level" (Gerzymisch-Arbogast 2008, 20). Descriptive terminological resources are not different from traditional terminological resources in this respect. By separating a term from its natural habitat – i.e. the text – a lot of valuable information on which translation decisions are based is lost, e.g. the topic of the text, the perspective from which the topic is approached, the text's communicative purpose, the stylistic features of the text, etc.

A second point why (structured) terminology resources are not able to fully cover the wealth of linguistic options in texts is because bi- or multilingual terminology work is primarily focused on finding direct or cognitive equivalents (in several languages) for a given term in the source language (Adamska-Sałaciak 2010) – i.e. terms in several languages that share the same meaning. In translations, however, terms may also be translated into other types of equivalents. Seen from a translation perspective, 'equivalence' is not always the same as 'equivalence' seen from a terminographical perspective.

We argue that the coverage of terminological options (in both source and target languages) in translation-oriented terminological databases can be improved if such resources are enriched with data derived from multilingual, parallel corpora. The problem of low 'coverage' in terminological resources will be illustrated on the basis of a case study in which we compared the occurrence of term variants and their translations between a multilingual parallel corpus and the EU multilingual terminological database IATE.

3. Term Variation in IATE

In order to conduct the comparative study of intra- and interlingual variation (see Section 4), it was essential to first acquire an understanding of the way term variation is structured in the IATE database. In particular, we needed to know where to look for term variants in each terminological record. In order to do this, we first analysed IATE's database structure. Based on that study, we managed to extract the different fields of information from a sample of about 1138 terminological records that were manually collected from IATE's on-line search system.

Term variation is accounted for in different ways in IATE's term records. Overall, a distinction can be made between field records which simply list the possible term variants (e.g. the 'Term' field), fields in which information is provided about specific contextual usages (e.g.. the fields 'Language Usage', 'Regional Usage', 'Notes' and 'Context') and fields providing additional features of the different term variants (e.g. the fields 'Grammatical info', 'Reliability' and 'Evaluation').

Different types of terms can enter the Term field. Form-related terms appear in the same 'Term Group'. Other possibilities are a term and its corresponding abbreviation or the common and full title of an agreement (IATE project meeting 2008, 11). Each term added to a record can receive a 'Reliability' score (a number ranging from 0 to 4) on which decisions for term preference in certain contexts can be based.

Apart from the reliability marker, status indicators provide an evaluation of the terms that are added to IATE. If a term is marked as 'Obsolete', it means that it is no longer in use, that a body has ceased to exist or that an instrument has been replaced. 'Preferred' means that the term should be used instead of the other equally correct (synonyms), for harmonisation purposes. Apart from those two categories, terms can also be marked as 'Admitted' – meaning that a term is accepted as a synonym of a preferred term – or 'Deprecated'. The latter is used for terms that have been rejected and should no longer be used (IATE project meeting 2008, 13).

Another field relevant for finding terminological variants in IATE is the 'LookUp Form'. Users are allowed to enter in this field any term or spelling variant that they wish to be searchable, but not visible to the common user: e.g. "common spelling mistakes, alternative spellings, generic forms of words used in the term field, etc." (IATE project meeting 2008, 18).

Lookup forms are written in any order. Different terms should normally be separated by semi-colons (IATE project meeting 2008, 18). In practice, however, this was not always the case. In our study of the IATE terminological records, we noticed that in IATE entry number 2230131, for instance, the lookup alternatives for 'carbon dioxide capture and storage' were listed without separation: "CO2 capture and storage carbon capture and storage carbon capture and sequestration carbon sequestration."

Apart from the aforementioned fields in which different types of terms (variants) are recorded, other fields (such as 'Note', 'Language Usage' and 'Regional Usage') can provide more information about the specific use of each variant in different communicative contexts.

The Note field is a mixture of different types of information which can also appear in different field records. Particularly relevant for this study is that also cases were observed in which additional terminological variants were placed in the 'Note' field. Examples of observed types of variants are: lexical variants, formulas, abbreviated forms and orthographic variants. An example listing lexical variants is found in the note "Syn.: catchment basin, river basin" referring to the term catchment area (IATE entry number 1084586). Formulas are found in the note "Symb.: °C; Cf.: kelvin(K)" linked to the term Celsius (IATE entry number 1084741). The abbreviated form 'JIA' for the term 'Joint Implementation Agreement' was found in entry 1747231. Finally, the orthographic variant 'flood-plain' as language usage note for 'flood plain' was found in entry 1857490.

Different types of information appearing in the 'Language Usage' field were observed in the IATE research material. For instance, the typical information about a term's usage was found in entry 1049292 where the term 'Least Developed Countries' is specified as: "A country may be described as 'one of the least developed countries', not as 'a least developed country'."

Also examples were found in which the 'Language Usage' data category contained additional terminological variants. For instance, in the following comment about language usage, several terminological variants of 'carbon dioxide capture and storage' are listed: "Sometimes called carbon capture and storage, carbon capture and sequestration, or carbon sequestration. See IATE:911523" (IATE entry number 2230131). A reduced form of the term 'EU Action Plan to 2010 and Beyond' was found in the following language usage note: "Sometimes referred to as "Agenda 2010"" (IATE entry number 2245706). An orthographic variant of runoff is specified in the following comment: "Can also be written with a hyphen: "run-off"" (IATE entry number 750406). From the language usage note in entry 779289, it can be derived that the singular form of bacteria is bacterium. The abbreviated form of 'Food and Agriculture Organisation of the United Nations' – i.e. FAO – is mentioned in entry 799023: "The abbreviation "FAO" is used without the definite article [...]." Finally, an example of a quasi-synonym can be found in the language usage note of entry 782821 where the term solar power is identified as a quasi-synonym of the term solar energy: "sometimes used loosely as a synonym for "solar energy"."

Information concerning the way a term is used in a particular geographical area is normally entered in the 'Regional Usage' field. An example can be found for French in term entry 2230131 in which it is stated that the term 'captage et stockage du dioxyde de carbone' ('carbon dioxide capture and geological storage') is an expression typically used in Canada.

From the discussion of IATE's field records, it can be derived that EU terminologists/translators are offered many different possibilities to account for terminological variants of different types in the IATE system. The different fields of information which potentially hold information about term variants, were extracted from a collection of 1138 terminological records and stored in a separate database. In order to create a basis for comparison between IATE and the parallel corpus (see Section 2), only terminological records were collected describing concepts that also formed the starting point for the analysis of intra- and interlingual variation in the parallel corpus (see Section 4).

Given the concept-oriented structure of the database, it was expected that IATE would not cover all types of interlingual variants that were observed in the parallel corpus. Results of the comparative study of interlingual variation between IATE and the corpus will be discussed in the next section.

4. A Comparative Study between IATE and a Parallel Corpus

The primary objective of the comparative study was to find out to what extent terminological choices (in both source and target texts) were also represented in the IATE terminological database. We first compiled a parallel corpus comprised of 43 English source texts and their translations into French and Dutch in order to examine and compare the patterns of variation for a predefined set of concepts in both subcorpora. The texts in the corpus dealt with environmental topics. Different text genres were taken into consideration, such as information leaflets published by the European Environment Agency or text types belonging to the EU legislative framework (e.g. opinions published by the European Economic and Social Committee, EC directives and staff working documents). IATE was used as a source of reference for all the translations in the corpus.

Our choice for different types of texts from different types of institutions was motivated by our interest in examining how similar concepts in the environmental domain are expressed in texts constituted on the basis of different situational parameters. For a more elaborate presentation of the corpus used for this study, we refer to Kerremans (2014).

The method for identifying terminological variants in the English source texts was based on co-referential analysis, similar to the method explained in Rogers (2007). Each concept was denoted by a cluster of terminological variants. Terms referring to the same concept were annotated according to the same unique identification code or cluster label. Once these variants were identified, we looked for all translation equivalents of the selected patterns in the translations. Terms and their translation equivalents were retrieved from the parallel corpus and stored in a separate file for quantitative and qualitative comparisons. For a more elaborate discussion of the extraction method, we refer to Kerremans (2013).

The study revealed no significant differences between the different texts types as to the degree of variation between source and target texts. Patterns of terminological consistency or change in the source texts tended to be reflected in the translations. The influence of the source texts on the degree of variation in the target texts was therefore apparent.

More relevant for the scope of this article was the fact that the clusters of variants retrieved for a given concept in French and Dutch were more lexically (or terminologically) diverse than the original English clusters. This suggested that interlingual variation – i.e. variation in the translation of terms – could be observed in all text types.

In the subsequent qualitative analysis, we examined how certain concepts in the source texts were exactly transferred to the target texts in Dutch and French. Apart from the many direct equivalents (resulting from literal translations) of English terms that were encountered in the translations, several occurrences were also found in which an English term (variant) was translated by means of an equivalent that was not the result of a direct transfer from the source to the target text. An example of such an indirect equivalent is shown in the following text sample:

English source: Reducing emissions in the EU would be beneficial for energy security and (1)**air pollution** and would stimulate competitive technologies.	
Fr	La réduction des émissions de l'UE sera bénéfique pour la sécurité des approvisionnements en énergie et pour la (1)**qualité de l'air**, et stimulera la mise au point de technologies compétitives.
Nl	Een verlaging van de uitstoot in de EU is gunstig voor de continuïteit van de energievoorziening en de (1)**luchtkwaliteit** en stimuleert competitieve technologieën.

This example is taken from a Commission staff working document on strategies for limiting global climate change to 2 degrees Celsius.[2] The first row contains the English text fragment. The second and third rows contain the French and Dutch translations, respectively. Looking up the possible Dutch and French translations of the English term 'air pollution' in IATE would typically reveal so-called cognitive equivalents. These are direct equivalents in the target languages that share the same semantic properties and point to the same concept as the term in the original language. Equivalents suggested by IATE for this particular example are 'pollution de l'air' and 'pollution atmosphérique' in French and 'luchtverontreiniging' in Dutch. In the example above, however, the English term was translated in both the French and Dutch versions as the conceptually related term 'air quality' ('qualité de l'air' in French and 'luchtkwaliteit' in Dutch). The choice for the indirect equivalents in both French and Dutch is probably due to the presence of the word 'beneficial' in the English context, which may cause interpretation problems in combination with 'air pollution'. The translators of the Dutch and French versions correctly interpreted in this case that the author of the original text probably meant 'beneficial for the reduction of air pollution' and therefore changed the word 'pollution' into 'quality' in order to reduce the risk of misinterpretations. The example shows that translators sometimes (need to) opt for a type of equivalent that is less likely to appear in the same terminological record as the term in the source language. This is due to the concept-oriented structure of the terminological database. The choice for a conceptually-related equivalent in the target language can be motivated by cognitive factors, such as conceptual

2 The reference of the English version of this document is: Commission of the European Communities, 2007. SEC(2007) 7 – Commission staff working document – Limiting global climate change to 2 degrees Celsius – The way ahead for 2020 and beyond – Impact assessment summary {COM(2007) 2 final} {SEC(2007) 8} /* SEC/2007/0007 */.

motivations or intentions as well as linguistic factors, such as collocational restrictions or discursive factors (Kerremans 2014).

One of the outcomes of the study of intra- and interlingual variation in the parallel corpus, is a classification of transfer procedures, showing how English terms in the corpus were translated into French and Dutch. As we mentioned before, apart from direct transfer (as a result of literal translations), also cases of indirect transfer were observed in the data. Such cases were marked when structural or formal differences were observed between the term in the source language and its equivalent (e.g. a change in part-of-speech (POS), singular *vs.* plural form; a term translated as a description; abbreviated form *vs.* full form; etc.) or when semantic differences were observed (e.g. the translation of a term into its conceptually related variant). An example of the latter was shown in the text fragment above.

5. Teaching Corpus-Driven Terminology Research

In the previous two sections, we discussed that intra- and interlingual variation appear in both the parallel texts as well as in IATE. The comparative study of variation between the parallel corpus and IATE also revealed that some deviations from literal translations of SL terms are difficult to represent in concept-oriented term records.

At Vrije Universiteit Brussel, we teach students how terminological resources can be enriched with data derived from multilingual, parallel corpora. The corpus-driven method that we applied in our comparative study (Kerremans 2013) is now implemented in the terminology course entitled 'Studie van Vaktaal en Terminologie' ('Study of Special Language and Terminology') that is part of the master programmes of translation and interpreting.

The course provides a theoretical introduction into terminology as an academic discipline. Several topics related to the study of terminology in domain specific languages are discussed in this theoretical part on the basis of a reader with selected articles. Examples of topics are cultural elements in domain specific languages, term variation, polysemy, metaphors, neologisms, the dynamics of understanding terminology in contexts, etc.

These theoretical discussions serve the practical part of the course in which students are asked to enrich existing IATE records on the basis of corpus-driven analyses of terms and their translations in multilingual, parallel corpora.

Such translation-oriented terminology projects can be carried out on an individual basis or in smaller groups. Students learn to compile a parallel corpus (comprised of EU texts), taking into account different communicative registers.

They learn how to identify terminological variants in the source texts and their corresponding equivalents in the target texts, using corpus analysis tools.

The result of each project is a terminology 'portfolio' and a report of the results obtained. The terminology portfolio is comprised of all collected material that students considered necessary to write the report.

6. Conclusion

The comparative study between IATE and a parallel corpus revealed that translators consulting the IATE database do not necessarily get to see a solution in the target language that is directly applicable to the specific text that they are translating (i.e. the 'translation context'). This is for instance because the equivalent found in the database was taken from a document that belongs to another 'register' (e.g. a legal document vs. a Commission's fact sheet) or 'source' (e.g. a term entered into IATE by a translator/terminologist from the Commission *vs.* a term entered by the Translation Centre for the Bodies of the European Union (CdT) than the text being translated. In this case, translators need to see examples of actual term use in order to check the appropriateness of the given term in the translation context. To this end, they can rely on multilingual corpora comprised of original texts in the source and target languages as well as on parallel corpora or translation memories.

Translation-oriented terminological resources should better account for terminological variation in actual discourse. This variation is determined by a combination of contextual parameters at different levels (situational, linguistic and cognitive). For translators, it is important to know the different terminological options in source texts and to know how these options can be translated, taking into account the different aforementioned contextual parameters.

We discussed how students in the master programmes of translation and interpreting at Vrije Universiteit Brussel are taught to turn principles of translation-oriented terminological research into practice. Advantages of the approach are that students learn to carry out terminological research on the basis of a contrastive, corpus-driven approach and learn to use different types of corpus analysis tools for terminological research (e.g. text alignment tools, bilingual concordancers or term extraction tools). By analysing the parallel texts, they acquire an understanding of the different translation possibilities of a given term in the source language (taking into consideration different linguistic, situational and cognitive factors influencing translation choices) and learn that terms are not always translated consistently. By writing a report on the tasks carried out, students are intellectually challenged because they need to reflect on their methodology and on the results obtained (e.g. 'How is 'translation equivalence' achieved in corpus X?').

References

Adamska-Sałaciak, Arleta. 2010. "Examining Equivalence." *International Journal of Lexicography* 23 (4): 387–409.

Cabré, Maria Teresa. 2003. "Theories of Terminology. Their Description, Prescription and Explanation." *Terminology* 9 (2): 163–99.

Collet, Tanja. 2004. "What's a Term? An Attempt to Define the Term within the Theoretical Framework of Text Linguistics." *Linguistica Antverpiensia* 3: 99–111.

Faber, Pamela. 2009. "The Cognitive Shift in Terminology and Specialized Translation." *MonTI* 1: 107–34.

Felber, Helmut. 1984. *Terminology Manual.* Vienna: Infoterm.

Fuertes-Olivera, Pedro A. 2011. "Equivalent Selection in Specialized E-Lexicography: A Case Study with Spanish Accounting Terms." *Lexikos, AFRILEX,* 21: 95–119.

Gerzymisch-Arbogast, Heidrun. 2008. "Fundamentals of LSP Translation." *MUTRA* 2: 7–64.

IATE project meeting. 2008. "IATE Manual."

Kerremans, Koen. 2013. "Improving Specialised Translation Dictionaries on the Basis of a Study of Terminological Variation." In *Translation and Meaning, Part 9. Proceedings of the Maastricht Session of the 5th International Maastricht-Łódź Duo Colloquium on "Translation and Meaning,"* edited by Marcel Thelen and Barbara Lewandowska-Tomaszczyk, 227–39. Maastricht: Hogeschool Zuyd, Faculty of International Communication, School of Translation and Interpreting.

— 2014. *Terminological Variation in Multilingual Europe. The Case of English Environmental Terminology Translated into Dutch and French.* PhD thesis, Brussel: Vrije Universiteit Brussel.

Picht, Heribert, and Jennifer Draskau. 1985. *Terminology: An Introduction.* Surrey: University of Surrey, Department of Linguistic and International Studies.

Rogers, Margaret. 2007. "Lexical Chains in Technical Translation. A Case Study in Indeterminacy." In *Indeterminacy in Terminology and LSP,* edited by B. Edem Antia, 8:15–35. Terminology and Lexicography Research and Practice. Amsterdam/Philadelphia: John Benjamins Publishing Company.

Temmerman, Rita. 2000. *Towards New Ways of Terminology Description: The Sociocognitive-Approach.* Amsterdam/Philadelphia: John Benjamins Publishing Company.

Wüster, Eugen. 1979. *Einführung in Die Allgemeine Terminologielehre Und Terminologische Lexikographie.* 3rd ed. Würzbburg: Ergon.

Barbara Lewandowska-Tomaszczyk

Principle of Cluster Equivalence and Parallel Corpora

Abstract: The paper focuses on providing corpus-based evidence for the *semantic approximation* (Lewandowska-Tomaszczyk 2012) between the SL version and its corresponding TL version in terms of *meaning re-conceptualization* (Lewandowska-Tomaszczyk 2010) and what can be called *cluster*-for-*cluster* equivalence, basing on the data from monolingual corpora (BNC and National Corpus of Polish) and relevant parallel corpora. The concept of semantic *similarity* is first discussed, structured around a multi-peaked radial category space with a number of *tertia comparationis*, or points of reference, which serve as similarity conditioning parameters. The translator can *manipulate* the distance – either by shortening or by lengthening it, depending on both external pragmatic and linguistic conditions as well as internal, individual preferences, not infrequently revealing particular translator's personal identity features. Examples are drawn from the concordance materials referring to a number of *Event Clusters* in English and Polish, inter alia *Emotion Events* (Lewandowska-Tomaszczyk and Wilson 2013), as well as from more constrained official EU reports, with collocational profiles of relevant items, which reveal high interconnectivity links between terms and structures within the same *meaning clusters*, forming cross-language categories of cluster-equivalence types. Relevance and possible applications of the results of the present study to translator education are discussed in the concluding part.

Keywords: cluster equivalence, collocational profile, construal, meaning approximation, parallel corpora, re-conceptualization, translation.

1. Translation as Re-Conceptualization

The product of translation is a result of a number of processes. As argued in Lewandowska-Tomaszczyk (2010), it comes into being through a number of cycles of *re-conceptualization* of the Source Language message. The translator's and eventually the TL receivers' *construal* of a scene (Langacker 1987), structured by relevant language convention, cultures and contexts, individual dispositions and preferences, contribute to a modified scene construal as identified in the target language text. Any syntactic variant of the TL text, which the translator considers a possible equivalent, brings about *a new re-conceptualization cycle*, responsible for particular *imagery effects*.

2. Communication Relies on Approximate (and Not Identical) Meaning Sharing

Semantic approximation (Lewandowska-Tomaszczyk 2012) does not take place exclusively between a Source Language and a corresponding Target Language version. Communication generally involves/relies on similar and not identical meanings in each interaction. Due to the partially indeterminate nature of meanings, communication is approximative and language users accommodate the meanings to one another in terms of a *multi-directional accommodation.*

On the basis of data from monolingual corpora (BNC and National Corpus of Polish) and relevant parallel corpora, used with corpus tools involving a collocation generator (pelcra.pl/hask_pl, Pęzik 2014) and an aligned concordancer (http://clarin.pelcra.pl/Paralela/#), it will be argued here is that communication takes place in terms of what can be called meaning *cluster-for-cluster equivalence*. This process can clearly be observed in juxtaposing a SL and TL text.

3. Typology of Communication

Communication among interactants may involve any of a number of inter-semantic correspondences:

(i) loose communication, Gestalt in nature,
(ii) aligned communication, typical of LSP texts, in which interactants aim at more exact correspondences of the content they convey,
(iii) particularized communication, which assumes a more thorough explanatory strategy to achieve communicative success.

Each of these types, above all loose, Gestalt communication, can be practiced by providing so-called more-or-less or else *almost* meanings.

3.1 More-or-Less solutions – Epistemological Vagueness

The term *more-or-less solutions* is used by mathematicians to mean 'an approximation of an exact solution', while an *almost solution* appears in such cases when no exact solution exists for a given equation (Sossinsky 1986). Adopting this terminology to linguistics, we can propose that some meanings are used in interaction as approximative more-or-less types. It takes place in situations in which there exist necessary/sufficient criteria of a given meaning but, due to some social, psychological, linguistic, or contextual, emergent reasons, they are used as approximate entities. We can name this state of affairs *epistemological vagueness* of the linguistic unit, as e.g. in examples 1–4 below, discussed before (Lewandowska-Tomaszczyk, Maastricht/Lodz Duo Colloquia, 2005, 2010).

(1)

TERMS: *general practitioner/general physician* (Svartvik & Quirk 1980)

- a 626 general science, eh, general medicine now I thought was the non-elitist –
- A oh NO, it's very ELITIST
- a I thought it was the specialists who are elitists
- A but general medicine is a SPECIALITY… I mean. m ….general MEDICINE. Eh people don't . it's very INTERESTING, everybody KNOWS what a general SURGEON is – I mean everybody knows what em – a paediatrician is or a GYNAECOLOGIST..but it's very INTERESTING people don't REALLY know what a general . PHYSICIAN is . it's a PHYSICIAN – it's dealing with TREATING people. who's got DISEASE who don't need SURGERY – and that includes –
- B it's quite different from a general PRACTITIONER
- A oh YEAH . m . a general PRACTITIONER will refer patients to – ehm a general PHYSICIAN – a general physician well – uses DRUGS . I mean that's his main . you know he doesn't CUT . he uses DRUGS. And he'll treat – he'll treat DISASEASES – such as – INITIALLY a duodenal ULCER . 656 ehm – cardiac FAILURE

3.2 *Almost* Meanings – Ontological Vagueness

Almost meanings are rooted in the fact that the exact, crisp, meaning of some concepts defining an entity, process, etc. does not exist as is typically the case with so-called vague meanings as e.g., *aesthetic* or *good* below:

(2) *aesthetic*

- There's a particular way you have to make the stroke for it to look good. An aesthetic thing has a certain set, a certain character, which I can't define. Because it couldn't be defined made me think there was nothing to it. But I learned from that experience that there is something to it – and it's a fascination I've had for art ever since.

(3) *good* as contrasted with *very good* and *average*
723 WELL – – I think there's no point in DOING something – . I think well I'm at the stage NOW where I'm trying to ASSESS what . what are my CAPABILITIES – -AND [ehm] I COULD do SURGERY – – . I would not be good at I'm not to I may be being YOU know . AVERAGE – – using GOOD to be ABOVE average – – using GOOD to be ABOVE average – well that's NOT quite true good is AVERAGE ISN'T it . but I wouldn't be VERY good

3.3 Parallel (More) Aligned (Typically Domain-Specific)

Parallel or, in other words, *aligned* meanings are typically used in a domain-specific communication type in specialist varieties of language. Parallel meanings are applied in monolingual specialist contexts, e.g., the concept of *notary public* in American English will be aligned in the circles of US specialists in law as well as will be shared, to a certain extent, by general public there. However, when used in translation contexts, it may invoke a *false friend*, e.g., in the form of Polish *notariusz*, the term which is applied to an educated lawyer, dealing with contract law.

To provide an aligned AmE > Pol term, one resorts to a *particularization* communication type.

3.4 *Particulate*, Fine-Grained, Explanatory Communication

Particulate or in other words *explanatory*, communication can be carried out by resorting to two types:

Depth particularization – in which one or more interactants provide a description or definition of an item by uncovering *deeper* semantic layers of particular meaning components in an original context (e.g. LSP or culture-specific items.

Width particularization – is identified in such contexts in which the original meaning is compared or contrasted with other senses (i.e. by using figurative language, or categorization hyper-/hyponymic, synonymic or antonymic relations) and *new* conceptual links created embrace wider cognitive areas:

(4) *wok*

- A wok
- b 1297 I [ha] overheard a man in Barkers today' asking for a wok – and – I apparently was the only other person there who knew what a wok was c- (. laughs)
- l…
- la 1299 what is a wok
- l b a wok is a [eh] one of those big
- l C FRYING-PAN
- lb Chinese frying-pans with a rounded bottom you know that they swizzle things around in
- l a 1302 oh I see . oh yes

Particularization, or *precisation* can be either self- or other-party stimulated:

(5)

– *this shows different sides of the matter or rather shows it in different light*

(6)

A: *He came in* B: *or rather slipped in*

4. Meaning Clusters

It is proposed in the present work that *meaning clusters* identified in various linguistic materials are mental areas structured around *similar content. Similarity* (Lewandowska-Tomaszczyk (2012:1) is determined by a multi-peaked radial category space with a number of *tertia comparationis*, or points of reference, which serve as similarity conditioning parameters. It is argued (cf. also Gärdenfors 2000) that, conceptually, similarity is a mapping of physical distance on a cline between the Speaker's and Addressee's conceptual spaces, containing objects, relations and events.

The translator can *manipulate* the distance – either by shortening or by lengthening it, depending on both external pragmatic and linguistic conditions as well as internal, individual preferences, not infrequently revealing particular translator's personal identity features.

4.1 Meaning Clusters Cross-Linguistically

As discussed in Sections 1 and 2 meanings are approximate both in monolingual contexts and in translation. One manifestation of approximation is so-called *displacement of senses* between languages (Lewandowska-Tomaszczyk 1996), as exemplified by the English form *go a*nd its various displaced correspondences in Polish:

(7)
Displacement of senses (Lewandowska-Tomaszczyk 1996)
Eng. *go (to school)* [Pol. iść/chodzić—
[Eng. *walk* –[Pol. spacerować

Eng. *go*—[

Eng. *go (by bus)* [Pol. jechać/jeździć—

[Eng. *drive (a car)* –

[Pol. jechać (kierować) (samochodem) / prowadzić (samochód)

[Eng. *ride (a horse, a bicycle)* –

[Pol. jechać na (koniu, rowerze)

4.2 Resemblance

The relationship between *go* and other English meanings and Polish cluster equivalents is that of semantic *resemblance*. Semantic resemblance can be established in terms of a number of shared features, i.e.,

> *shared Qualitative features* [phonetic, morphological, syntactic, semantic (shapes, topology, function, etc.), pragmatic]

and

> *shared Quantitative features* [near sets], i.e., the number of object feature values in common.

4.3.1 Allowable modulation & practical substitutions: re-conceptualization types

Cluster members are not identical, they show (degrees) of resemblance between one another. There are a number of properties that can be modulated by practical inter-substitution strategies, which can be contextually constrained but not fully predictable a priori. Below is a list of allowable substitutions, which invariably lead to smaller or larger reconceptualization of senses but which assume (the possession of) different degrees of resemblance between the input and target conceptualizations:

(8)

SL CONSTRUAL → TL Construal
PERSPECTIVE 1→ PERSPECTIVE 2
EVENT *figurative* → EVENT *literal*
SYNTACTIC Pressure *(Syntactic Selections) [e.g. case marking, for-to S, collocations]*
OBJECT 1 → OBJECT 2
Granularity/Schematicity *[addition/deletion of meaning i.e.,]*
Prototypical category member →Peripheral category member
(near) Synonyms
(near) Equivalents
Word → Definition
Word → Examples (list)
Prototypical category member →Peripheral category member

4.3.1 Sufficiently similar meanings

In discourse, sufficiently similar meanings are tolerated for practical reasons – more-or-less identical effects.

Similarity measures are based on the resemblance criteria as in the following. Practically substitutable lexical forms:

(9)
(i) *We're having/planning a sunny weather for tomorrow*
(ii) *A wok is you know this kind of thing, a frying pan, you sizzle things in*
(iii) *fajny no to taki trochę głupi no znaczy głupi taki. no głupawy trochę ten film* '[lit. all right, well, a bit silly, that means stupid, one that is stupifying a bit, this film'

4.4 Tolerance Space

Meanings, as proposed before (Lewandowska-Tomaszczyk 2012) must be networks, dynamically activated within a certain tolerance space, which are dynamically construed up to (context-specific) tolerance threshold, beyond which a miscommunication or a communicative boycott occurs. Verbal signals of these communicative problems are, for instance, requests for repetition *I beg your pardon?* or *What did you say?*

4.5 Constraints on Modulation – The Tolerance Threshold

As proposed in Lewandowska-Tomaszczyk (2010), the boundaries of meaning modulation are limited by the resemblance of particular linguistic signs used in communication, which is culture-, context- and speaker-specific. None of these variables can be predicted or determined outside of context, although, as proposed by Gärdenfors (2000) the original linguistic sign is, to a large extent, a determinant of the *width of the possible tolerance spaces with regard to particular attribute values.*

4.6 Cluster Equivalence

Although meanings are their semantic spaces are not fully predictable outside of context, they retain their core, prototypical senses, which can serve as a point of reference to compare degrees of similarity with other concepts. Sufficiently similar concepts can be predicted to belong to the same *cluster*. This membership, as is always the case with categorization, is dynamic and subject to modulation.

It is argued in the present study that *translation* activates the areas of *cluster spaces* in SL and TL and the translator resorts to them and applies cluster members of TL as equivalents of a form/meaning in SL.

5. Example Materials and Methods

Some parallel Polish-to-English corpus data is presented in the paper to support the claim that a translated text involves firstly equivalent structures from the core as well as successively more and more peripheral areas of the SL-TL similarity space. Examples are drawn from the concordance materials, both general language, literature and LSP, some of them referring to *Event clusters* in English and Polish, inter alia *Emotion Events* (Lewandowska-Tomaszczyk and Wilson 2013). The results reveal high interconnectivity links between terms and structures within the same cluster. It is eventually hypothesized that the translator is limited by an *approximation threshold*, which confines the area of *permissible* as opposed to a cline of *risky* TL for SL solutions.

In this part of the study examples of the analysis of the concordance materials in English and Polish will be presented, accompanied by:

collocational profiles of relevant items
construal (qualitative analysis)
questionnaire-based methodology.

The data used in this section are generated from monolingual national corpora (BNC and National Corpus of Polish), parallel (Polish-to-English & English-to-Polish) corpora and the corpus tools used are collocation generator (pelcra.pl/hask_pl) and aligned concordancer (http://clarin.pelcra.pl/Paralela/#) (Pęzik 2014).

6. Emotion Clusters

6.1 Language- and Culture- Specific Status of All Emotion Terms

Emotion studies conducted by Lewandowska-Tomaszczyk and Wilson (2011, 2013, 2014) reveal that not only social, self-conscious emotions but also such basic human emotions as fear, love or disgust are shaped by the language and culture the experiencer is brought up in. There are both differences in emotion perception, positive and negative evaluation and control, e.g. in Asian cultures pride is less valued than in American culture, while control over fear is more intense in British English than in Polish culture as visualized in the graph below:

Figure 1: Means of Pol. starch [S] 'fear' vs. BEng. fear [F] on the Potency-Control Dimension (Lewandowska-Tomaszczyk & Wilson 2013).

LOW POTENCY-----------HIGH POTENCY CONTROL

6.2 Gestalt Meaning Approximation in Translation

Lewandowska-Tomaszczyk (2012) presents the following results of a comparison of emotion terms in a Polish contemporary romantic novel and its English translated version. The cluster of words in the Polish *strach* 'fear' domain considerably outnumbers the set of its English equivalents as used in the translation:

(10)

Pol. original *S@motność w sieci* > Eng. translation *Loneliness on the net*

Polish original *strach* cluster

Strach* 'fear'	5	
Lęk* 'anxiety'	23	
Niepok* 'uneasi*'		29
Przestra* 'to fear (inchoative)'	10	
Obaw* 'fear/worry'		5
Bać 'to be afraid infinitive'		2
Boj* 'afraid 1person Sg/Pl, 3 person Pl'		5
Boi* 'afraid 2 person Sg/Pl, 3 person Sg'		6
Przeraż* 'terror'		14
TOTAL: 106		

(11)

English translation *fear* cluster

Fear* (noun and Verb)	38	
Afraid	35	
Anxiet*		16
Terror*		6

Terrified* 6
Uneas* 0
TOTAL: 101

A closer observation of the equivalence patters between the two languages reveals additional properties of the translation process, conforming to the *principle of Cluster Equivalence* defended here.

(12)
Examples
Polish to English

strach 'fear' took him > terror seized him	Więc wyszedł pośpiesznie na majdan, bo go w tej izbie strach brał.	He hurried to the square, for terror seized him in that room.
skoro niepokój stał się 6 powszechnym. Lit. 'un+peace'; anxiety	since the alarm had become universal	

English to Polish

23	Zajęty był fabrykowaniem piorunów w kopalni i zdradzał okropny strach	engaged in the manufacture of thunderbolts in a mine, and displaying great cowardice when his gigantic master came home (very hoarse) to dinner.

In the above examples, which represent a number of possible equivalence patterns identified in this and other texts the following equivalents are identified:

(13)
Strach go złapał 'fear caught him' > Terror seized him
Niepokój stał się powszechnym 'anxiety became universal' > *The alarm had become universal.*
displaying great cowardice > *zdradzał okropny starch* 'betraying terrible fear'

Even so few examples contain a number of practically equivalent cluster terms:

(14)
Fear > terror, alarm, anxiety, cowardice
Catch > seize
Display > betray
Great > terrible

The next question refers to the presence of a limit, constraints with regard to the extent of semantic modulation of the lexical forms that would plausibly be considered equivalent in translation.

6.3 Emotion Models: Tolerance Measures

The comparison between conceptual systems of Polish and English and the meanings SL and TL users communicate using their linguistic systems reveal *different ontologies of objects and events* the speakers develop and apply in interaction. In the emotion systems stronger links are uncovered between English *fear* and *sadness* clusters than in Polish, while Polish *strach* *'fear'* is indicated as closer to *złość/gniew* 'anger' cluster than observed in English.

Comparisons of collocational patterns across large corpora show more frequent collocations between Polish *fear* and concepts such as *sowiecki* 'Soviet', *niemiecki* 'German', *zachodni* 'Western', *wojna* 'war' than in English, which, as analysed in the context of respective concordances, indicate causes.

Communication thus establishes certain *tolerance measures* for meaning equivalence, primarily for prototypical sets & their values in a context (culture, situation) and for prototypical Event Scenarios. When used in new contexts, tolerance measures are first inherited from the prototypes as these new concepts can be generalized to *approximate* concepts based on tolerance measures.

6.4 Quantitative Criteria of Re-Conceptualization. Collocation Distribution

The quantitative criteria of meaning re-conceptualization (Lewandowska-Tomaszczyk 2010) are applied when, inter alia, collocational strings are compared for their textual distribution as e.g. for the Nouns *disgust* and *repulsion* in English and two of their possible Polish cluster equivalents *obrzydzenie* and *wstręt* in the BNC and the National Corpus of Polish respectively. The quantitative distributional criteria reveal additional semantic specificity of the items compared.

(15)
light disgust 'lekkie obrzydzenie' (14 occurrences) ?
light repulsion 'lekki wstręt'- not reported
vs. *deep repulsion* 'głęboki wstręt' (6)

The higher emotion arousal for *repulsion* vs. *disgust*, corresponds to Pol. *wstręt* – *obrzydzenie* distinction:

(16)
disgusting display (4)
repulsive force (14) (ambiguous)
vs non-reported *disgusting force* and *repulsive display.*

6.5 Conclusion

In effect of the analysis a few conclusions can be drawn so far. What is observed in the process and product of translation are the following properties:

(17)
- *cluster-for-cluster mapping*
- *higher schematization* of the Target as contrasted with the Source version,
- *Part-of-Speech re-categorization* (e.g. Noun – Verb correspondences: Eng. *disgust, aversion, nausea, distaste, horror, despise, to loathe, to shrink (from something), dirt, reluctance*, translated as Pol. *wstręt* 'repulsion', *brzydzić się* 'to loathe').

7. Meaning Clusters in LSP

The principle of *Cluster equivalence* can also be observed in LSP translation of terminology in restricted domains. Below the Polish term *zgoda* 'agreement' was identified in the texts of Polish-to-English administrative documents (776 instances identified in 4,798,309 segments of English – Polish parallel corpora):

(18)

English
consent
consensus
consent
authorization
concord
agreement
unanimity
assent
approval
acceptance

Polish *zgoda*

acquiescence
qualification
granting
designation
accreditation
licence
suport for
allowing
reconciliation
permission
permit

A wider range of the cluster area is identified for the same term in the language of EU press releases:

(19)
UE press releases

by decision [of the Commission]

[our] 'yes'

this cannot be refused

[political] go-ahead for

giving their backing

voting for

[veto] may be overridden by the majority

To investigate even further areas of the cluster English – Polish materials from spoken discourse were consulted:

(20)
Spoken discourse

Zgoda, powiedziałam		**Well,** I said
Na równość **zgoda**		Equality, **yes**!
Zgoda została zawartaa		They were **friends again**
Zgoda		**Very well**
Niech będzie **zgoda**		Let there be **peace**!
Zgoda między ludźmi		**Goodwill** among Flesh an' Blood
Zgoda, barankowie, **zgoda**!		**Harmony**, lambs, **harmony**!
	{	**That's what** we'll do
		That's right
Zgoda		**That's all right**
		So that all's settled
		Well then
No to **zgoda**		We **don't dispute** that

In the English-to-Polish translation texts, the cluster equivalence areas grew larger and covered terms from neighboring concepts:

(21)
English>Polish clusters *consensus*
1572 from 4,798,309 segments.

- porozumienie
- konsensus
- consensus
- konsens
- **zgoda (5)**
- powszechna/zgodna opinia, powszechne odczucie
- większość (głosów),
- jednomyślność, jednolita opinia
- zgodność, kompromis, poparcie, wsparcie
- ostateczna wersja, wspólna decyzja

8. Cluster Equivalence

The principle of *Cluster Equivalence* is a fact in translation practice. The area of a tolerance relation on more complex structures can be defined on particular domain elements in the following order, originating in Gärdenfors (2000) and elaborated on and extended here to cover cases of *Extended Equivalence*, which involves areas of presupposition, causality, and a number of implicational clues, and *Emergent Equivalence*, which is dynamically set up and often acts as a 'nonce' formation in the text.

(22)

Trivial tolerance spaces

- identifying equal elements and distinguishing elements different

Non-trivial tolerance spaces

- objects that most FULLY satisfy the similarity conditions [natural category members]: cluster members

Extended tolerance spaces

- objects that MIGHT satisfy the conditions: causes, presuppositions, results,
- objects are NOT LIKELY, but NOT IMPOSSIBLE to satisfy the conditions of meaning approximation

Emergent tolerance spaces

- unconventional, dynamically constructed Equivalence space between objects which fall outside conventional similarity/resemblance patterns

Some of the equivalent pairs discussed in the present study exemplify the categorization presented in (22) above.

(23)

- **Trivial tolerance**
  - *strach* – fear
- **Non-trivial CLUSTER tolerance**
  - *strach* – anxiety, terror, horror
- **Extended tolerance (presuppositional, causal, implicational):**
  - *strach* - cowardice
  - [stereotypical – more universal] *strach* – death, crime
  - [social] *strach* – Nazi, God
- **Emergent tolerance**
  - [individual] *strach* –dogs

9. Note on Translator Education

The role of the principle of *Cluster Equivalence* for translation training cannot be underestimated. Relevance and possible applications of the results of the present study to translator education can be considered a point of departure for the students' *semantic awareness* raising in contrasting the source and target languages. Batteries of creative tasks developed on the basis of translation data which are generated from parallel corpora and confronted with large monolingual corpus data in SL and TL are likely to become a source of new insights at translation classes.

References

Gärdenfors, Peter. 2000. *Conceptual Spaces – The Geometry of Thought.* Cambridge, Mass.: The MIT Press. A Bradford Book.

Langacker, R.W. 1987. *Foundations of Cognitive Grammar,* Vol. 1. Stanford University Press.

Lewandowska-Tomaszczyk, B. 2010. "Re-conceptualization and the emergence of discourse meaning as a theory of translation." In: B. Lewandowska-Tomaszczyk and M. Thelen *Meaning in Translation.* Peter Lang. 105–148.

Lewandowska-Tomaszczyk, B. 2012. "Approximative spaces and the tolerance threshold in communication." *International Journal of Cognitive Linguistics,* Volume 2, number 2. Nova Science publishers, Inc.

Lewandowska-Tomaszczyk, B. and P. Wilson. 2013. "English 'Fear' and Polish 'Strach' in Contrast: GRID Approach and Cognitive Corpus Linguistic Methodology." *Components of Emotional Meaning.* Oxford University Press. 425–436.

Lewandowska-Tomaszczyk, B. and P. Wilson. 2014. "Self-Conscious Emotions in Collectivistic and Individualistic Cultures: A Contrastive Linguistic Perspective." In: J. Romero-Trillo (ed.), *Yearbook of Corpus Linguistics and Pragmatics 2014: New Empirical and Theoretical Paradigms*, Yearbook of Corpus Linguistics and Pragmatics 2,© Springer International Publishing Switzerland. 123–149.

Pęzik, P. 2014. "Spokes – a search and exploration service for conversational corpus data." http://pelcra.pl/docs/lib/exe/fetch.php?media=spokes_sub_2.pdf

Sossinsky, A. B. 1986. "Tolerance space theory and some applications. *Acta Applicandae Mathematica.*" Volume 5, Issue 2. 137–167.

Svartvik, J. and R. Quirk. 1980. *A Corpus of English Conversation*. Lund : CWK Geerlup.

British National Corpus

National Corpus of Polish nkjp.pl

Parallel English-to-Polish and Polish-to-English Corpora, CLARIN Project, University of Lodz.

Munzhedzi James Mafela

Marking Plural Forms in Tshivenḓa and the Study of Translation and Mass Nouns

Abstract: Tshivenḓa, one of the indigenous African languages of South Africa, is characterised by noun classes. Among others, the function of noun classes is to mark the singular and plural forms of nouns. African languages use the prefix to mark the singular and plural forms. However, not all noun classes reflect the singular and plural forms in Tshivenḓa because some represent mass nouns. As a result, translating mass nouns from languages such as English into Tshivenḓa has recently become a problem. Translators add the prefix to mass nouns to mark the plural form, which in turn distorts the meaning of words. This paper seeks to demonstrate to translators and the public that Tshivenḓa mass nouns do not have plural forms. Examples from Tshivenḓa will be analysed to illustrate this argument.

Keywords: African languages, curriculum, Tshivenḓa, mass nouns, noun class, neologism, prefix, translator training, morphology, grammar.

1. Introduction

Tshivenḓa, like other indigenous South African languages, is characterised by noun classes that are ordered in pairs. The main function of these noun classes is in fact to distinguish singular from plural forms. Unlike languages such as English, which mark the plural forms by making use of infixes and suffixes; indigenous African languages use prefixes to mark both the singular and the plural forms of nouns. However, the regular rule that forms plural and singular nouns does not apply to non-countable nouns. Newman (1990) observes that plural formations are denoted differently across languages of the world. It is therefore not surprising to find that the marking of singular and plural forms differs in English and in Tshivenḓa. However, not all noun classes have singular and plural prefixes in Tshivenḓa. Mass nouns do not use prefixes to mark the singular or plural form, as they have no plural form.

Translating countable nouns from languages such as English into Tshivenḓa is not complicated. However, translating these nouns from English, for example, into African languages such as Tshivenḓa has recently become more difficult because some translators fail to understand that these are non-countable nouns. The result is that when they translate such nouns translators often add the prefix to indicate a plural form. Even when the table of Tshivenḓa noun classes does not provide for a plural form of the mass noun, some language users persist in adding the prefix to indicate this. For instance, a word such as *vhutshilo* (life) is a mass noun. *Vhutshilo* has no plural form in Tshivenḓa, while in English *life* may take the plural form *lives*. When translating from English into Tshivenḓa, some translators tend to replace the *vhu-* in *vhutshilo* (life) with *ma-* to denote the plural form *matshilo* (lives). This suggests that *vhu-* is the singular form, while it is not. There is no such noun as *matshilo* in Tshivenḓa. *Vhutshilo* is non-countable, hence it is a mass noun. The addition of prefixes to mark the plurality of mass nouns when translating into Tshivenḓa distorts the meaning of these words as they are not intended to be used in the plural. Translators who attribute plural forms to mass nouns have been influenced by spoken Tshivenḓa, which imitates the English forms of words. Such imitation of English corrupts the standard Tshivenḓa in this regard.

This inability among some Vhavenḓa translators to translate mass nouns accurately has arisen partly because the school curriculum, and even those of institutions of higher learning, does not emphasise the study of noun classes in the African languages. Plural formation in these languages has not been subject to comprehensive investigation. At the same time, translators seem to lack the necessary background in Tshivenḓa grammar; it may be that their training has been inadequate. This paper seeks to demonstrate that some Tshivenḓa mass nouns are single classes and do not have plural forms. As Maho (1999:3) notes: "Some noun classes occur in several pairings, while others do not pair at all; the latter concern mainly the non-countable, such as mass nouns and infinitives. Non-paired classes are usually referred to as 'single classes'". Tshivenḓa examples will be analysed to illustrate this argument.

2. Definition of Terms

Most languages of the world differentiate between nouns and other categories of words. Nouns are words used to identify entities, places, things or concepts. According to Ziervogel, Wentzel and Makuya (1981), the noun in African languages has a distinctive structure. The most common method of forming the singular and plural forms of nouns in African languages is by adding a prefix to a stem. These authors assert that:

> It consists of a stem to which a prefix is added. This prefix determines the noun class to which a noun belongs. The most important function of the class prefix, as it is generally called, however, lies in the fact that it is used for the deduction of the concords by means of which the noun is brought into concordial agreement with the remaining parts of the sentence (1981:12).

This assertion is endorsed by Poulos (1990), who observes that the noun in Tshivenḓa consists of two parts, namely a noun prefix and a noun stem. As indicated above, the prefix denotes the singular or the plural form. Fromkin and Rodman (1998) remark that prefixing is widespread in the languages of the world. Different prefixes are used to indicate singular and plural nouns (Maho, 1999:2–3).

There are different types of nouns, namely proper nouns, common nouns and abstract nouns. Fromkin and Rodman (1998:161) classify nouns further into two categories, namely, nouns that can be enumerated, count nouns, and those that cannot be enumerated, called mass nouns. Chierchia (2010:101) explains mass nouns as follows:

> A common way to put this is that mass nouns denote/refer to/are semantically associated with "substances" where the latter are to be thought as material aggregates that may be joined or split without changing their nature.

Barner and Snedeker (2003) argue that in many languages, a systematic distinction exists between count nouns and mass nouns. Mass nouns are nouns that refer to things that cannot be counted. They refer cumulatively to the sum of the parts of an entity. Whereas count nouns can occur in both singular and plural forms, mass nouns simply denote a set of ordinary individuals plus all the pluralities of such individuals (Chierchia, 1998:54).

3. Tshivenḓa Noun Classes

According to Ziervogel *et al.* (1987), every Tshivenḓa noun belongs to one specific class of nouns. These classes are numbered according to the system that is customarily used in the *comparative* study of the family of languages to which Tshivenḓa belongs (Poulos, 1990). Noun classes are classified according to their prefixes. Maho (1999) observes that noun classes in African languages are traditionally numbered according to a system originally devised by Willem Bleek (1851, 1869). Rijkhoff (2002) notes that whereas some languages have only two genders/classes, others may have more than a hundred. Following Poulos' (1990) classification we can identify about 21 noun classes in Tshivenḓa.

Class	Prefix	Example
1	*mu-*	*muthu* (person)
2	*vha-*	*vhathu* (persons)
1a	----	*makhadzi* (aunts)
2a	*vho-*	*vhomakhadzi* (aunts)
3	*mu-*	*muri* (tree)
4	*mi-*	*miri* (trees)
5	*ḽi-*	*ḽino* (tooth)
6	*ma-*	*mano* (teeth)
7	*tshi-*	*tshiṋoni* (bird)
8	*zwi-*	*zwiṋoni* (birds)
9	*n-*	*ndau* (lion)
10	*dzin-*	*dzindau* (lions)
11	*lu-*	*lufo* (wooden spoon)
14	*vhu-*	*vhutshilo* (life)
16	*fha-*	*fhasi* (down, below, on the ground)
17	*ku-*	*kuitele* (characteristic way of doing)
18	*mu-*	*murahu* (at the back)
20	*ku-*	*kutshila* (small tail)
21	*ḓi-*	*ḓanḓa* (big, clumsy hand)

It is clear from the noun classes tabulated above that there are nouns that are paired and those that are not. The first ten noun classes are paired; in each pair, the prefix of the first noun class denotes the singular form while the prefix of the second of the pair denotes the plural form. For example, *muthu* (person) is made up of the singular prefix *mu-* and the stem *-thu; vhathu* (persons) is made up of the plural prefix *vha-* and the stem *-thu.* The first ten noun classes, all contain countable nouns. Noun classes 11, 14, 16, 17, 18, 20 and 21 are not paired. Among them are those that have countable nouns, for example, noun class 20, *kutshila – zwitshila* (small tail – small tails), which uses the plural prefix of noun class 8, and noun class 11, *lufo – dzimpfo* (wooden spoon – wooden spoons), which uses the plural prefix of noun class 10. Then there are those that have non-countable nouns, for example, noun classes 14, 16, 17 and 18. Many mass nouns in Tshivenḓa occur in these classes because they are non-countable. Poulos (1990) observes that this class consists mainly of abstract nouns and a few concrete nouns. Abstract nouns are grammatically treated as mass nouns or non-countables (Maho, 1999:72). The examples given above demonstrate that in Tshivenḓa there are no plural forms for mass nouns.

In languages such as English, nouns such as *life* and *pain* can be used in the plural forms *lives* and *pains* respectively. This is not the case in Tshivenḓa, there are no plural forms of these words because they are mass nouns.

4. Translation of Mass Nouns in the vhu- class

As indicated above, some nouns in the *vhu-* class are countable while others are non-countable; the latter are known as mass nouns. In this section we demonstrate that mass nouns do not have different singular and plural forms. Therefore, when translating them, one should not attach prefixes that denote the plural form. The discussion will be illustrated by an analysis of the non-countable nouns *vhutshilo* (life), *vhutsi* (smoke), *vhuṭungu* (pain) and *vhusiku* (night).

In their dictionary, Wentzel and Muloiwa (1982:72) define *vhutshilo* as *life.* The definition indicates that this lexical entry does not have a plural form. They define *vhutshilo* as follows:

> **vhutshilo** (*geen mv* | *no pl*) lewe | life (Wentzel & Muloiwa, 1982:72)

Geen mv and *no pl* means that there is no plural of the word *vhutshilo.* However, there are translators who provide a plural form for this word. In instances where some Vhavenḓa priests or preachers preach the word of God in church, *vhutshilo* (life) is pronounced as *matshilo* (lives), by replacing the *vhu-* in *vhutshilo* with *ma-*, forming *matshilo.* In reality, there is no such word as *matshilo* in Tshivenḓa as it is not part of the Tshivenḓa lexicon. In fact, the word *matshilo* is meaningless in Tshivenḓa. It is believed that the use of the prefix *ma-* to form the plural *matshilo* is the result of the influence of English. The fact that English has a plural form for *life* leads those who are familiar with English to think that the same rule applies in Tshivenḓa. The English equivalent of *vhutshilo* is *life*; in Tshivenḓa, this word does not allow the formation of the plural form. In English, however, adding the suffix -s to *life* creates the plural noun *lives.* In addition to the fact that *matshilo* is meaningless in Tshivenḓa, those who use it as the plural of *vhutshilo* are mistaken in thinking that *vhutshilo* is a singular noun. *Vhutshilo* is neither singular nor plural, but a mass noun. The noun class *vhu-* does not denote the singular form. Translators should not make use of *matshilo* as a plural form of *vhutshilo* because it is not part of the Tshivenḓa lexicon. Notwithstanding the fact that lexicographers have indicated in dictionaries that the word *vhutshilo* does not have a plural form, current translators and ordinary speakers in their daily conversation, use *matshilo* as the plural form of *vhutshilo*. Masala (2013:1) states:

> U rina madzina ndi zwa ndeme kha **matshilo** a vhathu. Kanzhi madzina a hone a vha a tshi goḓa, u kaidza, u eletshedza, u ṭuṭuwedza na zwiṅwe zwinzhi zwine zwa kwama **matshilo** a vhathu ḓuvha na ḓuvha.

> Naming is important in people's **lives**. In many instances the names will be functioning as instruments of mocking, reprimanding, advising and so on, that affect people's daily **lives**.

In this extract, Masala provides the plural form of *vhutshilo* as *matshilo* which is highlighted in bold. This extract is taken from Masala's MA dissertation. This is to show that even students in institutions of higher learning are not aware that some mass nouns in Tshivenḓa do not have plural forms.

The same applies to *vhutsi* (smoke), which is occasionally given the plural form *mitsi*. As in the example above, *vhutsi* does not have a distinctive plural form. Wentzel and Muloiwa (1982:72) define *vhutsi* as follows:

> **vhutsi** (*geen mv* | *no pl*) rook | smoke

Again, lexicographers use *geen mv* and *no pl* to mean that there is no plural. In this case the noun class *vhu-* in *vhutsi* is replaced with the noun class *mi-* to form a plural *mitsi*. In English, likewise, the mass noun *smoke* does not have a plural form because it is non-countable. It is thus unclear why some Tshivenḓa speakers have created a plural form of *vhutsi*. Perhaps it is because some confuse noun classes 3 (*mu*) and 4 (*mi*) with noun class 14 (*vhu-*). For these speakers, *vhutsi* can be replaced by *mutsi*. They attach the prefix *mu-* to *-tsi* to create a singular form *mutsi*, and then the plural form *mitsi* is created by adding the prefix *mi-* to *-tsi*. However, Wentzel and Muloiwa (1982:78) provide the equivalent of *vhutsi* as *smoke*, and further indicate that the lexical entry does not have a plural form. At the same time, *mitsi* is indicated by Wentzel and Muloiwa (1982:78) as the plural form of *mutsi* (smoke) because *mutsi* and *mitsi* are used in other dialects of Tshivenḓa, which are not part of the standard language. The correct Tshivenḓa equivalent of *smoke* is *vhutsi*. Those who can translate the word *vhutsi* into Tshivenḓa with a coined plural form are not acquainted with standard Tshivenḓa. Unlike *matshilo* above, *mitsi* is in the Tshivenḓa vocabulary because it is a form used in Tshivenḓa dialects that are not standard; this is recorded in Wentzel and Muloiwa's (1982) dictionary.

One further example that is frequently used incorrectly is *vhusiku* (night). *Vhusiku* denotes both the singular and the plural meaning of this word. Wentzel and Muloiwa (1982) indicate the English equivalents of the lexical entry *vhusiku* as *at night, night,* and *nights*. They define *vhusiku* as follows:

vhusiku (*mv selfde* | *pl same*) snags, nag, nagte | at night, night, nights

Mv selfde and *pl same* means that the plural form is the same. These equivalents reveal that *vhusiku* represents both singular and plural meanings. Whereas in the first two examples, *vhutshilo* and *vhutsi* have no plural meaning, *vhusiku* differs because it represents both a singular and a plural meaning, as in phrases such as *last night* (*vhusiku ha mulovha*), and *two nights* (*vhusiku huvhili*). Those who can translate the second phrase incorrectly, will translate it as *masiku mavhili* (two nights). This is not correct. In reality, *vhusiku* in the first phrase has a singular meaning, whereas in the second phrase it has a plural meaning. In English the singular form is differentiated from the plural by affixing the suffix *-s* to the noun *night*. There is no such word as *masiku* in the Tshivenḓa vocabulary; the word *masiku* is meaningless and should not be used as a plural form of the word *vhusiku*.

Another interesting example occurs in the translation of the words *pain* and *pains* into Tshivenḓa. *Pain* can be translated as *vhuṱungu* in Tshivenḓa. However, according to Van Warmelo (1989), the word *vhuṱungu* has a number of equivalents, i.e. *poison*, *venom*, *physical pain*, *anguish*, and *sorrows*. We talk of *physical pains* and *sorrows* in English. However, *venom*, *poison*, and *anguish* do not have plural forms in this language. The same applies to Tshivenḓa; we cannot talk of singular and plural forms of the word *vhuṱungu*. The equivalent of both *pain* and *pains* in Tshivenḓa is *vhuṱungu*, not *maṱungu*. The English equivalent of *maṱungu* is *sorrows*, and not *pains*. Van Warmelo (1989:183) indicates the English equivalents of *maṱungu* as *pains, sorrows, tribulations* and further observes that *maṱungu* is the plural form of *vhuṱungu*. Hereunder is Van Warmelo's definition of *maṱungu:*

maṱungu, 6 (*pl. of vhuṱungu*) pains, sorrows, tribulations

The Tshivenḓa equivalents of *pain*, *poison*, *venom* and *anguish* cannot be *maṱungu* as none of these words have plural forms. Chiercia (1998:53) argues that mass nouns come out of the lexicon with plurality already built into them. This means that plurality is intrinsic to the word *vhuṱungu;* there is no need to create a plural form. *Pain* and *pains* are both translated as *vhuṱungu* in Tshivenḓa. Only *sorrows* and *tribulations* can be translated as *maṱungu*. Those who provide the equivalent of *pains* as *maṱungu* have been influenced by the English equivalents of these words. Besides the influence of other languages when marking plural forms of mass nouns, however, there are other factors involved, as discussed below. Thus the translation of English words such as *lives* and *pains* into Tshivenḓa can be difficult.

5. Discussion

As indicated in the preceding paragraphs, some mass nouns of the class noun *vhu-* do not have plural forms, partly because they are non-count nouns. However, there is a tendency among some translators to mark the plural forms of these mass nouns. Some of these invented plural forms render the words meaningless because the words do not actually exist in the Tshivenḓa lexicon. Where such words do exist in Tshivenḓa, they have different meanings to the ones they are intended, such as *vhuṱungu* and *maṱungu*. For instance, *vhuṱungu* means *pain, poison, venom*, whereas *maṱungu* means *sorrows*. *Pain* and *sorrows* have related but different meanings.

Translators and interpreters who mark the plural forms of mass nouns as discussed above have been influenced by, among others, the existence of plural forms in other languages such as English and by a lack of training in translation skills. South Africa is a multilingual society. The interaction between language groups plays a considerable role in promoting multilingualism. In such a situation, underdeveloped languages are influenced by developed ones such as English, in this case resulting in the formation of plural forms where none exist. It is possible to have plural forms for mass nouns in English. As a result, translators coin plural forms for equivalent mass nouns in indigenous African languages, such as Tshivenḓa. Although this type of neologism is used in standard speech, it is not accepted in the written standard Tshivenḓa.

Furthermore, many translators among the Vhavenḓa translate documents, not because they have the necessary translation skills, but because they happen to be Tshivenḓa speakers. A translator should have flair and feel for his own language (Newmark, 1995). Being a native speaker of a particular language does not necessarily mean that one is a translator. Without the necessary translation skills one will be unable to differentiate between the spoken and the standard language. The spoken language is influenced by processes in other languages, as indicated above.

This problem is exacerbated by the fact that the school curriculum does not pay much attention to the study of aspects such as phonetics, phonology and morphology in African languages. Very little is taught in the way of noun classes, including how they are created. The study of the morphology of noun classes would assist learners in differentiating between count nouns and non-count nouns and they would be able to form a deeper understanding of noun classes and their associated words. This should be emphasised both at school and tertiary levels.

6. Conclusion

This discussion has sketched the formation of African language nouns, Tshiveṋda nouns in particular, both singular and plural forms. The types of Tshiveṋda nouns, divided into count nouns and non-count nouns, were discussed. Many non-count nouns are mass nouns, which are characterised by the absence of plural forms. A challenge arises when the public and translators in particular mark plural forms of mass nouns, creating words that are in fact meaningless or not of the same meaning as the "singular" form. This problem should be addressed if high quality translations are to be produced. Language users, translators in particular, should refrain from copying language usage from other languages, especially when there are existing terms in their language. They should respect the language rules of the target language, particularly in the case of African languages. By so doing they will avoid creating plural forms where they are not necessary and coining meaningless words. Furthermore, translators should be better trained in the acquisition of translation skills. Translation skills should be applied professionally if we are to preserve the standard form of the language. Not everybody can become a translator. Newmark (1995:6–7) states:

> Whilst accepting that a few good translators (like a few good actors) are "naturals", I suggest that the practical demands on translators are so wide, and the subject still so wrapped up in pointless arguments about its feasibility, that it would benefit students of translation and would-be translators to follow a course based on a wide variety of texts and examples.

The Education Department should make a concerted effort to emphasise the teaching of phonetics, phonology and morphology in the school curriculum. This will help to raise learners' awareness of mass nouns and their meaning. They will then be in a better position to note that mass nouns in African languages, and Tshiveṋda in particular, do not have plural forms. As Newmark (1995:73) notes: "The basic-carrying element of language is its grammar. But since the grammar is expressed only in words, we have to get the words right." Sometimes a word has no plural form, as in the case of mass nouns.

References

Barner, D. & Snedeker, J. (2003), *The Use of Mass Nouns to Quantify Over Individuals*. Csjararchive.cogci.rpi.edu/proceedings/2003,pdfs/43.

Chierchia, C. (1998), *Plurality of Mass Nouns and the Notion of 'Semantic Parameter'*. scholar.harvard.edu/files/chierchia/files/1998.semanticparameter.pdf.

Chierchia, C. (2010), "Mass Nouns, Vagueness and Semantic Variation." *Synthese*. 174: 99–149.

Fromkin, V. & Rodman, R. (1998), *An Introduction to Language, Sixth edition.* Orlando: Harcourt Brace College Publishers.

Maho, J. (1999), *A Comparative Study of Bantu Noun Classes.* Gothenburg: Acta Universitatis Gotoburgensis.

Masala, M. *Tsenguluso nga ha Mishumo ya Madzina a mvelele kha Vhavenḓa.* Unpublished MA Dissertation. University of Limpopo. Turfloop.

Newman, P. (1990), *Nominal and Verbal Plurality in Chadic.* Dordrecht/Providence RI: Foris Publication.

Newmark, P. (1995), *A Textbook of Translation.* London: Phoenix ELT.

Poulos, G. (1990), *A Linguistic Analysis of Venda.* Pretoria: Via Afrika.

Rijkhoff, J. (2002), *The Noun Phrase.* Oxford: Oxford University Press.

Van Warmelo, N.J. (1989), *Venda Dictionary: Tshivenḓa – English.* Pretoria: Van Schaik.

Wentzel, P.J. (1982), *Improved Trilingual Dictionary: Venda – Afrikaans – English.* Pretoria: University of South Africa.

Ziervogel, D., Wentzel, P.J. & Makuya, T.N. (1987), *A Handbook of the Venda Language.* Pretoria: University of South Africa.

Lucia Salvato

Functionalism in Literary Translation. The Use of a Functionalist Approach in Translating Contemporary Swiss-German Poetry

Abstract: The paper explores the potential of a functionalist approach in *interlingual* translations of literary texts. The theoretical perspective is provided by Christiane Nord's introduction to the theory and methodology of translation-oriented ST analysis. The viewpoint refers to the concept of translation as an *action*, that is, as an intercultural communicative act with the ST functioning as an offer of information, and with which the translator must always reckon. The paper describes the main steps of the translation process as formulated in Nord's model, by illustrating the linguistic choices of the Italian translation of poems by Swiss-German writer Werner Lutz. Lutz's poetic language is examined through the presentation of the main translation problems as outlined by Nord. Focus is on the *intra-textual* factors of the ST, specifically on lexis (word creations) and (cultural) presuppositions, which thoroughly engage and challenge the Italian translator.

Keywords: German-Italian Translation; Swiss-German Poetry; Werner Lutz; Functionalist Approach; Christiane Nord; translation process; translation problems; word creations; word compounds; presuppositions.

1. Introduction

The paper focuses on a translating project concerning poems written by Swiss-German writer Werner Lutz (1930 –) and translated into Italian by the Author[1]. The translating project is highlighted using a functionalist approach that is considered useful for all types of *interlingual* translation and text typologies. The theoretical perspective is provided by Christiane Nord's introduction to the theory, methodology, and teaching of translation-oriented source-text (ST henceforth) analysis (Nord 1997, 1988/2005) derived from the *Skopos theory* introduced by Hans Vermeer and Katharina Reiss (1984). Functionalism will here be applied to the literary translation of Lutz's poems in line with the central pillar of functionalism (Nord

1 The Italian translations presented in the paper have been made by the Author of the article and will be published subsequently.

1988/2005, 10): what operates the translation process is not the ST as such, but the intended function or *skopos* of the target text (TT henceforth).

The reason at the basis of this attempt was indicated by Nord in an article on the importance of scientific approaches in literary translations (Nord 1991). According to Nord, the majority of translators of literary texts approach them as an art, that is, too instinctively and not enough with the mind ("zu wenig mit dem Kopf und zu viel 'aus dem Bauch'"; Nord 1991: 61). Consequently, their translations can present problems which derive from the use of intuition alone and the rejection of scientific approaches. Nord tries to demonstrate that for a satisfactory solution of translation problems, translators should use a methodical, scientific procedure that starts from the analysis of the ST features and plans the translation strategy through the interpretation of the translation *brief*, i.e. the *assignment* (cf. Nord 1997[a]). The aim of the paper is thus to show the main steps of Nord's approach used as a foundation that may assist in the evaluation of the Italian translation of Lutz's poems and the resolution of the resultant problems.

2. Theoretical Background

The *theoretical* starting point of Nord's approach is a pragmatic "action-oriented concept of textuality", according to which texts and translations are considered along with a functional communicative perspective. It follows that a *text* is an element of a communicative interaction which takes place in a communicative situation (cf. Nord 1988/2005, 13–17; Nord 1997, 22–23) and that a text *translation* is an action which makes it possible for a new text to fulfil certain functions for other participants in a new communicative situation (Nord 1988/2005, 257). Translating is hence "a purposeful activity" (1997), in which a functional TT is produced by maintaining a strict relationship with the ST and according to the translation *skopos*.

From a *methodological* viewpoint, in Nord's "looping model" translation is metaphorically seen as a circular process, whose starting point is the TT *brief* assigned by the *initiator*, who starts the process and determines its course (cf. Nord 1988/2005, 9–11). The process then develops through a *prospective* analysis of the TT-in-situation defined by the translation brief, and through a *retrospective* analysis of the ST-in-situation, which implies the analysis of both *extra-textual* and *intra-textual* factors. Moreover, the circular path contains a number of smaller circular movements ("loops") between ST and TT which help translators confirm or correct the solutions gained (cf. 2005, 36–39). Within the whole process, translators thus play a decisive role by making a progressive comparison between the result of the ST analysis and the result of the analysis of the TT *skopos*. The comparison allows them to decide whether, and in what respect, the ST should be adjusted to the TT situation by determining the procedures of adaptation, the intention, and the type of translation.

Based on strictly functionalist terms, Nord actually distinguishes between two translation types by differentiating between the function of the translation process and the function of the TT as the result of this process (cf. Nord 1997, 47–52). However, both types are more or less related to the traditional differentiation between the *source-oriented* and *target-oriented* translation, thus not appearing to be particularly innovative. The *documentary* type aims, in fact, at producing in the target language (TL henceforth) a kind of *document* of the communicative interaction in the ST by exposing its linguistic and stylistic features. On the other hand, the *instrumental* type aims at producing in the TL an *instrument* for a new communicative interaction between the source culture sender and the target culture audience, using the ST as a preceding "offer of information" (Nord 1997, 32).

3. Following the Main Steps

The following paragraphs describe the main steps of the translation process as outlined in Nord's model, by illustrating the Italian translation of Lutz's poems.

The first part of the translating activity is dedicated to the planning of the translation strategy. The first step consists of the analysis and interpretation of the TT purpose (*skopos*), which is "the prime principle determining any translation process" (Nord 1997, 27). The purpose is normally assigned within the *brief* by the initiator who provides as many detailed features as possible regarding the TT *profile* (*sender, intention, receiver, medium, place, time, motive, message, function*). In the case of Lutz's poems, the translation has followed the personal *intention* of the Author to translate Lutz's poems into Italian for the first time to raise the awareness of the poet and his poems, even in Italy. The intended *receiver* is the Italian public, whose German knowledge is not assumed but actually requested, being the *communicative function* directed to activate a sort of "intercultural co-operation" (Nord 1988/2005, 31). Among the four functions indicated by Nord (*referential, expressive, appellative, phatic,*; Nord 2001, 8), the Italian translation focuses on the *expressive* and *appellative* varieties. On the one hand, the translated poems intend to be a personal expression of the subjective attitude of the poet, of his feelings, and attitude towards things, phenomena, and realia. On the other hand, they appeal to the receivers' sensitivity in order to spark their interest in the German language and for the poet's linguistic and stylistic choices in comparison with their Italian translation.

The second part of the translation process is dedicated to the analysis of the ST, that is, its *extra-textual* and *intra-textual* factors. The first ones regard the communicative situation and the distinctive factors of the ST (*sender, intention, receiver, medium, place, time, motive, message, function*). The intra-textual factors regard the author and the linguistic and stylistic features of the original text (*subject matter, content, presuppositions, text-composition, non-verbal elements, lexis, syntax, supra-segmental features*). Lexis and presuppositions in particular will be considered in the following paragraphs.

4. Translation Problems

The transfer of the content from the ST to the target situation usually causes translation problems, whose classification can be "useful for structuring teaching and learning aims in the field of transfer competence" (Nord 1988/2005, 174). The classification is supposed to offer a guideline in dealing with the main aspects of translation and to distinguish the (subjective) translation difficulties from the (objective) translation problems. Nord classifies them into four different groups according to the extra-textual and intra-textual factors from which the main challenges arise (cf. Nord 1988/2005, 174–177).

The "pragmatic translation problems" (*Pragmatische Übersetzungsprobleme – PÜP*) regard extra-textual factors, such as the contrast between ST and TT receivers, medium, and function, and can be identified using the text-analytical model.

The "convention-related problems" (*Konvention Übersetzungsprobleme – KÜP*) are the result of the differences in culture-specific habits, norms, and conventions, which are often difficult to transfer from one language to another.

The "linguistic translation problems" (*Sprachliche Übersetzungsprobleme – SÜP*) regard structural differences between languages, especially in lexis and syntax. Their solution is strictly linked to the translator's awareness of their relationship to the text's factors.

The "text-specific translation problems" (*Textspezifische Übersetzungsprobleme – TÜP*) regard all special cases linked to a particular text. Word creations or figures of speech are hence due to the specific text in which they occur and consequently do not allow generalization.

4.1 A Focus on Lexis

Lutz's poems challenge Italian translators, provoking a great deal of linguistic and cultural effort. A first example is set by the many word compounds and word creations that the poet conceives in the same way as a painter would do with new pictures and images. A prototype can be seen in the titles of his anthologies. *Kussnester* (2009), *Farbengetuschel* (2004), *Treibgutzeilen* (2013), *Schattenhangschreiten* (2002) are a challenge especially for Italian and English translators who cannot easily find parallel linguistic constructions. *Kussnester*, for instance, is composed of two words (*das Nest*, *der Kuß*): it has been translated into English with a two-word phrase, *kissing nests* (Lutz 2013[b]) and in Italian it would correspond to a two- or three-word phrase, *Nidi bacianti*, *Nidi di baci*. The same happens with *Farbengetuschel* and *Treibgutzeilen*, which cannot be rendered with one-word compounds (Ital. *Mormorìo di colori*, *Versi alla deriva*; Engl. *Color whispering*, *Drifting verses*)[2].

However, even more challenging in Lutz's poems are the unusual three-word creations. A title like *Schattenhangschreiten* is composed of three lexemes (*der Schatten*, *der Hang*, *schreiten*) and is reworded with difficulty into Italian without the application of long phrases such as *L'incedere lungo il pendìo ombreggiato* (Engl. *Walking solemnly down the shaded slope*). Further challenging three-word creations are those compounds, such as the title *Zuckersalzwind* (2013[a]), which curb the potential of their cultural and linguistic implications to be easily conveyed into a foreign language. Translators can thus appeal to the aesthetic value of the ST and try to reproduce it in the TT. The following poem, for example, contains two word-creations, *herzwindzerzaust herzblattverwirrt*, that form a type of anaphor, the second being complementary to the first:

Möglich
dass Frühlingsregen beginnender
Verliebtheit gleicht
herzwindzerzaust
herzblattverwirrt
und oft im Fallen schon geknickt (Lutz 2006, 34)[3]

The parallelism of both terms derives from their complementary structure: lexical (three lexemes with two nouns and a verb, *Herz/Wind/zerzaust*; *Herz/Blatt/verwirrt*), syllabic (four syllables), morphological (*zer-zaus-t*, *ver-wirr-t*), and metric (two stressed and two unstressed syllables). The impossibility of finding a corresponding Italian compound causes mostly linguistic translation problems and can generate different solutions. One is to privilege the "compensation process"

2 In the absence of a specific reference to official translations, all verses and full poems reported in English or Italian are the result of translation by the Author.

3 Ital.: *Possibile / che la pioggia primaverile / assomigli all'innamoramento /* ***sconquassato dal vento del cuore / scompigliato come foglia d'amore*** */ e spesso nel cadere già spezzato* (All bold emphasis in the poems are by the Author).

(cf. Hervey and Higgins 1992, 248) by using a paraphrase. The Italian translation uses, for example, two verses (*sconquassato dal vento del cuore, scompigliato come foglia d'amore*; Engl. *upset by the heart's wind / ruffled like a love leaf*) that are characterized by phonetic expedients: the rhyme of the last two words (*cuore – amore*) and the rhythm resulting from the three accented words of both verses (*sconquassáto – vénto – cuóre; scompigliáto – fóglia – amóre*). The Italian version thus tries to phonetically compensate the impossible word-for-word translation by using elements that are parallel not only in the content (an upset love as a leaf, ruffled by the wind), but also in the form (the onomatopoetic word *sconquassato* with the repeated, unvoiced dental fricative [s], and the palatal lateral approximant [ʎ] in *foglia* and *scompigliato*).

Another example regards the first part of a poem, in which Lutz created three terms whose translation can create both semantic (*TÜP*) and linguistic difficulties (*SÜP*):

> *Nacht*
> *braun und warm von Tieren*
> ***Tropfentürme Brunnenwiegen***
> ***Gurgelgeister*** […] (Lutz 2004, 28)

In Switzerland, water springs are caught in cavities (*Quellmulden, Quelltöpfe*), where loud, unpleasant noises and other sounds are produced. Lutz must have been amazed by the singularity of such sounds and hence used onomatopoeic and semantically bizarre word creations to describe them linguistically. The impossibility of finding corresponding Italian word compounds drives the translator toward another compensation process by looking for corresponding onomatopoeic terms. The voiceless plosive alveolar [t] that characterizes both lexemes in the first German compound (***T**ropfen**t**urm*; *dropping towers*) can, for example, be rendered into Italian with the voiceless velar plosive [k] which is actually present twice in the plural Italian *simplex* (***c**as**c**ate*). The three-times occurring voiced alveolar nasal [n] in the second word compound (*Bru**nn**e**n**wiege**n***; *springs' cradles*) can be translated with a word that presents the long consonant [l:] (*cu**ll**e*). Lastly, the three-times occurring voiced velar plosive [g] in the third German word-compound (***G**ur**g**el**g**eister*; *throat's gargling*) makes it evidently an onomatopoeic sound which best reproduces the unpleasant noises heard in water spring cavities. This word has provoked in Italian the idea of a three-word phrase containing the same and three-times occurring voiced velar plosive (***g**ar**g**arismi della **g**ola*). The translation of the first part of the poem may therefore sound as follows:

Notte
bruna e calda di animali
cascate di gocce culle di sorgenti
gargarismi della gola [...]

4.2 A Focus on Presuppositions

A provoking challenge for translators is usually caused by the many presuppositions contained in original texts. Lutz's poems are not an exception and the many presuppositions hidden in them regard different cultural fields, such as Swiss customs, Italian, French, or Jewish culture, Christian faith, irony, as well as botany and entomology.

As Nord highlights by quoting Garner (1971), the notion of *presupposition* is rather complex because there are "several radically different concepts, all of which have been related to the word presupposition" (Nord 1988/2005: 105). What the German theoretician means by presupposition is neither the logical nor the philosophical notion[4]. In line with Schmidt (1976, 105), Nord refers to "pragmatic presuppositions" as "situational presuppositions", which comprise "all the information that the sender expects (= presupposes) to be part of the receiver's horizon". Focus is therefore on the sender, who "will only presuppose information which the receiver can be expected to be able to 'reconstruct'" (Nord 1988/2005, 106).

However, in Nord's "sender-oriented" concept of presupposition, the implicit part of the communication seems to remain at the level of the utterance without involving any deeper level of implication. The importance attributed to translators in the identification of presuppositions simply regards "the level of explicitness" that should be adjusted to the background knowledge of the intended TT audience using expansion or reduction procedures. As a result, for the right interpretation of the cultural implications contained in a text, this concept does not seem to be enough. Oswald Ducrot's notion (1991) involves, for example, even a deeper logical level of the *sous-entendus* which coincides with the condition of existence of the utterance (*l'implicite fondé sur l'énonciation*). For the French linguist, language involves an indefinite number of human interactions that also imply themes, topics, and subjects (such as feelings) that are somehow protected from a sort of "law of silence" (*loi du silence*, Ducrot 1991, 5). In addition, to convey such *implicit* information, the sender prefers to use some other way, which thus involves a deeper inference by the receiver, who also plays a decisive role in the identification of presuppositions.

4 Cf. Strawson (1950); Frege (1892).

Interesting presuppositions are present in the first part of a poem by Lutz in which the narrating voice wishes to experience three different extreme situations:

> *Müsste schön sein*
> ***so eine Schussfahrt auf einem Davoserschlitten***
> *den höchsten Berg hinunter*
> *müsste schön sein*
> ***aus Quellwasser einen „Premier cru" zu machen*** [...] [Lutz 2006, 45]

A first implication is contained in the desire to experience a ride "on a Davos sled" down the highest mountain. Sledding, sledging, or tobogganing is a well-known winter activity. However, the reference to Davos presupposes something more by associating the activity to the famous "Davos sledge" which is effectively the original amongst toboggans (the first official toboggan race was held in Davos in 1883).

The second implication is a mixture of French culture and Christian faith and is expressed through the wish to transform source water into a *Premier cru*. The French name refers to a vineyard of recognized quality and therefore to the French distinction of producing some of the best wines in the world. A *documentary* translation would maintain the original French name, while an *instrumental* one would maybe reword it into *Barolo* or *Brunello*. For the reference to the transformation of source water into wine, instead, the translator should infer the relationship to the Christian faith bound to Jesus' miracles. In particular, Jesus performed the first during a wedding at Cana in Galilee, where he transformed the water from six stone jars into "good wine" (John 2:1-12).

Further presuppositions can be grasped within a rather long poem dedicated to "Liliane" (Lutz 2004, 64), in which the poet thanks her for the many experiences they have lived through together. One of these experiences is conveyed in a verse (*für Stein an Stein im jüdischen Friedhof*; Engl. *for stone near stone in the Jewish cemetery*) which needs some reflection because of the hidden implication. The first part of the verse – *für Stein an Stein* – would imply the simple laying of stones, one near another in such a way as to create a pavement. In the second part of the verse – *im jüdischen Friedhof* – the stones may instead refer to the many gravestones that are put one near another in cemeteries. However, the reference to Jewish culture is a relevant attribute and must be examined closely. In this regard, the final color scene of the black and white film "Schindler's list" by Steven Spielberg (1993) is an illuminating example. Actual *Schindlerjuden* – the Polish-Jewish refugees saved by the German businessman, Schindler during the Holocaust by being employed in his factories – are accompanied by the actors who portrayed them in the film to the cemetery in Jerusalem and they place stones on Schindler's grave. Unlike Christians, Jews actually renounce floral decoration and prefer to place a small stone on the grave-headstone of their dead relatives and friends. The association of Jewish culture to the stones in Lutz's poem hence evokes an ancient custom of the Israelites in the desert. As they were not able to construct graves with marble slabs, they formed a small heap of stones to mark the place where their dead lay, in order to be able to find them again and to prevent the corpses from being dug out by wild animals.

4.3 A Focus on Irony

Irony is a mark of Lutz's candid way of looking at himself and at the features of human beings. A first example of this is contained in a poem, which is a naïve request to the Lord to receive one single hair on his head in order to be revered by his colleagues, with the proviso that the hair be "green":

Herr lass wachsen
ein einziges grünes Haar
auf meinem Haupt

dann werden ***Karl***
und seine Kollegen sagen
wir haben ihn unterschätzt
diesen Kerl [Lutz 2004, 31]

In line with Nord's model, it is worth focusing on the *KÜP* translation problem – here emphasized in bold – which regards a German masculine proper name. *Karl* is probably derived from the old Germanic form (ahd.) *karal* meaning "(free) man". It is known as the name that was historically given to seven emperors of the Holy Roman Empire, and that other famous bearers of this name include German philosophers as well as kings of Austria, Sweden, and Norway. For this reason, between the end of the 19th and the beginning of the 20th centuries the name was an extremely popular boys' name, whose popularity rose again at the end of the 20th century. In the case of a *documentary* translation type, the translator would therefore maintain the German historical effect by using *Karl*, or maybe by using an analogous historically relevant name such as Umberto or Vittorio Emanuele (corresponding to Italian kings in pre-war Italian history). An *instrumental* translation, instead, would maybe provide common names frequently used in general statements like *Luigi* or *Paolo*, which usually aim at leaving the reference unknown.

A quite difficult poem, which may provoke possible misunderstanding, is *Verehrte Ferne*. This poem challenges the translator in a thought-provoking way, because irony hides in an atmosphere of sweetness and reverence that can even distract the careless reader from a correct interpretation:

Verehrte Ferne

***ihre** luftige Meinung*
ist auch meine Meinung
*und so grüsse ich **sie***
in unvergänglicher Liebe
*über **Hügeleien***
*und **Tälereien** hinweg*

und bleibe für immer
***ihr** Werner Lutz* (Lutz 2009, 100).

The anti-poetic quality of Lutz's diction works here with irony on conventional images. The poem is a short leg-pull of formal letters with redundant expressions, that is, empty rhetorical phrases that mechanically recall repeated expressions with no real content. The short letter is addressed to a female figure, personified by a "revered distance" which – like a muse – could even remain as a sort of delicate thought worthy of a sweet tribute. In this case, the translation difficulties regard conventions, that is, the evident differences in culture-specific habits and norms.

There are two linguistic expedients in the poem through which Lutz expresses his irony. The first coincides with the pronouns and possessive adjectives that the poet uses in the polite form without capital letters as would be proper in German (*ihre* instead of *Ihre; sie* instead of *Sie; ihr* instead of *Ihr*). However, even the careful reader might misunderstand the poem by intending it as a somewhat eccentric, but possible, love poem to a person who could actually be far away.

The second expedient coincides with two bizarre terms, *Hügeleien* and *Tälereien*, which are nominal derivations created with the addition of the German suffix *-ei(en)* to the proper terms *Hügel* and *Täler* in standard German. Like most of the suffixes in many European languages, *-ei* adds meaning to the term and is almost stressed in the pronunciation. Moreover, the suffix *-ei(en)* usually signals that the action expressed in the nominal form is repeated, so that the term assumes a pejorative connotation by designating a negative situation or activity. The same occurs with derived substantives marked by the variance of the suffix, *-erei*. This is often used in verbal derivations like *Plauderei* (from the verb *plaudern, to chat*) and *Rennerei* (from the verb *rennen, to run*) which often express behavior or an event that is repeated or continues for some time and can hence be redundant or superfluous (cf. Weinrich 1993, 963–964).

For both linguistic expedients, the Italian translation should convey the same ironic effect. By avoiding the capital letter for personal pronouns, which should also be capitalized in formal epistles, the Italian translator is able to convey an ironic effect even to the TT reader[5]. The same occurs with the suffix *-ate* (*vallate*, *collinate*) which is the plural form of the feminine singular *-ata* that renders the pejorative effect of the German suffix *-ei* in *Hügeleien* and *Tälereien*[6]. On the other hand, the English translation does not render the bizarre linguistic choice of the original version, and prefers to use plain terms (*hills* and *valleys*) which therefore make the poem lose a part of the ironic feature of the original version[7].

5. Concluding Remarks

The focus of this paper was on a translating project concerning poems written by the Swiss-German writer Werner Lutz (1930 –) and translated into Italian for the first time by the Author. The translating project has been highlighted by Christiane Nord's functionalist approach, which provides a theoretical, pedagogical, and methodological introduction to translation-oriented ST analysis. The aim of the paper was to show the main steps of Nord's approach applied to the Italian literary translation of Lutz's poems in order to evaluate it and to help solve any resulting problems.

The starting point is a pragmatic concept of textuality, according to which both texts and translations are key elements of the communicative interaction which takes place between author and ST addressee, as well as between author and translator/interpreter, and between translator/interpreter and TT addressee. Texts and translations are thus communicative acts that need to be analyzed according to their focus, the communicative intention and function.

Nord's methodical procedure begins with the planning of the translation strategy through the interpretation of the translation brief and the study of the TT profile, and it goes further into the crucial analysis of the ST and of its *extra-* and *intra-textual* factors. The central paragraphs of the paper (4.1-4.3) have been therefore committed to those *intra-textual* factors – lexis and presuppositions – that are considered to be relevant both for the interpretation of Lutz's lyrics and for the solution of the most appealing translation problems. The translation of the numerous word creations and cultural presuppositions in Lutz's poems has been

---

5 *Illustrissima lontananza / il **suo** arioso pensiero / è anche il mio pensiero / perciò **la** saluto / colmo d'intramontabile amore / superando **vallate** / e **collinate** / per sempre / **suo** aff. mo Werner Lutz.*

6 Cf. Dardano (1996, 208–241) and Bisetto and Scalise (2008).

7 *Revered distance / **your** spacey opinion / is also my opinion / and I greet **you** / in everlasting love / over the **hills** / as far as the **valleys** / and remain always / **yours** / Werner Lutz* (Lutz 2013[b], 85).

evaluated through Nord's classification of the main translation problems, which aims to demonstrate that, for their satisfactory solution, translators should use a methodical scientific procedure.

However, after following Nord's theory through all its fundamental steps of the translation process, decisive questions inevitably arise. Is it convenient to follow all the steps of a scientific theory even for literary translations? Can translators of literary poems consider their translation only from a scientific point of view? Translators cannot forget that a rewording of a literary text also implies a creative, almost instinctive factor, other than the plain scientific implication of a translation science. In this regard, Nord's requirement of a scientific approach even in literary translations can hardly be considered as definitive. Literature – and lyrics in particular – is essentially an art, which, as such, needs to be approached not only with the mind but also with the intuitive capacities of a subjective person, the translator.

References

Bisetto A. and Scalise S. (2008). *La struttura delle parole.* Bologna: Il Mulino.

Dardano M. (1996). *Manualetto di linguistica italiana.* Bologna: Zanichelli.

Ducrot, O. (1991). *Dire et ne pas dire. Principes de sémantique linguistique.* Paris: Hermann.

Frege, G. (1892). "Über Sinn und Bedeutung", in *Zeitschrift für Philosophie und philosophische Kritik,* 100: 25–50.

Garner, J. (1971). "'Presupposition' in Philosophy and Linguistics". In Fillmore, C.J. & Langendolm, G.T. (eds.): *Studies in Linguistic Semantics,* New York.

Glück, H. (Hrsg) (2005). *Metzler Lexikon Sprache.* 3. Auflage. Metzler, Stuttgart & Weimar.

Hervey, S. and I. Higgins (1992). *Thinking translation.* London/New York: Routledge.

Lutz, W. (2002). *Schattenhangschreiten.* Frauenfeld: Waldgut Verlag.

Lutz, W. (2004). *Farbengetuschel.* Frauenfeld: Waldgut Verlag.

Lutz, W. (2006). *Bleistiftgespinste.* Frauenfeld: Waldgut Verlag.

Lutz, W. (2009). *Kussnester.* Frauenfeld: Waldgut Verlag.

Lutz, W. (2013). *Treibgutzeilen.* Frauenfeld: Waldgut Verlag.

Lutz, W. (2013a). *Zuckersalzwind.* Viganello: Alla Chiara Fonte.

Lutz, W. (2013b). *Kissing Nests.* Translated by M. Vincenz. New York: Spuyten Duyvil.

Nord, C. (1991). "Literarisches Übersetzen zwischen Kopf und Bauch". In E. Feldbusch, R. Pogarell und C. Weiß (eds.): *Neue Fragen der Linguistik. Akten des 25. Linguistischen Kolloquiums Paderborn 1990, Bd. 2: Innovation und Anwendung, 2 Bde.,* Tübingen: Niemeyer, 61–67.

Nord, C. (1997). *Translating as a Purposeful Activity. Functionalist Approaches Explained.* New York: Routledge.

Nord, C. (1997a). "Defining Translation Functions. The translation Brief as a Guideline for the Trainee Translator". In Ilha do Desterro (Brasilien), *Special Issue Translation Studies in Germany.* Ed. W. Lörscher, 2/39–53.

Nord, C. (2001). *Lernziel: Professionelles Übersetzen Spanisch-Deutsch.* Wilhelmsfeld: Egert Verlag.

Nord, C. Nord, C. (1988/2005). *Text Analysis in Translation. Theory, Methodology, and Didactic Application of a Model for Translation-Oriented Text Analysis.* New York: Rodopi.

Reiss, K. and H.J. Vermeer (1984). *Grundlegung einer allgemeinen Translationstheorie.* Tübingen: Niemeyer.

Schmidt, S.J. (1976). *Texttheorie.* München.

Strawson, P.F. (1950). "On Referring", in *Mind, New Series,* Vol. 59, No. 235, 320–344.

Rita Temmerman

Researching and Teaching the Translatability of Neologisms

> *Over the past decades, English has become the predominant language for the transfer of specialized knowledge, which conditions the creation of new lexical units in other codes. This conditioning can result in terminological dependency, a linguistic phenomenon arising from a unidirectional transfer of specialized denominations between two languages.* (Ibáñez Sánchez, Miguel and Joaquin García Palacios 2014:107).

Abstract: Nowadays, in most scientific domains, neology creation takes place first and foremost in English. In this contribution we discuss some primary neologisms that were coined in English by specialists in molecular biology. Wanting to gain an insight into how translatable these English neologisms are, we did a unit of understanding (UoU)[1] analysis of some scientific publications on recent developments of cognition in the field of molecular biology, more specifically in protein synthesis in eukaryotic cells. We then looked for secondary terms in French and Dutch in publications on the same scientific developments.

We discovered that despite an explicit language and terminology policy in France with a tradition in making deliberate efforts to create genuine French neologisms for all phenomena, in recent years French-speaking molecular biologists borrowed and incorporated more and more English neologisms. In the Dutch-speaking world such language policy is absent and English loan terms are customary.

Two case studies are presented here and discussed from a translator's educational perspective. The first case study deals with how translators into French or Dutch as well as French-speaking and Dutch-speaking text writers on molecular biology deal with English neologisms that came into being in a metaphorical cognitive context. We wonder to what extent terminology creation, based on domain-metaphorical understanding is language-and-culture-bound and therefore difficult to translate. In the second case study we consider newly created English abbreviations in molecular biology and consider whether and how they are translated into French and Dutch. Our overall claim is that students enrolled in translation training classes should learn to distinguish between primary and secondary terminology creation and should know how to deal with secondary term creation.

Keywords: Neology creation, primary neologism, secondary neologism, translating texts on molecular biology, language policy, units of understanding (UoUs), translation of terminological metaphors, translation of abbreviations.

---

1 As explained in Temmerman (2000) 'units of understanding' come to life in discourse. They are characterized by prototype structure and evolve over time.

1. Primary and Secondary Neologisms

Domain specialist in molecular biology who do not have English as their first language but e.g. Dutch or French, as well as text writers and translators in both languages engage in secondary term creation. This means that they will create neologisms in Dutch or in French, based on their understanding of new terminology that was originally coined in English (nowadays the lingua franca in molecular biology, as in most scientific fields). Alternatively, they may borrow terminology from English. Whereas primary term creation (Sager 1990:80) occurs in the thought- and communication processes of a group of domain specialists exchanging ideas within the same language, secondary term creation implies finding an equivalent in language B (e.g. Dutch or French) for a unit of understanding that has already been expressed in language A (e.g. English). The new term gets translated from language A into language B or, alternatively, it is borrowed from A into B. In this article we discuss differences in translation culture between French and Dutch regarding neologisms. We look for primary neology creation in the English language textual archives of the domain of molecular biology and we investigate how the units of understanding concerned are expressed in French and Dutch texts (secondary neologisms). In both languages we expect to find "terminological dependency on English" (Ibáñez Sánchez, and García Palacios 2014).

Our research demonstrates that there are reasons why a number of English neologisms cannot be easily expressed in Dutch or in French. One of these reasons is metaphorical thinking giving rise to metaphorically underpinned neologisms that appear to be culture-bound (see section 2). A second reason for borrowing English forms instead of creating original language specific terminology in molecular biology is the high number of abbreviated forms in this discipline (see section 3), some of which take the shape of acronyms. Most of these abbreviations are taken over in both French and Dutch. Whereas Dutch has a tradition in borrowing acronyms from English, in French this is a recent phenomenon as there used to be a tradition in finding real French equivalents for whatever foreign form the French culture was confronted with. Because there has been a different language policy for French as compared to Dutch, our observations must be framed differently within different language political traditions (section 4).

2. Metaphorical Neologisms in English and Their French and Dutch Translations

Primary term formation is part of a process of understanding within the confines of one language, in a specific domain (e.g. molecular biology) and a particular setting (e. g. Melissa Moore's research group on 'spliceosomal factors', see infra). As the domain of molecular biology has been in full expansion in recent decades, many processes of new understanding leading to innovation have been described and the coining of many neologisms have been part of this process of understanding. In this section we will go into the creation of a neologism embedded in metaphorical understanding within a particular domain (molecular biology) in English (spliceosome) and we will discuss the translatability of the neologism into French and Dutch. Indeed, metaphorical understanding led to the creation of the English culturally embedded term spliceosome in the highly specialized domain of molecular biology as illustrated in the following quote:

> *The removal of noncoding regions or introns and the splicing together of the protein-coding regions or exons from precursor messenger ribonucleic acid (pre-mRNA) transcripts is fundamental to metzoan cell development, as well as its maintenance. The nuclear process of pre-mRNA splicing is a complex phenomenon catalysed by the* 'spliceosome'. The spliceosome *consists of greater than a hundred protein and RNA molecules. Integral to the* spliceosome *are five RNA-protein complexes, the U1, U2, U4, U5 and U6 small nuclear ribonucleoproteins (snRNPs). The numerous proteins and the U snRNPs that make up the* spliceosome *come on and off during the* spliceosome's *reaction cycle. This article places an emphasis on our current understanding of the dynamics, composition and structure of the* spliceosome. (Anthony and Pomeranz Krummel: 2013).

In order to understand this text fragment some historical knowledge on molecular biology and on the role metaphor played in the development of the discipline is needed. In 1953 Watson and Crick found that DNA has the shape of A DOUBLE HELIX ROPE LADDER and that it consists of a code of four letters that represent the bases thymine (T), adenine (A), cytosine (C) and guanine (G). DNA holds instructions for making proteins within the cell. DNA contains genes, meaningful sequences of nucleotide bases. These genes code for proteins, which are in turn used to build cells. Two domain metaphors are used simultaneously in this understanding of protein synthesis, namely DNA IS A DOUBLE HELIX ROPE LADDER and DNA IS A CODE TO EXPRESS GENETIC INFORMATION. These metaphors are at the basis of a long series of neologisms e.g. the four-letter code of DNA gives rise to the terms *transcription* and *translation* of the *information* in different steps of protein synthesis and to *mRNA* (*messenger* RNA), *the editing of the text*, etc. (Temmerman 2008). After DNA is transcribed into RNA, *editing* must be done to the nucleotide chain to make the RNA functional. *Introns* (intervening sequences) — non-functional segments of DNA — are spliced out of the chain. *Exons*, segments of DNA that code for proteins, are then re-joined by the *ligase enzyme*, a process called *mRNA splicing*. In their attempt to better understand this process, researchers discovered that it was a large complex that carries out RNA splicing. This large complex was called spliceosome because the process of the excision of introns followed by the joining of exons had been called splicing earlier on (figure 1). The underlying reason was that the metaphorical understanding of the double helix structure of DNA resembling a two-stranded string of rope continued to play a role in the further understanding and in the continuing neology creation process that is part of increasing cognition concerning protein synthesis.

Figure 1: The spliceosomal machinery.

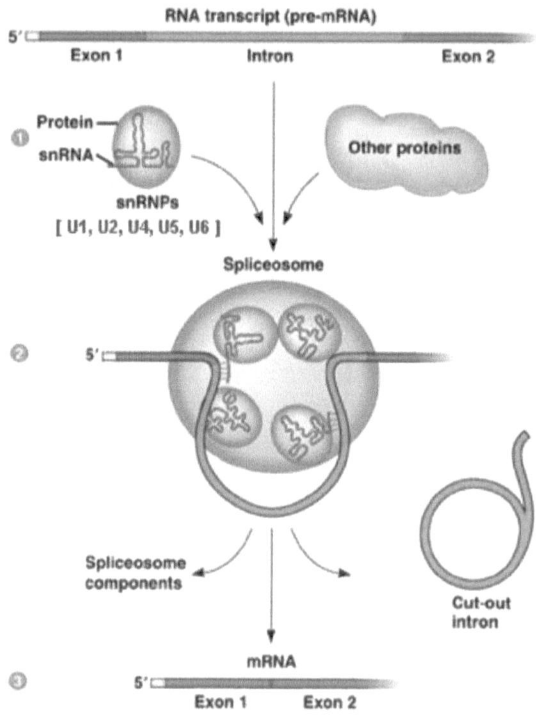

Source: http://carolc13.files.wordpress.com/2010/12/c7-17-11-spliceosome.jpg

A third metaphor was introduced in 1993 when the "machinery" of the spliceosome was understood (THE SPLICEOSOME IS A MACHINE). The complexity of this machinery is being unravelled in a long process of improved understanding.

Melissa Moore[2], one of the American specialists in spliceosomal activity and structure, co-authored an article in which the spliceosome is referred to as "a flexible, reversible macromolecular machine". Together with her colleagues, Moore engages in research looking for more insights into the spliceosome e.g. by using single molecule fluorescence microscopy (Hoskins and Moore *et al.* 2012). The point is that the understanding of protein synthesis in eukaryotic cells has been a process spanning several decades. It involved acquiring insight into an increasing number of units of understanding. Scientists gradually discovered the machinery of protein synthesis in eukaryotic cells. They understood that eukaryotes are cells with a nucleus; that DNA is the genetic code; that DNA is in the nucleus of the cells; that cells synthesize proteins; that protein synthesis is a process that involves the passing on of information from DNA to mRNA to protein; that mRNA plays a role in protein synthesis by the cell; and that in mRNA the introns are removed and exons are joined (splicing) by the spliceosome.

Whereas in the first phase (before 1970), the terminology in the discipline of molecular biology was largely based on classical Greek and Latin terminology and nomenclature (nucleus, protein, enzyme, etc.), we see that the English language gradually takes over as a cognitive tool contributing to and facilitating the improving understanding of protein synthesis. The splicing and spliceosome case furnish proof of this. A spliceosome is a complex of specialized RNA and protein subunits that removes introns from a transcribed pre-mRNA (hnRNA) segment. It "splices out" the introns from the mRNA. Spliceosome is a motivated term in English. We will see that this term is borrowed in French and in Dutch where it loses its metaphorical motivation. Rope can be spliced (a technique for repairing it) and when scientist found out that in protein synthesis double helix structured DNA is first transcribed into mRNA that is then cut and pasted (spliced) before being translated into protein, the term mRNA splicing was assigned. This understanding in terms of splicing was going to inspire to more neologisms like spliceosome.

Beyond doubt, the English neologism spliceosome is a motivated term. In French the repair of rope is named épissage, and *mRNA splicing* is referred to by épissage ARNm, which shows that the basic metaphors are part of the French language and culture as well. However, in French publications the term splicéosome seems to have become customary and is used more often than the variants particule d'épissage or complexe d'épissage. Logically, the creation of a new term *épissag(e)osome might have been considered, but this did not materialize. By

2 website Melissa Moore : http://labs.umassmed.edu/moorelab/Moore_Lab_Website/research.html.

borrowing the English term and transforming it into splicéosome (adding the accent), the metaphorical motivation of the term's meaning is lost in French as is made explicit is shown in the following text fragment.

> *L'épissage est assuré par un ensemble de complexes ribonucléoprotéiques (RNP) appelé collectivement splicéosome (épissage se dit splicing en anglais). Le splicéosome contient des particules snRNP (small RNP particles) et hnRNP (heterogeneous RNP particles).* (Monneaux and Muller 2007: 726)

In Dutch splicing, mRNA splicing and spliceosome are three loan words that have no genuine equivalents in the Dutch language (see Temmerman 2015).

One wonders whether a different understanding might have happened if a language other than English had been used for cognitive development in molecular biology. This is a hypothetical question that we will never be able to answer, since the term spliceosome has been borrowed by other languages e.g. French splicéosome, Dutch spliceosoom. The new and innovative understanding was given shape in English and it remains anchored in culturally embedded metaphorical thinking in English, which is likely to imply that further metaphorical reasoning on this subject in other languages is less evident.

3. Letter Words and Abbreviations in English, French and Dutch

Concerning letter words and abbreviations French, unlike Dutch, had relatively little interference from English until recently. Examples of abbreviated terms in English, French and Dutch can be found in figure 2.

Figure 2: English, French and Dutch abbreviations and examples of core terminology in molecular biology.

English	**French**	**Dutch**
DNA	ADN	DNA
mRNA	ARNm	boodschapper RNA mRNA
tRNA	ARNt	tRNA
protein	protéine	eiwit
mRNA-splicing	épissage ARNm	mRNA-splicing

As illustrated (see supra) French has secondary neologisms for all primary English neologisms (protéine, épissage ARNm) and it has its proper abbreviations (ADN, ARNm, ARNt). Dutch has some genuine terms (boodschapper RNA, eiwit) and borrows some terms from English (mRNA-splicing) including abbreviations (DNA, tRNA).

This is illustrated in the following quotes:

> *Bij RNA- splicing worden gedeelten introns verwijderd van het transcript dat na synthese van een eukaryotisch primair transcript niet in het mRNA zal komen.*
> *(...)*
> *Een spliceosoom is een groot complex dat is opgebouwd uit eiwitten en RNA-moleculen Een spliceosoom voert RNA-splicing uit door een wisselwerking met de uiteinden van een RNA-intron. Het intron wordt hierbij losgekoppeld en de extrons worden gekoppeld.*
> Source: http://www.genetica.webwetenschap.nl/index.php/rna-processing (April 2015)
> *Polynucelotide, dat de basen cytosine, guanine, adenine en uracil bevat. Boodschapper-RNA (mRNA) transporteert de informatie voor de synthese van een eiwit van de kern (chromosoom) naar de ribosomen.*
> Source: http://www.digischool.nl/bi/pbb/search.php (April 2015)

As molecular biology progressed, several types of RNA were differentiated as shown in figure 3.

Figure 3: Some of the principal types of RNAs produced in cells (English terminology and definitions). Sources: http://smart-therapeutics.com/Technology/RNAs-Role-in-Protein-Synthesis and https://en.wikipedia.org/wiki/List_of_RNAs (15 April 2015).

mRNAs	messenger RNAs, code for proteins
rRNAs	ribosomal RNAs, form the basic structure of the ribosome and catalyze protein synthesis
tRNAs	transfer RNAs, central to protein synthesis as adaptors between mRNA and amino acids
snRNAs	small nuclear RNAs, function in a variety of nuclear processes, including the splicing of pre-mRNA
snoRNAs	small nucleolar RNAs, used to process and chemically modify rRNAs
scaRNAs	small cajal RNAs, used to modify snoRNAs and snRNAs
miRNAs	microRNAs, regular gene expression typically by blocking translation of selective mRNAs
siRNAs	small interfering RNAs, turn off gene expression by directing degradation of selective mRNAs and the establishment of compact chromatin structures

In the first of a series of three review articles on « Le monde complexe et mouvant des ARN » by J. Lamoril, N. Ameziane, J.-C. Deybach, P. Bouizegarène, M. Bogard, entitled « Immuno-analyse et biologie spécialisée » (2010), we have systematically traced back all the short forms. The article is written in French, but it is sprinkled with English terms, phrases, and abbreviations. We find French terms and acronyms for English deoxyribonucleic acid (DNA), namely acide désoxyribonucléique (ADN), and for English ribonucleic acid (RNA), namely acide ribonucléique (ARN). Consequently, messenger RNA (mRNA) becomes ARN messager (ARNm). Lamoril *et al.* describe how gradually the world of RNA is being unveiled by science. New types or RNA are discovered:

> *Actuellement, on distingue les ARN codants (en pratique, les ARNm, ARN messagers) et les ARNnc. Parmi ces ARNnc, on distingue les longs ARN dont la taille est supérieure à 200 nucléotides qui fonctionnent sans prétraitement particulier et les petits ARNnc issus d'un prétraitement de longs précurseurs (6)*

We witness a mix of loans from English, blends (of English and French elements), and newly created French abbreviated forms.

In the following list the types of "ARN" are enumerated as they occur in Lamoril *et al.* 2010. (See also figures 3 and 4)

> *1. les petits ARN: un certain nombre de petits ARN contribuent à divers processus biologiques en association avec des complexes de ribonucléoprotéines (RNP), par exemple les petits ARN nucléaires (snRNA, small nuclear RNA).*

The term petits ARN nucléaires is genuine French but English synonyms are given in the text between brackets.

> *2. les snoRNA (small nucleolar RNA, petits ARN nucléolaires): ces petits ARN contribuent aux modifications de séquences ARN des ARN ribosomaux.*

The English abbreviated term snoRNA is borrowed and at the same time the full form is given in French (petits ARN nucléolaires) and English (small nucleolar RNA).

> *3. les microARN (miARN): ce sont de courts ARN de 21 — 23 pb dont le rôle de régulateur de l'expression est fondamental. Ils provoquent la dégradation de l'ARNm ou la répression de la traduction.*

The form microARN (miARN) is genuine French.

> *4. les siARN (small interfering RNA, petits ARN interférents): leur rôle est similaire à celui des microARN, mais ils dégradent systématiquement l'ARN cible.*

SIARN is a blend of English "small interfering" and French ARN.

> *5. les piARN (piwi-interacting RNA, piRNA, ARN interagissant avec les protéines piwi): ces ARN jouent aussi un role dans la régulation de l'expression des gènes.*

PIARN is a blend of English "piwi-interacting" and French ARN.

In the publication by Lamoril *et al.* (2010) we found several examples of English abbreviated forms that are borrowed in French and for which the full forms are given between brackets, e.g. UTR, untranslated region and ORF («appellée aussi 'open reading frame'»)

> *6. Sur le plan structurel, un ARNm est schématiquement constitué d'un chapeau en 5'(ajout en 5'du pré-ARNm d'un nucleotide G méthylé non codé par l'ADNg), une partie non traduite, la partie 5'non codante (5'NC ou 5'UTR, untranslated region), une séquence codante appellee aussi open reading frame (ORF) et constituée de nucléotides dont l'association par triplet est dénommée codon.*

There are more examples of loan terms and blends that occur in the same article by Lamoril *et al.* (2010):

P-TEFb: positive transcription elongation factor b (LOAN)
rasiARN : repeat-associated siARN (BLEND)
rARN: ARN ribosomique (the r is in front, like in English) (BLEND)
snARN: small nuclear ARN (petits ARN du noyau) (BLEND)
SRP: signal recognition particle (LOAN)
tmRNA: transfer messenger ARN (LOAN)
tARN: ARN de transfert BLEND

Blends and loan terms can be observed in French. Some English short forms are kept (P-TEFb, SRP, tmRNA), and sometimes the position of the defining particle is kept like in English (tARN, siARN, snARN, rARN, rasiARN).

Figure 4: Visual representation of the types of ARN (French for RNA) based on Lamoril et al. 2010.

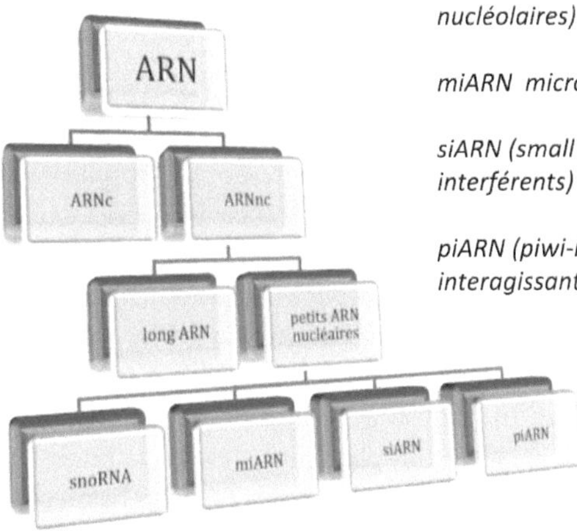

snoRNA (small nucleolar RNA, petits ARN nucléolaires)

miARN microARN

siARN (small interfering RNA, petits ARN interférents)

piARN (piwi-interacting RNA, piRNA, ARN interagissant avec les protéines piwi)

Whereas in the first of the following fragments all terminology is French, in the second fragment the terminology is hybrid (French and English):

> *Chez les eucaryotes, les gènes codant pour des protéines sont constitués d'une suite d' exons et d'introns alternés. Lors de la transcription, un* pré-ARN messager *(ARNm) est synthétisé, celui-ci va être épissé (excision des introns et ligature des exons) pour donner un* ARNm *dit mature. Cet* ARNm mature *est alors exporté du noyau vers le cytoplasme pour être traduit en protéine.* (Monneaux and Muller 2007: 726)

> *L'épissage est assuré par un ensemble de complexes ribonucléoprotéiques (RNP) appelé collectivement splicéosome (épissage se dit splicing en anglais). Le splicéosome contient des* particules snRNP *(small RNP particles) et hnRNP (heterogeneous RNP particles). (Monneaux and Muller 2007: 726)*

In summary, what we observed in French scientific articles is that French abbreviated terms occur alongside English abbreviations and blends. In Dutch there is more consistency as right from the beginning of the development of the discipline, abbreviated terminology was taken over from English (e.g. DNA, RNA, mRNA (the Dutch full form *boodschapper RNA* is not found as an abbreviated form: *bRNA does not occur in Dutch but *mRNA* does)).

4. Teaching the Translatability of Neologisms in Distinct Language Policy Traditions

In this contribution we discussed the cognitive role of language by zooming in on the coining of neologisms in the domain of molecular biology. Sapir's idea (1947) on *language habits* of groups of people (in this case the group of specialists in the domain of molecular biology) was illustrated with terminology creation that plays a role in knowledge extension in molecular biology. Summarizing the history of understanding *DNA*, *messenger RNA* and *protein synthesis in eukaryotic cells* enabled us to illustrate neology creation as a process in time. We explained the process of understanding *mRNA splicing* and the discovery of the *spliceosome*. We also showed that understanding is language-and-culture-bound. Despite the active language policy in the French speaking world, molecular biologists expressing themselves in French recently appear to have no choice but to import loan words from English to express newly discovered knowledge in the French language. The in vivo analysis of their publications brought out some reasons why this is the case. We realized that English is very much part of the language habits of these French specialists who read and publish in English as well as in French. The language habits of the speakers of French are gradually changing. Nowadays, English terms are borrowed and integrated into the French language on a regular basis. Our data indicate that the language habits of present-day French molecular biologists are hybrid, i.e. strongly influenced by the English language and still trying to comply with the tradition of creating genuine French terms.

Our case studies on metaphorical understanding and abbreviations in molecular biology indicate that French translators need to know about the limits of secondary term creation. It is not their task to search for new secondary terms. They need to take stock of the language habits of French speaking molecular biologists. If these specialists use English terminology in their French language publications, translators should be aware of this. When translating English texts on molecular biology into French, translators should be advised to check whether possible French equivalent neologisms are actually used by specialists in their French language publications.

French had relatively little interference from English in the domain of molecular biology until a few decades ago. DNA (deoxyribonucleic acid) is consistently named ADN (acide désoxyribonucléique) in French, RNA (ribonucleic acid) is ARN (acide ribonucléique) and mRNA splicing is called épissage mARN. For centuries, the official French language authority (Académie française) raised the awareness of all speakers of the French language (*la francophonie*) on the importance of « *le mot juste* ». This attitude has changed in recent times with the discovery of e.g. the spliceosome (1993) (FR: splicéosome), snurportines (FR: snurportines), snoRNA (small nucleolar RNA), called in French petits ARN nucléolaires, (but the abbreviation snoRNA is kept in French), ORFs (open reading frames, also ORF in French), and UTR (untranslated region, also UTR in French). In recent years, French-speaking molecular biologists have borrowed and incorporated more and more English neologisms into their language. English, the lingua franca of science, influences their language habits, regardless of language political efforts to find *le mot juste* in French. Speakers of French experience terminological dependency on English.

Student translators should learn about this terminological dependency (Ibáñez Sánchez, and García Palacios 2014:107) on English and how to deal with it when translating (awareness raising). Their awareness should also be raised concerning cultural dependency and tradition in neology creation. Translators in training should learn that French authors also struggle with neology creation in French and that hybrid terminology (a mixture of French and English) is created and loan words are introduced for pragmatic reasons (internationalisms). Trainers in translation and terminology should illustrate the process of neology creation in French and demonstrate the language- and-culture-boundness (Temmerman & Van Campenhoudt 2014)of terminology creation based on e.g. metaphorical understanding of a domain. They should discuss the problems in finding French equivalents for English abbreviated forms. Translators into French need to be aware that French-speaking countries have a tradition in language policy (*aménagement linguistique*). Aspiring translators should know that in France several terminology planning initiatives were launched e.g. the Centre de Terminologie et de Néologie (CTN), which was created in 1987. One of the CTN's tasks is to watch for technical terminology and neologisms. Awareness is recommended of the fact that there is a dominant linguistic policy explicitly stating:

> *Pour demeurer vivante, une langue doit être en mesure d'exprimer le monde modern dans toute sa diversité et sa complexité*[3].

The language policy for Dutch, however, is rather a *laissez-faire, laissez-aller* attitude, characterized by a lack of interventionism. *Nederlandse Taalunie* (the Dutch Language Union is an organization based on a political agreement between The Netherlands and Flanders on the Dutch language since 1980) does NOT have the objective to prescribe or regulate Dutch terminology[4].

The lesson to be drawn from our observations is that translators in training will need to be guided in at least two types of awareness raising. First they need to realize that French and Dutch (as many other languages) are subject to *terminological dependency* on English. Second, trainers should raise translation students' awareness of *cultural dependency*, i.e. language planning principles that may be present or absent in the target languages and in the cultural heritage they are an expression of.

References

Sager, Juan Carlos. 1990. *A Practical Course in Terminology Processing.* Amsterdam: John Benjamins.

Ibáñez Sánchez, Miguel and Joaquin García Palacios 2014 "Semantic characterization of terms as a trace of terminological dependency" *Terminology* 20(2) 171–197.

Sapir, Edward. 1949. Mandelbaum, David, ed. *Selected writings in language, culture and personality.* Berkeley: University of California Press.

Temmerman, Rita. 2000, *Towards New Ways of Terminology Description. The Sociocognitive Approach,* Amsterdam/Philadelphia: John Benjamins.

3 http://www.culture.fr/Resources/FranceTerme/Enrichissement-de-la-langue.

4 http://taalunie.org/wat-doet-taalunie/activiteiten/terminologie.

Temmerman, Rita. 2008, "Sociocultural situatedness of terminology in the life sciences: The history of splicing", in Frank, R. M., Dirven, R., & Ziemke, T. (2008), *Sociocultural Situatedness*, vol. 2, Berlin: Walter de Gruyter, p. 327–360.

Temmerman, Rita. and Van Campenhoudt Marc. 2014. "Dynamics and terminology: An interdisciplinary perspective on monolingual- and multilingual culture-bound communication", in Rita Temmerman and Marc Van Campenhoudt (eds) *Dynamics and Terminology,* 1–14. Amsterdam Philadelphia: John Benjamins.

Temmerman, Rita. 2015. "How multilingual primary neologisms and multilingual secondary neologisms shape European culture" In Jana Engelbrechtova (ed.), 2015. *Proceedings of the International Conference for Cultural Studies (Searching for Culture—SEFOC), 16–17 October 2014. Palacký University in Olomouc (Volume 6)* 133–146.

Publications in the Field of Molecular Biology

Anthony K. C. and Pomeranz Krummel D., 2013, "Spliceosome" eLS. John Wiley and Sons, Ltd. www.els.net.

Hoskins A. A., Gelles J., Moore M. J., 2011, "New insights into the spliceosome by single molecule fluorescence microscopy", *Current Opinion in Chemical Biology,* Volume 15, Issue 6, December, Pages 864–870.

Hoskins A. A., and Moore M. J., 2012, "The spliceosome: a flexible, reversible macromolecular machine", *Trends in biochemical sciences* 37.5 : 179–188.

Lamoril J., N. Ameziane, J.-C. Deybach, P. Bouizegarène, M. Bogard, 2010, "Le monde complexe et mouvant des ARN. Première partie", *Immuno-analyse & Biologie Spécialisée,* volume 25, issue 1, February 2010, Pages 4–25.

Monneaux F., and S. Muller, 2007, "Le splicéosome et son intérêt dans la recherche thérapeutique sur le lupus", *La Revue de Médecine interne,* volume 28, issue 10, October.

Pomeranz Krummel D. A. and Nagai K., 2005, "Spliceosome" eLS, John Wiley & Sons, Ltd. www.els.net.

Sergiy Tyupa

Cognitive Debriefing of Patient Questionnaires: How to Capture Meaning as Understood by Respondents?

Abstract: Patient questionnaires are widely used in clinical trials as instruments for measuring the efficacy of new drugs or treatments. Therefore, the requirements with respect to the quality of translation of such questionnaires are extremely high. The paper describes the results of a linguistic experiment that was carried out in order to evaluate the advantages and disadvantages of an alternative method for testing the comprehension of patient questionnaires by respondents. Preliminary results show that the new method may be used as an optional tool together with the existing methods. More research is needed in order to investigate possible cultural differences between respondents from different cultural and linguistic groups.

Keywords: clinical trials, cognitive debriefing, cognitive interviewing, language of medicine, linguistic validation, medical translation, patient questionnaires, patient-reported outcomes (PRO), PRO questionnaires, translation quality assessment.

1. Introduction

Few would disagree that medical translation belongs to the most challenging types of translation, both in terms of the required subject matter expertise and the associated ethical and legal considerations. There is a wide variety of source texts that belong to the field of medical translation, including patient information leaflets, user manuals for medical devices, pharmacovigilance reports, clinical trial protocols and many others. Some medical documents, e.g. investigator brochures and summaries of product characteristics, are intended for an expert audience only, whereas others, such as informed consent forms and patient information leaflets, are developed for the general public. *Patient questionnaires* belong to the latter group; however, they have some unique features that make them particularly challenging for translators. The primary purpose of patient questionnaires – more specifically, patient-reported outcomes[1] (PRO) questionnaires – is to measure the

1 Patient-reported outcome (PRO) — A measurement based on a report that comes directly from the patient (i.e., study subject) about the status of a patient's health condition without amendment or interpretation of the patient's response by a clinician

outcomes (results) of a treatment as experienced by patients, usually in a clinical trial setting. Therefore, such questionnaires contain disease-specific information and terminology together with special vocabulary referring to patients' subjective feelings and impressions, usually represented by idiomatic and colloquial phrases.

Since the overwhelming majority of clinical trials are conducted in multiple countries and with multilingual target groups, the problem of translating questionnaires is of paramount importance – the responses provided by patients serve as one of the most important indicators of the efficacy and safety of a new drug or treatment evaluated during a given clinical trial. The volume of required translation is more than considerable: ClinicalTrials.gov, a registry and results database of publicly and privately supported clinical studies of human participants conducted around the world, currently lists 193,310 studies conducted in all 50 US states and in 190 countries worldwide[2].

Regulatory authorities generally acknowledge the importance of translation: thus, the US Food and Drug Administration (FDA) states that '[r]egardless of whether the instrument[3] was developed concurrently in multiple cultures or languages or whether a fully developed instrument was adapted or translated to new cultures or languages, we recommend that sponsors provide evidence that the content validity and other measurement properties are adequately similar between all versions used in the clinical trial' (FDA 2009: 22). Although FDA *Guidance for Industry* says very little about specific methods of translation to be applied, it does contain one specific recommendation: '…the appropriateness of the content should be addressed in cognitive interviewing in each language group tested' (FDA 2009: 13).

Cognitive interviewing is a general method used for critical evaluation of instruments (including questionnaires) developed for data collection from respondents (definition based on Willis 2005: 3). In the field of medical translation for clinical trials, cognitive interviewing (more widely known as cognitive debriefing or linguistic validation) is a process whereby translated questionnaires are piloted on a small group of respondents (normally from 5 to 8) who belong to the target language population and have the disease or condition that is the subject of the questionnaire. After the respondents fill in the questionnaire, they are asked to reword (paraphrase) each item in the questionnaire. Their rewording is then

---

or anyone else. (FDA 2009: 32). <http://www.fda.gov/downloads/Drugs/Guidances/UCM193282.pdf > accessed 29 June 2015.

2 ClinicalTrials.gov, <https://clinicaltrials.gov> accessed 29 June 2015.

3 *Instrument* in this context refers to PRO questionnaires.

compared against the original English wording and conclusions are made about the equivalence of the translation.

It can be reasonably claimed that little research has been carried out on the efficacy and effectiveness of cognitive debriefing . Unfortunately, it was not possible to find references to cognitive debriefing/interviewing in available Translation Studies publications, whereas reports published in medical journals usually only mention the fact that cognitive debriefing was used for the translation of a patient questionnaire without discussing in detail possible problems connected with the cognitive debriefing process (e.g. Brzoza *et al.* 2011).

The author of the present paper has worked as a medical translator from English into Ukrainian and Russian for Ukraine since 2001, and over this time he has translated about 190 patient questionnaires and conducted over 1,100 cognitive debriefing interviews. A number of shortcomings of the cognitive debriefing process can be singled out based on his long-term personal experience with cognitive debriefing, namely:

1. Most respondents feel stressed and nervous because of the interview situation, which inevitably affects their performance during the interview;
2. Some respondents lack the language skills necessary to paraphrase questionnaire items;
3. Cognitive interviewing involves code-switching from the written mode of a questionnaire to a spoken mode of an interview, which often affects the performance of respondents;
4. Respondents commonly have problems with memory span, especially with longer questionnaire items;
5. Overall, untrained respondents are expected to perform a highly complicated operation that may be interpreted as a case of intralingual translation (cf. Jakobson 2004 [1959]): situations when an interviewer reads a given item to respondents and asks them to paraphrase it may be compared with consecutive interpreting, whereas situations when a respondent reads an item and paraphrases it aloud may be compared with on-sight translation; both these translation activities require special training and adequate language skills, which cannot be required nor expected from untrained respondents.

The author believes that the five problems described above can be mitigated if a written mode of paraphrasing is introduced in addition to the spoken mode. The purpose of the present article, therefore, is to describe the results of a linguistic experiment that was carried out in order to compare written and spoken modes of paraphrasing and establish whether the existing cognitive debriefing methods could be improved with the help of the new approach.

2. Methods

A number of methodological and practical challenges had to be accounted for in the experiment design. Firstly, in order to establish whether a respondent understood a given questionnaire item the way it was intended by the questionnaire author it was important to obtain access to an instrument that would have a detailed description of items constructed by the author (a document known as 'concept elaboration' or 'list of concepts'). Secondly, the interviews had to be conducted in English with native speakers of English as the introduction of a translated version would have introduced an additional and uncontrollable source of bias. On the practical side, due to visa restrictions the author was not able to carry out interviews in an English-speaking country and had to look for English-speaking respondents in Poland – the country where he has a temporary residence permit. Moreover, the questionnaire needed to focus on symptoms that could be experienced and understood by the general population and not only by respondents with a specific disease, as the latter would be even more difficult to find.

The questionnaire chosen for the experiment was the Schizophrenia Quality of Life Scale Revision 4 (SQLS-R4) (Oxford Outcomes 2004). The SQLS-R4 measures psychosocial feelings, cognition, and vitality in individuals diagnosed with schizophrenia. The questionnaire contains instructions for respondents, 33 items and 5 response options applicable to all items. Table 1 offers sample items from the questionnaire together with the concept elaboration prepared by the instrument authors.

Table 1: Sample SQLS-R4 items and concept elaboration

	Questionnaire item	**Concept elaboration**
1	We are interested in finding out about the quality of your life OVER THE PAST SEVEN DAYS, INCLUDING TODAY.	The study team are asking the following questions because they're interested in finding out about the patient's quality of life (their overall health, emotional health, how they cope and feel and so on). The questions should be based on the previous week (past seven days), and the respondent should include TODAY when answering.
2	I lacked the energy to do things.	The respondent felt that they did not have as much physical energy to do things (activities, tasks, routines of daily life, hobbies etc.) as usual/as necessary. Lacked = absence of deficiency

	Questionnaire item	Concept elaboration
3	I couldn't be bothered to do things.	The respondent could not be bothered (could not make themselves do something though not from physical problems – e.g. they were too unhappy to do something). Do things: activities, hobbies, socialising etc.
4	I was worried about my future.	The respondent felt worried (troubled, anxious, concerned) about their future/ about what will happen to them in future.

During the 3 months of recruitment, only 4 native speakers of English volunteered for the experiment. Only volunteers who had spent fewer than 6 months in Poland were invited to take part in the experiment. Their demographic data is presented in Table 2.

Table 2: Demographic data of respondents

	Sex	Age	Nationality
1	M	38	Ireland
2	M	22	UK
3	M	25	UK
4	M	55	UK

All interviews were carried out individually with each respondent. They were given an explanation of the purpose of cognitive debriefing interviews in the context of clinical trials and were informed that the experiment was linguistic and not medical in nature. Each respondent received a printed copy of SQLS-R4 and was given adequate time to fill it in. On completion of the questionnaire, the respondents were asked general questions about comprehensibility and ease of completion, and then interviewed on each item. The questionnaire items were divided into 2 groups: group 1 (from the instructions to item 16) and group 2 (from item 17 to item 33). The cognitive debriefing with each respondent was made up of 2 parts: a spoken interview and re-writing. The re-writing was carried out on A5 paper cards that contained one item each and slightly modified questions that are normally asked by the interviewer during the spoken part. The sequence of 2 parts was mixed: 2 respondents first filled in the cards and then answered interview questions; 2 respondents completed the spoken interview first and then filled in the cards. All spoken interviews were recorded on a voice recorder and a transcript was subsequently prepared. On completion of both parts all respondents were asked about the part that they preferred and the reasons for such preference.

3. Results

All respondents completed both parts of the cognitive debriefing process and demonstrated good understanding of the questionnaire items. Table 3 summarizes the time taken by respondents to complete both parts of the cognitive debriefing.

Table 3: Time spent on cognitive debriefing

Respondent	Interview	Re-writing
1	6	12
2	8	18
3	7	12
4	7	13

The mean time for completing the interview was 7 minutes, whereas the mean time taken for re-writing was 13.75 minutes. The mean time spent on the cognitive debriefing process was 21.5 minutes. No items were missed or left unexplained during the interview part. In the re-writing part, respondent 2 missed 6 items; the remaining three respondents produced paraphrases for all items. As for the number of words that respondents used for paraphrasing the items, there were no considerable differences between the interview and the re-writing part. Since respondent 2 missed 6 items, it was not possible to compare the word count for all 34 items; however, a 10-item sample (from item 24 to item 33) demonstrated that the mean word count for the interviewing part was 90 words (respondents 2 and 3), whereas the mean word count for the re-writing part for the same items was 75.5 words (respondents 1 and 4).

The analysis of the transcript of the interviews and the re-writing part shows that respondents tended to use more colloquial and idiomatic phrases during the interviews than in the re-writing part. Table 4 offers examples for items 1 and 2.

Table 4: Sample paraphrases for items 1 and 2

Original item 1	**I lacked the energy to do things**
Concept elaboration	The respondent felt that they did not have as much physical energy to do things (activities, tasks, routines of daily life, hobbies etc.) as usual/as necessary. Lacked = absence of deficiency
Respondent 1 (interview)	I felt unmotivated, I felt lack of motivation, a lethargy
Respondent 2 (re-writing)	I lacked the energy to do day-to-day tasks
Respondent 3 (re-writing)	I had no energy
Respondent 4 (interview)	I didn't feel energetic about my tasks, I lacked energy for doing my tasks
Original item 2	I couldn't be bothered to do things
Concept elaboration	The respondent could not be bothered (could not make themselves do something though not from physical problems – e.g. they were too unhappy to do something). Do things: activities, hobbies, socialising etc.
Respondent 1 (interview)	I couldn't be arsed, I felt no compulsion, no desire
Respondent 2 (re-writing)	I had a clear lack of desire to do anything
Respondent 3 (re-writing)	I had no desire to do anything
Respondent 4 (interview)	I felt lazy about doing things

Three respondents confirmed that they preferred interviews to re-writing because it was easier to clarify things, and only one stated that he liked the re-writing part more than the interview.

4. Conclusions

Due to a limited number of respondents, lack of females in the sample, and the fact that the interviews with native speakers of English were conducted outside of an English-speaking country, it is not possible to draw definitive conclusions about the advantages and disadvantages of the suggested alternative for cognitive interviews. Therefore, only the most non-controversial conclusions will be suggested.

First of all, re-writing takes about twice as much time as interviewing. This may not be an issue in the case of small questionnaires but would require careful planning with larger instruments. Secondly, it is more likely that a respondent will leave an item unexplained during the re-writing. However, even then it is still possible for the interviewer to contact the respondent again and debrief the items that were not paraphrased by the respondent. The advantage of re-writing that was mentioned by two respondents is that there is more time for thinking over items, whereas during the interview a more immediate answer is expected.

The experiment did not prove the initial hypothesis that respondents would be less nervous and stressed when writing their paraphrases. There are two possible explanations for this: either the respondents were not stressed because they were volunteers and knew that they were taking part in a linguistic experiment, or there is a clear cultural difference between Ukrainian and British/Western European respondents in such situations. This means that a new improved experiment is needed that would involve a representative sample of respondents from various linguistic and cultural groups. Nevertheless, it can be claimed with a certain degree of confidence that re-writing may be suggested as an optional cognitive debriefing tool.

References

Brzoza, Z., K. Badura-Brzoza, A. Młynek, M. Magerl, I. Baiardini, G.W. Canonica, K. Weller, E. Kocatürk, D. Kalogeromitros, A. Zalewska-Janowska, T. Zuberbier, and M. Maurer. (2011). "Adaptation and initial results of the Polish version of the GA2LEN Chronic Urticaria Quality of Life Questionnaire (CU-Q2oL)", *Journal of Dermatological Science*, 62, 36–41.

FDA (2009). *Guidance for Industry. Patient-Reported Outcome Measures: Use in Medical Product Development to Support Labeling Claims.* <http://www.fda.gov/downloads/Drugs/Guidances/UCM193282.pdf> accessed 29 June 2015.

Jakobson, R. (2004 [1959]). 'On linguistic aspects of translation'. In L. Venuti (ed.), *The Translation Studies reader. Second edition,* pp. 138–143. London & New York: Routledge.

Oxford Outcomes Ltd. (2004). *The Revised Schizophrenia Quality of Life Questionnaire (SQLS-R4): User's Manual for the SQLS-R4.* Cassington, Oxford: Oxford Outcomes.

Willis, G.B. (2005). *Cognitive interviewing: a tool for improving questionnaire design.* Thousand Oaks, London, New Delhi: SAGE Publications.

Authors

Marcos Aranda

Marcos Aranda holds a Ph.D. in Translation and Interpretation from Universidad Pontificia Comillas in Madrid, where he teaches Translation German-Spanish, Technical Translation, Localisation and Project Management. He currently serves as Secretary for the Spanish Association of Certified Translation Agencies. He owns TRIDIOM, one of the top 15 translation companies of Spain. His fields of specialisation are Project Management and CAT tools.

Henri Bloemen

Henri Bloemen (1957) is professor at the KU Leuven Campus Antwerp, where he teaches literary translation, legal translation, Translation Studies and German cultural history. His main research topics are theory of translation, ethics of translation, and didactics of translation. He is a member of the steering group of the PETRA-E-Project that develops a Europe wide 'Framework for the Education and Training of Literary Translators', and of the editorial board of the TS Series 'Approaches to Translation Studies' (Brill).

Łukasz Bogucki

Łukasz Bogucki is director of the Institute of English Studies at the University of Łódź and Head of the Department of Translation Studies. His academic interests include the theory of audiovisual translation, Translation Studies as an academic discipline, interpreting, specialised and computer-assisted translation, as well as localisation. Łukasz Bogucki is a member of the International Communication Association, as well as ŁTN (the Łódź Scientific Association) and the Łódź Section of the Polish Academy of Sciences. Since 2014 he has co-edited the Lodz Studies in Language series published by Peter Lang.

Eleanor Cornelius

Eleanor Cornelius is a senior lecturer in the Department of Linguistics at the University of Johannesburg. Her research focuses mainly on legal translation, legal language and the use of plain language in public and private spheres. She teaches, amongst others, text editing and psycholinguistics on undergraduate and postgraduate levels. She serves on the council of the South African Translators' Institute (SATI) and on the council of the International Federation of Translators (FIT). She is a SATI accredited simultaneous interpreter (Afrikaans-English/English-Afrikaans).

Linda Dewolf
Linda Dewolf is a professional translator and graduated in interpreting/literary translation (English – German – French), terminology. She holds a PhD in Linguistics, and a post graduate in cultural studies (VUB). Her research interests focus on Austrian and German literary translation, subtitling opera and drama, terminology, legal interpreting/translation and cross-cultural adaptation/translations of psychometric measures. She teaches French and translation at the Dept. of Applied Linguistics of Vrije Universiteit Brussel.

Montserrat Franquesa
Montserrat Franquesa is Associated Professor of History of Translation at Universitat Autònoma de Barcelona and Researcher in the Contemporary Catalan Translation Study Group. Her research focuses on the history of translation into Catalan, a branch in which she has especially dealt with the reception of Ancient Greek and Latin Classics. Among her recent studies is the book *La Fundació Bernat Metge, una obra de país (1923-1938).*

Elsa Huertas Barros
Dr Elsa Huertas Barros is a Lecturer in Translation Studies at the University of Westminster. Her PhD focuses on the role of interpersonal competence in translator training, and her main research interests include: translator training, student-centred approaches, collaborative learning, assessment practices and translator competence.

Iwona Jacewicz
Iwona Jacewicz, PhD, is associate professor at the Institute of Specialised and Intercultural Communication at the University of Warsaw. She completed the study of Applied Linguistics at the University of Warsaw (Translation and Interpretation Studies in German-Russian-Polish), and has a doctorate in Translation Studies at the Centre for Translation Studies at the University of Vienna. Her main fields of scientific research and interests are translation didactics, translation theory, legal translation and terminology studies.

Koen Kerremans
Koen Kerremans obtained an MA in Germanic Philology (Dutch-English) at Universiteit Antwerpen in 2001, an MA in Language Sciences at Universiteit Gent in 2002 and his PhD degree in Applied Linguistics at Vrije Universiteit Brussel in 2014. His research addresses several topics pertaining to translation and communication in specialised registers. He currently holds a position as a post-doctoral research and teaching assistant at the Department of Applied Linguistics (Faculty of Arts and Philosophy) of Vrije Universiteit Brussel (VUB).

Don Kiraly

Don Kiraly has been educating translators at the School of Translation, Linguistics and Cultural Studies of the University of Mainz, Germany, since 1983. He has also held visiting lecturer positions at ESIT (Université de Paris III) and the Monterey Institute of International Studies. Having written his dissertation in the area of cognitive translation processes (University of Illinois, 1989), his two main areas of research since then have been collaborative translator education and naturalistic second language acquisition.

Hendrik Kockaert

Hendrik J. Kockaert is an Associate Professor of French Linguistics, Terminology, Legal Translation, and Translation Technology at KU Leuven, Faculty of Arts, in Antwerp, and is the Chairperson of ISO TC 37 SC 1. Since August 2015, he is Dean of the Faculty of Arts on Campus Sint Andries in Antwerp. He is a Research Associate at the University of The Free State, Bloemfontein, Republic of South-Africa. He publishes in the areas of Terminology, Legal Translation and Translation Technology.

Barbara Lewandowska-Tomaszczyk

Professor Dr habil. Barbara Lewandowska-Tomaszczyk has been active as professor ordinarius at the University of Lodz for many years and at present she holds the position of professor ordinarius in English Language and Linguistics at the State University of Applied Sciences in Konin, at the Department of English and Translation. Her research interests are primarily in cognitive semantics and pragmatics of natural language, corpus linguistics and their applications in Translation Studies, lexicography and discourse analysis. She has published books and papers in those areas and organized cycles of international conferences and seminars. Over the years she has been invited to read papers at various international conferences and to lecture and conduct seminars at universities in Europe, Asia and Americas.

Donata Lisaitė

Donata Lisaitė is a teaching assistant at the Department of Translation, Interpreting and Communication at Ghent University. She teaches academic writing, professional business communication and translation into English. Besides her teaching assignment, she works at the moment on a research project related to student peer feedback activities and translation competences.

Munzhedzi James Mafela

Munzhedzi James Mafela is a professor of African Languages at the University of South Africa in South Africa. His fields of specialisation include African literature, lexicography and translation, and intercultural communication studies. He has published widely in the fields of his research and his upcoming title, which he edited, entitled *Nelson Rholihlahla Mandela: Reflections Through the Eyes of Poets* is due for publication during December 2015.

Armando Adriano Magaia
Armando A. Magaia graduated from Eduardo Mondlane University in 2005 and holds an MA in Linguistics (Translation Studies) from the University of South Africa. He taught English for nearly 8 years at the Language Institute of Maputo, where he was initially trained as an English Language teacher in 1990. Since 2006, he has taught English and Translation at Eduardo Mondlane University.

Bruce Maylath
Bruce Maylath, professor of English at North Dakota State University, USA, teaches courses in linguistics and international technical communication. His current research takes up translation issues in professional communication and has appeared in *connexions*, *IEEE Transactions in Professional Communication*, *Journal of Business and Technical Communication*, and *Technical Communication Quarterly*, among others.

Patricia Minacori
Dr. Patricia Minacori is the director of the Professional Masters Department in Applied Languages at University Paris Diderot, France. Former technical translator, she is now an associate professor. She has been teaching translation from English to French for over 27 years. She published articles on the different phases of translation: comprehension, expression, research, and revision. She also wrote articles on assessment, exchanges between technical communicators and translators, and competences. She is currently working on the notion of complexity, as defined by Edgar Morin, in technical communication and translation.

Birthe Mousten
Birthe Mousten has a PhD and MA in translation/localization, and a BA in German. She is an English/Danish certified translator and interpreter. Her research areas are: translation, localization, global studies. She lectures at Aarhus University, Aarhus; Aalborg University, Aalborg; Southern Denmark University (SDU), Odense as well as NUUK University, Greenland. Her specialisation is LSP and LGP translation, technical and legal writing, web translation, negotiation theory and intercultural communication. She carries out course activities for trade and industry.

Lucia Salvato

Lucia Salvato is Assistant Professor in the Department of Linguistic Sciences and Foreign Literatures at the Catholic University of Milan. Her research interests lie in the area of Applied German Linguistics, in particular, Translation Studies (German-Italian Translation) in German Language and Literature, Text as Communicative Act, Text and Discourse Analysis, and Rhetoric Analysis. She has been a lecturer of German Linguistics in graduate and undergraduate courses since 2002.

Winibert Segers

Winibert Segers is affiliated to KU Leuven, where he lectures in administrative, cultural and medical translation. He publishes in the following research areas: translation evaluation, translation didactics, translation ethics, translation philosophy, translation theory and translations of travelogues.

Rita Temmerman

Rita Temmerman is professor in translation, multilingual intercultural communication and terminology studies in the Master of Arts in Translation of Vrije Universiteit Brussel. Her research contributed to the sociocognitive approach in terminology management, and focuses on the translation of special language and terminology, more specifically application-oriented terminology analysis; neology creation; terminological variation; terminology and cognition; terminology harmonization within the EU; understanding terminology in cognitive, linguistic, situational and cultural contexts; metaphor studies; dynamic systems in language; culture-bound understanding.

Marcel Thelen

Marcel Thelen holds a PhD from Vrije Universiteit Amsterdam on *The Structure of the Lexicon. Incorporating a cognitive approach in the TCM lexicon, with applications to lexicography, terminology and translation*. He is a senior lecturer of terminology and translation at the Maastricht School of Translation and Interpreting in The Netherlands, where he was Head of School from 2007 to 2012. He is co-founder and co-organiser of *International Maastricht-Łódź Duo Colloquium on "Translation and Meaning"*, and vice-chairman of NL-Term. He publishes widely on translation, terminology, lexicology, quality management, translation didactics and curriculum building.

Sergiy Tyupa

A professional English-Ukrainian translator since 1997, Sergiy Tyupa obtained his MA in English Philology from Precarpathian National V. Stefanyk University in Ukraine in 2002. Ten years later he defended a PhD thesis at Jagiellonian

University in Kraków. His research interests are defined by his experience as a medical translator: translation quality assurance and quality assessment, back-translation as a QA tool, cognitive aspects of QA processes, patient interviewing as a QA tool, etc.

Susana Valdez
Susana Valdez is a Scientific-technical translator (since 2004), an Invited Assistant at NOVA University and a Translation Studies researcher at ULICES. She holds two Postgraduate courses, one in Translation Studies (Lisbon University) and another in Terminology (Universitat Pompeu Fabra) and a MA in Translation Studies (Lisbon University). She is currently working on her PhD on Scientific-technical translation (Lisbon University and Ghent University).

Sonia Vandepitte
Sonia Vandepitte is a full professor at the Department of Translation, Interpreting and Communication at Ghent University and head of its English section. She teaches English, Translation Studies, and translation into and from Dutch. Publication topics include causal expressions in language and translation, methodology in Translation Studies, translation competences, anticipation in interpreting, international translation teaching projects and the translation process.

Gys-Walt van Egdom
Gys-Walt van Egdom holds a doctor's degree in Linguistics and Literary Studies and a master's degree in Translation Studies. He is a lecturer and researcher at Zuyd University of Applied Sciences (Maastricht School of Translation and Interpreting) and is also affiliated to Vrije Universiteit Brussel. He is researcher at the Centre of Expertise Translation Didactics & Centre of Expertise International Relationship Management. His research interests include literary translation, philosophy of language and translation didactics.

Hildegard Vermeiren
Hildegard Vermeiren is professor at the Department of Translation, Interpreting and Communication of the University of Ghent. She teaches Conference Interpreting and Community interpreting Dutch -Spanish, Interpreting Techniques and Technologies, Interpreting Deontology and Audiodescription. Her main research interests are interpreting technology, history and sociology of interpreting, the right to an interpreter and interpreting strategies. She supervises student work placements.

Juliet Vine

Juliet Vine is a lecturer in Translation and Interpreting at the University of Westminster's Department of Modern Languages and Cultures. She translates Chinese into English. Her research interests include translation pedagogy and comparative rhetoric.

Index of Names

Index of Subjects

U

W

Z

ŁÓDŹ
Studies in Language

Edited by
Barbara Lewandowska-Tomaszczyk and Łukasz Bogucki

Vol. 1 Barbara Lewandowska-Tomaszczyk / Patrick James Melia (eds.): PALC'99: Practical Applications in Language Corpora. Papers from the International Conference at the Universtiy of Łódź, 15-18 April 1999. 2000.

Vol. 2 Lou Burnard / Tony McEnery (eds.): Rethinking Language Pedagogy from a Corpus Perspective. Papers from the Third International Conference on Teaching and Language Corpora. 2000.

Vol. 3 Barbara Lewandowska-Tomaszczyk / John Osborne / Frits Schulte: Foreign Language Teaching and Information and Communication Technology. 2001.

Vol. 4 Piotr Cap: Explorations in Political Discourse. Methodological and Critical Perspectives. 2002.

Vol. 5 Ewa Waniek-Klimczak / Patrick James Melia (eds.): Accents and Speech in Teaching English Phonetics and Phonology. EFL perspective. 2002.

Vol. 6 Barbara Lewandowska-Tomaszczyk / Kamila Turewicz (eds.): Cognitive Linguistics Today. 2002.

Vol. 7 Barbara Lewandowska-Tomaszczyk (ed.): PALC 2001: Practical Applications in Language Corpora. 2003.

Vol. 8 Corpus Linguistics by the Lune. A Festschrift for Geoffrey Leech. Edited by Andrew Wilson, Paul Rayson and Tony McEnery. 2003.

Vol. 9 Barbara Lewandowska-Tomaszczyk (ed.): Practical Applications in Language and Computers. PALC 2003. 2004.

Vol. 10 Imagery in Language. Festschrift in Honour of Professor Ronald W. Langacker. Edited by Barbara Lewandowska-Tomaszczyk and Alina Kwiatkowska. 2004.

Vol. 11 Seana Coulson / Barbara Lewandowska-Tomaszczyk (eds.): The Literal and Nonliteral in Language and Thought. 2005.

Vol. 12 Piotr Cap (ed.): Pragmatics Today. 2005.

Vol. 13 Jacek Waliński / Krzysztof Kredens / Stanisław Goźdź-Roszkowski (eds.): Corpora and ICT in Language Studies. PALC 2005. 2007.

Vol. 14 Krzysztof Kosecki (ed.): Perspectives on Metonymy. Proceedings of the International Conference "Perspectives on Metonymy", held in Łódź, Poland, May 6-7, 2005. 2007.

Vol. 15 Barbara Lewandowska-Tomaszczyk / Tomasz Płudowski / Dolores Valencia Tanno (eds.): The Media and International Communication. 2007.

Vol. 16 Krzysztof Kredens / Stanisław Goźdź-Roszkowski (eds.): Language and the Law: International Outlooks. 2007.

Vol. 17 Barbara Lewandowska-Tomaszczyk (ed.): Corpus Linguistics, Computer Tools, and Applications – State of the Art. PALC 2007. 2008.

Vol. 18 Barbara Lewandowska-Tomaszczyk / Katarzyna Dziwirek (eds.): Studies in Cognitive Corpus Linguistics. 2009.

Vol. 19 Barbara Lewandowska-Tomaszczyk / Marcel Thelen (eds.): Meaning in Translation. 2010.

Vol. 20 Łukasz Bogucki / Krzysztof Kredens (eds.): Perspectives on Audiovisual Translation. 2010.

Vol. 21 Piotr Stalmaszczyk (ed.): Turning Points in the Philosophy of Language and Linguistics. 2011.

Vol. 22 Stanisław Goźdź-Roszkowski: Patterns of Linguistic Variation in American Legal English. A Corpus-Based Study. 2011.

Vol. 23 Kamila Ciepiela (ed.): Identity through a Language Lens. 2011.

Vol. 24 Stanisław Goźdź-Roszkowski (ed.): Explorations across Languages and Corpora. PALC 2009. 2011.

Vol. 25 Krzysztof Kosecki / Janusz Badio (eds.): Cognitive Processes in Language. 2012.

Vol. 26 Alina Kwiatkowska (ed.): Texts and Minds. Papers in Cognitive Poetics and Rhetoric. 2012.

Vol. 27 Paul A. Wilson (ed.): Dynamicity in Emotion Concepts. 2012.

Vol. 28 Piotr Pęzik (ed.): Corpus Data across Languages and Disciplines. 2012.

Vol. 29 Mikołaj Deckert: Meaning in Subtitling. Toward a Contrastive Cognitive Semantic Model. 2013.

Vol. 30 Łukasz Bogucki: Areas and Methods of Audiovisual Translation Research. 2nd Revised Edition. 2016.

Vol. 31 Janusz Badio / Kamila Ciepiela (eds.): Language, Action, Interaction. 2013.

Vol. 32 Barbara Lewandowska-Tomaszczyk / Krzysztof Kosecki (eds.): Time and Temporality in Language and Human Experience. 2014.

Vol. 33 Iwona Witczak-Plisiecka (ed.): Cognitive and Pragmatic Aspects of Speech Actions. 2014.

Vol. 34 Małgorzata Anna Kamińska: A History of the *Concise Oxford Dictionary*. 2014.

Vol. 35 Łukasz Bogucki / Mikołaj Deckert (eds.): Accessing Audiovisual Translation. 2015.

Vol. 36 Joanna Jabłońska-Hood: A Conceptual Blending Theory of Humour. Selected British Comedy Productions in Focus. 2015.

Vol. 37 Krzysztof Kosecki / Janusz Badio (eds.): Empirical Methods in Language Studies. 2015

Vol. 38 Katarzyna Stadnik: Chaucer's Choices. Through the looking-glass of medieval imagery. 2015.

Vol. 39 Paulina Pietrzak / Mikołaj Deckert (eds.): Constructing Translation Competence. 2015.

Vol. 40 Małgorzata Fabiszak / Karolina Krawczak / Katarzyna Rokoszewska (eds.): Categorization in Discourse and Grammar. 2016.

Vol. 41 Marcel Thelen / Gys-Walt van Egdom / Dirk Verbeeck / Łukasz Bogucki / Barbara Lewandowska-Tomaszczyk (eds.): Translation and Meaning. New Series, Vol. 1. 2016.

www.peterlang.com

www.ingramcontent.com/pod-product-compliance
Ingram Content Group UK Ltd.
Pitfield, Milton Keynes, MK11 3LW, UK
UKHW041825100926
8556IPUK00002B/33

9 783631 663905